S0-BZE-712

HANDS-ON GUIDE SERIES®

Hands-On Guide to

Flash Video

The Focal Press Hands-On Guide Series

The Hands-On Guide Series serves as the ultimate resource in streaming and digital media-based subjects for industry professionals. The books cover solutions for enterprise, media and entertainment, and educational institutions. A compendium of everything you need to know for streaming and digital media subjects, the series is known in the industry as a must-have tool of the trade.

Books in the series cover streaming media-based technologies, applications and solutions as well as how they are applied to specific industry verticals. Because these books are not part of a vendor-based press they offer objective insight into the technology weaknesses and strengths, as well as solutions to problems you face in the real-world.

Competitive books in this category have sometimes been criticized for being either technically overwhelming or too general an overview to actually impart information. The Hands-On Guide Series combats these problems by ensuring both ease-of-use and specific focus on steaming and digital media-based topics broken into separate books.

Developed in collaboration with the series editor, Dan Rayburn, these books are written by authorities in their filed, those who have actually, been in the trenches and done the work first-hand.

All Hands-On Guide books share the following qualities:

- Easy to follow practical application information
- Step-by-Step instructions that readers can use in real-world situations
- Unique author tips from "in the trenches" experience
- Compact at 250–300 pages in length

The Hands-On Guide Series is the essential reference for Streaming and Digital Media professionals!

Series Editor: Dan Rayburn (*www.danrayburn.com*)

Executive Vice President for StreamingMedia.com, a diversified news media company with a mission to serve and educate the streaming media industry and corporations adopting internet based audio and video technology. Recognized as the "voice" for the streaming media industry" and as one of the internet industry's foremost authorities, speakers, teachers, and writers on Streaming and Digital Media Technologies.

Titles in the Series:

- *Hands-On Guide to Webcasting*
- *Hands-On Guide to Windows Media*
- *Hands-On Guide to Video Blogging & Podcasting*
- *Hands-On Guide to Streaming Media*
- *Hands-On Guide to Flash Video*
- *Hands-On Guide to Creating Flash Advertising*

HANDS-ON GUIDE SERIES®

Hands-On Guide to

Flash Video: Web Video and Flash Media Server

STEFAN RICHTER

JAN OZER

ELSEVIER

AMSTERDAM • BOSTON • HEIDLEBERG • LONDON
NEW YORK • OXFORD • PARIS • SAN DIEGO
SAN FRANCISCO • SINGAPORE • SYDNEY • TOKYO
Focal Press is an imprint of Elsevier

Senior Acquisitions Editor: Angelina Ward
Publishing Services Manager: George Morrison
Senior Project Manager: Paul Gottehrer
Assistant Editor: Doug Shults
Marketing Manager: Christine Degon Veroulis
Book Production: Borrego Publishing (www.borregopublishing.com)

Focal Press is an imprint of Elsevier
30 Corporate Drive, Suite 400, Burlington, MA 01803, USA
Linacre House, Jordan Hill, Oxford OX2 8DP, UK

Copyright © 2007, Elsevier, Inc. All rights reserved.

No part of this publication may be reproduced, stored in a retrieval system, or transmitted in any form or by any means, electronic, mechanical, photocopying, recording, or otherwise, without the prior written permission of the publisher.

Permissions may be sought directly from Elsevier's Science & Technology Rights Department in Oxford, UK: phone: (+44) 1865 843830, fax: (+44) 1865 853333, E-mail: permissions@elsevier.com. You may also complete your request online via the Elsevier homepage (http://elsevier.com), by selecting "Support & Contact" then "Copyright and Permission" and then "Obtaining Permissions."

 Recognizing the importance of preserving what has been written, Elsevier prints its books on acid-free paper whenever possible.

Library of Congress Cataloging-in-Publication Data

Richter, Stefan, 1973-
  Hands-on guide to Flash video : Web video and Flash media server / by Stefan Richter and Jan Ozer.
    p. cm. -- (Hands-on guide series)
  ISBN-13: 978-0-240-80947-2 (pbk. : alk. paper)
  ISBN-10: 0-240-80947-5 (pbk. : alk. paper) 1. Digital cinematography--Handbooks, manuals, etc. 2. Computer anima-tion--Handbooks, manuals, etc. 3. Digital video--Handbooks, manuals, etc. 4. Webcasting--Handbooks, manuals, etc. 5. Flash (Computer file)--Handbooks, manuals, etc. 6. Streaming technology (Telecommunications)--Handbooks, manuals, etc. I. Ozer, Jan, 1955- II. Title.
  TR860.R53 2007
  778.5'3--dc22

                                    2007007929

British Library Cataloguing-in-Publication Data
A catalogue record for this book is available from the British Library.

ISBN 13: 978-0-240-80947-2
ISBN 10: 0-240-80947-5

For information on all Focal Press publications
visit our website at www.books.elsevier.com

07 08 09 10 11 5 4 3 2 1

Printed in the United States of America

Working together to grow
libraries in developing countries

www.elsevier.com | www.bookaid.org | www.sabre.org

ELSEVIER   **BOOK AID** International   **Sabre Foundation**

Stefan Richter
Dedication

To my wife Joanna and my daughter Heidi.
This book wouldn't have been possible without your support—
and occasional efforts to drag me away from the computer.

Jan Ozer
Dedication

This one is for my folks, Jack and Margo Ozer.
My life has been blessed by their health and wisdom.
May they spend every cent of my inheritance.

Table of Contents

Chapter 1: Quick Start

Chapter 2: The Streaming Media Landscape

Chapter 3: Designing Your Set

Chapter 4: Lighting the Set

Chapter 5: Streaming-Related Shooting Skills

Chapter 6: Correcting Video and Audio Problems

Chapter 7: Preparing for Compression

Chapter 8: Producing Alpha Channel Video

Chapter 9: Encoding Your Video

Chapter 10: Flash Video Concepts

Chapter 11: Deploying Progressive Flash Video

Chapter 12: Customizing the FLV Playback Component

Chapter 13: Using Cue Points

Chapter 14: Controlling Your Content

Chapter 15: Advanced Effects and Playback Options

Chapter 16: Introduction to Flash Media Server

Chapter 17: Streaming Video with Flash Media Server

Chapter 18: Advanced Flash Media Server Techniques

Chapter 19: Case Studies

Index 353

Acknowledgments

Stefan Richter

Every software book is a team effort and this one is no exception. In particular I would like to thank my coauthor Jan, whose experience and guidance were invaluable and who went out of his way with help, advice and encouragement.

Thanks to Simon Bailey at nutrixinteractive.com for hours of reading and testing code samples, and to Dan Rayburn for the opportunity to make this book happen.

I'd also like to thank countless friends and developers for their help and support over the years and their willingness to share their knowledge. A few of the names that come to mind include Will Law, Bill Sanders, Ray Camden, Brian Lesser, Graeme Bull, Daz Lee, Steven Tew, Kevin Sutherland, Burak Kalayci, Renaun Erickson, Owen van Dijk, Jake Hilton, Tink, Phil Elias, Alex Dahlem, and Jerome Klingbeil.

Thanks to my family for putting up with me, especially at times when writing a book, moving home and Christmas all seemed to happen at once!

Jan Ozer

As you probably would guess, acknowledgments are written last, during the post-writing, runner's-high kind of glaze. It's quite a lovely feeling, and you do truly want to thank the world. Excuse me if I drone on.

Let me start with a few words of appreciation for Stefan, my coauthor. First books are seldom fun for either author or editor (I helped edit Stefan's chapters), but he worked tirelessly and with consistent good humor. We had the opportunity to meet at a conference in London, which helped, but it was his dedication and high-quality work during crunch time that was most impressive. Thanks, Stefan.

Next is Eric Schumacher-Rasmussen, my editor at StreamingMedia.com, who supports my creative efforts with wonderful assignments and insightful editing that allow me to learn on the job. I really couldn't have done this book without him. Thanks also to Dan Rayburn, series editor, who sponsored my presentations at StreamingMedia conferences and the codec reports I've written for streamingmedia.com.

There are many levels of knowledge; first you learn how to do something, and do it many times. Then you present it to a group of peers, and relearn it, to avoid embarrassing yourself. Then, you write an article, where you have to address (or at least knowingly dismiss) all the ancillary questions that seem to pop up and survive a much wider peer review. Then you put it all in a book, which adds another layer of detail. Eric and Dan helped sponsor the middle two layers of knowledge, without which this book might never have been written.

Finally, thanks to Angelina Ward, the Focal Press editor who put Stefan and I together with a germ of an idea that became this book.

Good technology books don't get written without the support of the hardware and software vendors that provide the base technology and infrastructure. Many thanks to Adobe in general and Giles Baker specifically for help during this project. I also appreciate the prompt assistance from On2's John Luther and Randon Morford and David Parkinson from Sorenson.

On the hardware front, I perform all Windows-related testing on workstations from Hewlett Packard and Dell that provide great performance and reliability. I write and test on a Dual G5 from Apple with a 23" Cinema display that's to die for. In my soccer-mom existence, I could not have gotten this book done without my 17" MacBook Pro, surely the best notebook computer ever made. Crack it open, and you're instantly productive, and 15- and 20-minute chunks of time really add up over the course of a few months.

Public relations professionals are the unseen grease that keeps the wheels turning. On this project, I'd like to thank Adobe's Sandra Nakama and my dearest Cara Porchia, surely the most charming PR person I've ever met.

On the home front, my wife and daughters endured many, many hours of me holed up in the "cave," my windowless office a few yards from the house. I'm coming, guys, let's go play hoops all the way, all the way.

Thanks to the folks who let me put their videos in this book, including the No Speed Limit band (Stevie Barr, Ryan Blevins, Amber Collins, Jacob Eller and Josh Pickett), Congressman Rick Boucher, David Kupsky, Gary McLennan, Whatley Ozer, Doctor Don T. Sumie, Taimo Toomast and Lisa Voelkel. Can't write books about video without video.

As always, many thanks to Pat Tracy for technical and other assistance.

Introduction

Flash video has taken the world by storm since the introduction of the VP6 codec with Flash 8. Finally, Flash video quality matched that of other streaming technologies like Real and Windows Media, which can't come close to Flash's design flexibility and player ubiquity.

Internet broadcast trophy sites like ESPN, CNN, YouTube, MySpace and many others adopted Flash en masse, and it's hard to find a Fortune 500 company that doesn't use Flash somewhere in its web presence. Truly, in 2006, the question changed from "Why use Flash video?" to "Why aren't you using Flash video?"

The answer is: you probably should be. And we're here to help.

Who Should Read This Book

The purpose of this book is to help you learn to produce and deploy Flash video. If you're already producing streaming video in other formats, the book will help you optimize your workflow for Flash, and choose the best encoding tools and codecs. If you're not producing streaming video in any format, the book will take you from set design to the optimal camera settings.

If you're on the programming, deployment or design side, the book will give you a gentle introduction to Flash and ActionScript, using examples that require only very basic prerequisite knowledge and which keep the focus very much on the video elements.

After covering some essential Flash video concepts, you will learn about progressive as well as streaming Flash video, its deployment and customization methods. You will also gain some essential knowledge that will help you get started with Flash Media Server so you can hit the ground running.

Introduction to the Video Creation Section

Most producers approach streaming video from two directions: either skilled videographers familiar with producing for television, film and DVD, or computer jocks, perhaps training IT or web developers, who are now tasked with producing streaming video. This book is designed to serve both groups.

How? First of all, it covers the gamut from choosing a background and framing your shot to allocating streaming data rate between audio and video streams. That's because if you don't know basic videography, your videos will, at best, look amateurish and, at worst, be unusable due to poor lighting or sound. If you lack computer-related knowledge, like how bandwidth deleteriously affects streaming video, you'll blissfully follow traditional TV or DVD production procedures until you encode your video and find it a bleary, blocky and/or blurry mess.

Of course, if you're coming from the video side, you'll probably be familiar with most of the materials contained in the chapters involving setup, shooting and perhaps even editing your video. For this reason, when appropriate, I'll identify those concepts that are identical with traditional videography, so you can ignore or skim over them, and highlight where different concepts are required for streaming video.

For example, you may know how to produce flat lighting and shadows on the set, but may not know which is preferred for streaming. You'll probably be familiar with how to choose a background for your videos, but may not know which backgrounds are compression-friendly.

If you're coming from the computer side, concepts like bandwidth and allocation of bit rate are old hat, so feel free to skim over these. However, recognize that if you don't produce "good video" before you start encoding, it won't be "good video" after encoding. There's quite a lot to producing a clear, well-lit image with good sound, and that's what your viewers expect.

What's Inside the Video Creation Section

Let's review the major sections of the video creation portion of the book. The first chapter introduces you to the streaming media environment, which isn't as hostile to video as it once was, but still contains lots of quicksand. Work *with* these principles and you can produce very good streaming video at nearly any data rate; work *against* them and you'll produce sub-optimal-quality video.

Next I'll describe setup issues like designing your set, including choosing the optimal background, which turns out to be one of the most important factors to producing high quality video. I also cover how to light your set, and how to choose and use microphones to achieve optimal audio quality. These last two aren't *War and Peace*-length sections, but they provide sufficient direction to get novices up to speed.

Then comes the shooting chapter. Here I describe traditional techniques for framing and shot composition, which will help video novices avoid amateurish video. I also cover optimal camera settings for streaming, including how to check lighting on the set to ensure good exposure. Another fun topic is whether shooting in progressive mode, produces better results than shooting in interlaced mode, which is one of the most widely raging debates in streaming video today.

Next comes editing, where you'll learn to adjust brightness and color, and to avoid introducing effects that degrade compressed video quality. Then I cover how to choose the target resolution, frame rate and data rate for your video, drawing upon what I've gleaned from Internet-based Flash streaming producers.

Once you've chosen your target encoding parameters, it's time to scale your video to the target, and I'll explain the magical concept of square vs. rectangular pixels (PAL and NTSC) to help you do so without distortion. I'll also address how to identify and address deinterlacing artifacts, and when to try noise filtering (and what to expect if you do).

One of the coolest new-ish features of Flash is alpha channel video. The next chapter discusses how to shoot and produce FLV files with an alpha channel.

The last video chapter addresses encoding. Here, I'll explain why and when you should abandon the Spark codec in favor of VP6, how to encode in Final Cut Pro and Premiere Pro, and when to consider third-party encoders like On2's Flix Pro or Sorenson Squeeze. I'll also describe the optimal workflow for producing your videos using these tools.

I've assumed that you want specific direction, not amorphous theory, and tried to approach these chapters with that in mind. You'll learn a lot about *what* to do, less so about *why*. Nice to know the whys, of course, but not when a client, boss (or editor) is breathing down your neck.

How to Use These Sections

You can use these sections on a standalone basis, jump in, learn what you need, and get on with your work. That said, failure in any one area can lead to irreparable damage to your overall video quality. Light incorrectly, and your video will look grainy, use the wrong background and compression artifacts will appear like unwelcome ants at the company picnic.

I'm not the first to say that streaming video is a garbage in/garbage out proposition, but it's definitely worth a reminder. If you have the time, you should strongly consider skimming through all the video production chapters, if only to learn what you don't know.

Introduction to the Deployment Section

After having read the first half of the book you will be very much ready to get your nicely-produced video out in front of your target audience and this is what the deployment section and second half of the book focuses on.

Just like Jan did in the first part of the book, I also try to cater to a wide variety of audiences and everyone—be it a video professional, Flash developer, DVD author or web newbie—should be able to follow the examples easily and walk away with a serious amount of new knowledge and skill. I have kept the use of ActionScript to a minimum in order to allow Flash novices to follow along. At the same time I aimed to offer a rich mix of different applications which even more experienced developers will find useful and which can be used as a starting point for more complex projects.

This also means that some readers will be able to skip over certain sections in the book, and if you have already deployed Flash video content in the past and are a skilled ActionScript programmer, then the basic video players you will build in Chapter 11, for example, may be less than challenging to you. On the flipside, I have no doubt that the Flash Media Server chapters contain plenty of new information for everyone.

What's Inside the Deployment Section

The aim of this part of the book is twofold: to give newcomers to Flash video a gentle introduction, yet a solid understanding of, the technology, while adding to existing skills of video professionals and experienced Flash developers alike. This is a challenging undertaking and in my opinion best served by breaking the subject matter down into the following sections, most of which are accompanied by code samples and fully functional demo applications.

I start with an introduction of the basic Flash video concepts including Flash's origins, its file formats and what the future may hold for the platform. After a brief look at the available Flash video codecs, I will guide you through the different delivery options available to you.

Next, you will learn about the different ways of deploying progressively-downloaded Flash video content, including the use of video components as well as more code-based approaches. I will introduce you to SWFObject as well as Dreamweaver's Flash video features.

The next chapter focuses on the design of the user interface around the video content and in particular, you will learn how Adobe's FLV Playback component can be customized, skinned or enhanced with uniquely-designed controls.

Cue points are covered next. They provide a powerful way of tying video content to other assets within your Flash application. Learning and leveraging this feature will help you build highly-interactive experiences that are very hard to replicate using any other technology.

Then, I describe how to enhance your completed Flash video applications by feeding external data into them, making them more versatile and reusable. You will learn about Flash-Vars, the LoadVars Object, as well as XML configuration, all of which play an important role in many Flash video applications. We finish the chapter by looking at ways to detect the end of a video, as well as how to play multiple clips back to back.

After taking a detailed look at some of Flash's more advanced playback options and effects, including creating a glow effect, alpha channel video, full screen Flash video and generating video snapshots, we move to Flash Media Server-related topics.

I will introduce you to Flash Media Server, and guide you through the complete installation process on Windows. You will also learn more about the server's folder structure and its connection procedure.

Next, I will describe how to stream Flash video using the popular FLV Playback component, including its support for SMIL files. You will also learn how to achieve the same result using ActionScript alone. The chapter concludes with a look at live Flash video.

The following chapter digs deeper into Flash Media Server's features and you will learn about virtual directories, server-side Flash Player detection via virtual keys and more advanced features like bandwidth detection. Also covered are the server's logging and reporting features alongside an introduction to SharedObjects.

The common thread throughout this entire section is very much that of supplying you with a detailed overview of progressive and streaming Flash video, alongside a little tool chest of working applications that you can learn from and build upon.

How to Use These Sections

The deployment sections take a very similar approach to the first half of the book. Each chapter is self-contained to a certain degree and while some chapters are loosely based on previous ones, they can be read in whichever order you see fit or most closely fits your skill set.

However, to get the most out of the book, I recommend that you read the entire section in the order it is written. If you are very familiar with a certain subject matter, then it is preferable to skim these parts rather than skip them entirely. This is particularly true for the chapters on Flash Media Server, starting at Chapter 16 and finishing at Chapter 18.

Sidebars

There are three types of sidebars used in this book: "Author Tip," "Inside the Industry," and "Alert." Each is separated from the text and gives you quick, helpful information that is easy to find.

 Author Tip: Gives tips that are directly from the author's experience in the field.

 Inside the Industry: Relays information about companies, behind the scenes happenings, quotes from people in the industry, a bit from a case study, statistics, market research, anything to do with the topic's industry that doesn't necessarily come from the author's experience.

 Alert: Spells out important information such as technical considerations, troubleshooting, warning of potential pitfalls, and anything else that needs special attention.

Conclusion

Well, as we pull together the final chapters, corrections and galleys, our work is done, and yours is about to begin. We both hope you find this book illuminating, immensely helpful and perhaps just a teensy-weensy bit of a good time.

All the best.

About the Authors

Stefan Richter

Stefan is one of the early adaptors of Flash video, having delivered his first live broadcast via Flash Communication Server in 2002. He was the driving force behind Europe's first Flash-centric video hosting provider and now runs one of the largest resources on the subject at Flashcomguru.com. As well as holding the position of VP of Application Development at Dallas-based POPview, he handles a variety of projects from his home office in the UK, specializing in Flash video and Rich Internet Applications for clients that include CNET, USA Network and Unilever. A well-known industry expert, Stefan is the author of a series of Adobe Developer Center articles, has spoken at several industry events and contributes a regular column on Flash video to Streaming Media Magazine.

Jan Ozer

Jan has worked in digital video since 1990, joining PC Magazine as a contributing editor in 1996, and EventDV in 1994. Jan has written twelve books on digital video, translated into seven languages, including the *PC Magazine Guide to Digital Video* (John Wiley, 2003), and the *Adobe Digital Video How-Tos: 100 Essential Techniques with Adobe Production Studio* for Adobe Press (2006). In addition to frequently teaching short courses at seminars and expositions, Jan shoots concerts and produces concert and training DVDs for local musicians and music associations. In 1994, Jan's company, Doceo Publishing, released the Video Compression Sampler, the first comparison of CD-ROM compression technologies. In January, 2006, Jan released two white papers through StreamingMedia.com that rigorously compared the quality and usability of the Windows Media, Real, Apple's H.264 and Flash codecs (Proprietary Codecs, 2006: Choosing and Using the Optimal Video Codec) and solely Flash codecs (Flash Codecs, 2006: Choosing and Using the Optimal Flash Codec).

CHAPTER 1

Quick Start

Certainly one of the most common tasks when publishing Flash video content is repurposing existing footage for online usage. While you can produce optimal quality by shooting exclusively for Flash delivery, this isn't always a realistic option, sometimes due to time constraints and other times due to budget.

As we're trying hard to "keep it real" in this book (there's a reason why this series is called *Hands-On Guide Series*), you will now jump right in and:

- Encode some existing footage to FLV format
- Bring it into Flash for configuration
- Export the application as a SWF file
- Upload the content to deploy it online.

Creating the FLV File

Here's the scenario. I (Jan) shot an interview with a local band named No Speed Limit. Local for me means Galax, Virginia, which is deep, deep southwest Virginia. The footage was originally targeted for DVD distribution, but then the band remembered their MySpace account and their own website. From DVD to streaming delivery in the flip of an idea.

Fortunately, I edit a lot in Adobe Premiere Pro, which can directly output Flash video files via a Flash encoding module borrowed from the Flash video encoder. It's fast, easy, looks great on low motion footage and, best of all, free.

Deinterlacing in Premiere Pro

I shot the interviews in HDV, which is an interlaced format, while Flash, of course, is frame based. To avoid interlacing artifacts, I needed to deinterlace before encoding. Once I finalized the clips to produce, I right clicked each and chose Field Options (**Figure 1-1**) to open that window. Then, I clicked the Always Deinterlace checkbox.

I had to do this for every clip, but the quality was worth it.

Figure 1-1
Choosing Always Deinterlace in this Field Options window ensures that all footage gets deinterlaced.

Outputting an FLV File Using Premiere Pro's Flash Encoder Module

Then it was time to output the file. To use Premiere Pro's Flash Video Encoder module, follow these steps:

1. Click File > Export > Adobe Media Encoder. Premiere Pro opens the Export Settings window (**Figure 1-2**). There's Josh, the lead guitar player, in the preview.

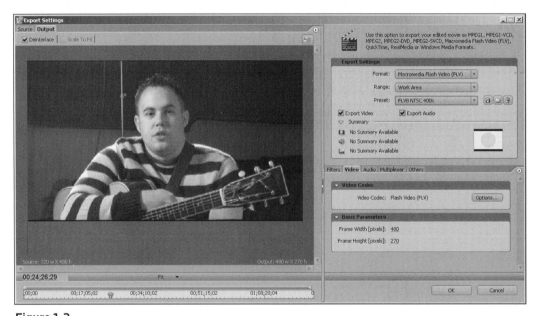

Figure 1-2
The Export Settings window of the Adobe Media Encoder. Choose Flash output, then a preset, and you're good to go.

2. In the Format list box, choose Macromedia Flash Video (FLV).

3. In the Preset drop-down list, choose FLV8 NTSC 400k. This is a preset with a data rate of 400 kbps video and 96 kbps audio, which should work just fine for our quick example.

4. In the Basic Parameters area, type the target Frame Width and Frame Height. A resolution of 480×270 was a nice big widescreen frame size, and I entered that.

5. I could mess with some options by clicking the Options button, but digging into detail before we . . . well, dig into details . . . doesn't seem like a good idea.

So click OK to close the Flash Video Encoding Settings Window, then OK again to close the Export Settings window. Name and save your file as normal.

In a few moments, I had the file Josh.flv ready to send off to Stefan in the UK to get it online.

Importing the FLV File into Flash

Now that you hold the FLV video file in your hands, it's time to import it into Flash. In this lesson you will use Adobe's FLV Playback component to play the video. This component supports progressive and streaming video, as well as live and on-demand video. The component also supports cue points, bandwidth-detection features (when used in combination with Flash Media Server), understands SMIL (for Synchronized Multimedia Integration Language) and you can customize its look and feel. Even better, it also includes all the ActionScript source code, which you can tweak if required.

 ALERT This chapter uses Adobe Flash CS3 Professional (alternatively you may use Adobe Flash Professional 8). To follow along with the examples, which I recommend, you will need a copy of the program installed on your computer. Should you not own a copy of the program, note that Adobe offers a free 30-day trial version on its website.

To import the FLV file into Flash, follow these steps:

1. Open Flash and create a new file by choosing File > New from the menu bar. Select Flash File from the window as shown in **Figure 1-3**.

Choose ActionScript 2.0 if you are using Flash CS3. Flash 8 will not offer this option and ActionScript 2.0 is simply implied.

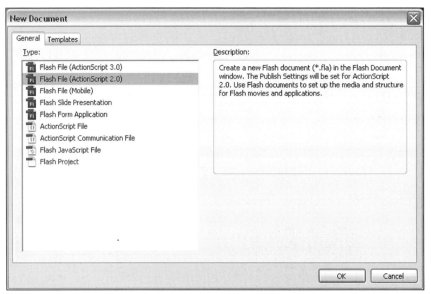

Figure 1-3
Flash's New Document window.

2. Click OK to close the window.

3. Name this file video_publish.fla and save it to the same folder as the FLV file that you just encoded.

4. Next, choose File > Import > Import Video from the menu bar. The Import Video window opens.

5. Click the "On your computer" radio button and browse to the encoded Josh.flv file, as shown in **Figure 1-4**.

6. Click Next to select a deployment method.

7. Click the radio button with the Progressive download from a web server label if not already selected.

8. Click Next to reach the Skinning window.

9. Select a skin of your choice from the Skin dropdown menu. The graphics in the preview window show what the finished player will look like. For this example, I chose the SteelExternalPlaySeekMute.swf skin file, as shown in **Figure 1-5**.

Figure 1-4
The FLV file has been selected.

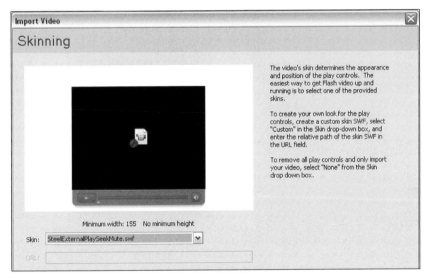

Figure 1-5
The Skinning page allows you to preview different skins for the Flash Player.

10.   Click Next to continue.

11.   You may now review your chosen settings. Click Finish when ready to import the file.

12.   The video wizard exits and you will be presented with a fully configured FLV Playback component in Flash. To review the optional configuration parameters, you may select the component and check the Parameters tab of the Properties panel, as shown in **Figure 1-6**.

Choose Window > Properties > Parameters from the menu bar if you cannot see the Parameters tab.

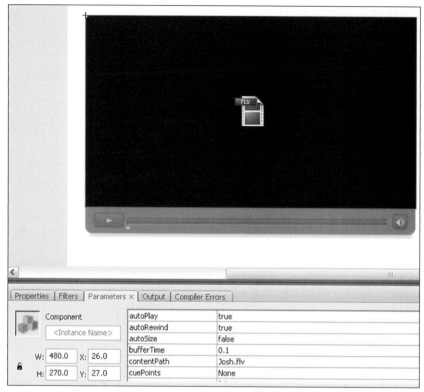

Figure 1-6
An instance of the FLV Playback component has been added.

Author's Tip

To jump to the specific Help files for a particular component, do the following:

- Select the component on Stage by clicking it

- With the component selected choose Window > Properties > Parameters from the menu bar to open the Parameters tab if it is not already showing

- On the Parameters tab, click the small question mark symbol on the right

- From the flyout menu that opens, choose "Help on this Component."

The specific Help files for the selected component will open in the Help panel.

From the Parameters tab, you can review and set additional playback options, including autoPlay, autoRewind and many more. Consult the Flash Help files for a full list of parameters.

Exporting the Application

You can now produce the application. This will compile the FLA source file into a SWF file, which is the target format that you will deploy, alongside other associated files.

1. Choose File > Publish from the menu bar. Flash will compile the FLA project into SWF format and also generate the necessary HTML files in the same folder in which the FLA was previously saved. If you are using Flash CS3 then a JavaScript is also generated. It aids the embedding of the SWF into the HTML page and doesn't require any attention.

2. To preview the completed application locally, open the file video_publish.html that was generated by Flash in your favorite web browser, as shown in **Figure 1-7**.

Figure 1-7
The FLV video plays inside the SWF file, embedded in the HTML page.

Deploying the Application

Now you can upload all files to a public URL, ready to be accessed over the Internet. Using your favorite FTP tool, upload all generated files (but not the FLA source file) to a location of your choice.

The list of files you should deploy is:

- Josh.flv (the actual video)
- AC_OETags.js (if you are using Flash CS3)
- SteelExternalPlaySeekMute.swf (or whichever skin file you chose previously)
- video_publish.html (the HTML page in which the SWF is embedded)
- video_publish.swf (the SWF which loads and plays the FLV video).

Create a link from your website to the HTML file, and start sending the link to your buddies for their viewing.

Conclusion

Well, folks, if it was up to me (Jan), this heading would say *Beginning*, not *Conclusion*, because truly you are just getting started. The next eight chapters describe the video production and encoding side of Flash video, while in Chapter 10 Stefan takes over and shows you what to do with all the picture-perfect FLV files that you've just created.

Enjoy the ride.

CHAPTER 2

The Streaming Media Landscape

Intuitively, you know that low-motion talking-head videos look better after compression than high-motion sports videos. This chapter explains why and, more importantly, how to use that knowledge to maximize production quality. After reading this chapter, you will:

- Understand the concepts of bandwidth and data rate and how they affect video quality

- Understand how interframe compression works and why that is important

- Learn how, when and why to limit motion in your videos during shooting and editing

- Learn that you need to set a target data rate for the video before you start shooting and/or editing.

Those coming from more traditional videography roles will understand the shooting and editing techniques you'll have to modify to produce high-quality, low-data-rate streaming video.

Bandwidth and Data Rate

In the beginning there was bandwidth and it was king. Essentially, bandwidth was the transfer capacity of the smallest pipe between your video data and the remote user's computer, typically expressed in kilobits per second (kbps), kilobytes per second (kBps), or if you're really lucky, megabytes per second (MBps).

For example, a 28.8-kbps modem can transfer a maximum of 28.8 kilobits per second. Similarly, a 128-kbps ISDN connection can transmit 128 kilobits of data per second. As long as your video "fits" within that pipe, your computer could play the video without stopping, a process that is now called *streaming*.

To accomplish this, you compressed your file to a certain *data rate*, or amount of data per second of video, also expressed in kbps, kBps or Mbps. In the early days of streaming, your job was to produce your video at a data rate under the bandwidth of the pipe between your video and the remote viewer.

For example, **Figure 2-1** is the Audio/Video Compression Settings screen from Sorenson Squeeze, a popular compression tool detailed in Chapter 8. In the screen's upper left-hand corner, you'll note the Name 56K_Dial_Up. This indicates that this template should be used for encoding files viewed via a 56-kbps modem. On the upper right is the Total Data Rate of 31 kilobits/sec.

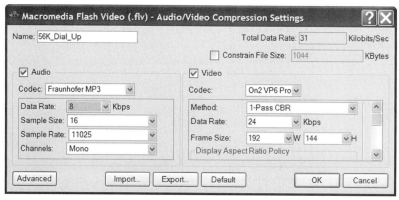

Figure 2-1
The Audio/Video Compression Settings Screen from Sorenson Squeeze.

Author's Tip

Bits and Bytes and Everything Nice

Though the streaming industry is improving in this regard, we still tend to recklessly interchange the terms bits and bytes, which can get confusing. Let's clear that up.

Briefly, one byte equals eight bits. To convert bytes to bits, you *multiply* by eight, so a video with a data rate of 150 kilobytes per second (kBps) also has a data rate of 1200 kilobits per second (kbps). To convert from bits to bytes you *divide* by eight, so an 8-megabit-per-second stream (Mbps) is also 1 megabyte per second (MBps).

Back when we were producing for CD-ROMs, most data rates and bandwidths were expressed in kilobytes per second, primarily because the original CD-ROM drives had a transfer speed of 150 kBps. Thus, we encoded files to 150 kBps or less to fit within that bandwidth.

As Internet-based streaming took hold, the industry shifted to bits per second, primarily because most communications devices, like modems and network cards, were rated in bits per second. As a practical matter, virtually all bandwidths and data rates are now expressed in bits per second, so a modem is 28 kilobits and a network 100 megabits.

To be clear, using these settings, Squeeze will compress the file so that the data rate is 31 kbps or below. In most instances, this file should stream, or play without interruption, when viewed via 56-kbps and faster connections.

Interestingly, the concept of bandwidth, once inexorably tied to actual transfer capabilities of devices like modems or CD-ROMs, is now much more subjective. Corporate LANs can support at least 100 megabits per second (Mbps), if not a gigabyte, but stingy network administrators limit video usage to a fraction of that capacity. Conservative webmasters take the same approach, allocating only a fraction of their available bandwidth to video to ensure speedy access to JPEGs, PDFs and other content on the website.

Either way, whether the data rate is subjectively assigned or tied to the bandwidth of a piece of hardware, virtually all video is compressed to a fixed data rate. Hold that thought while we briefly explore intraframe and interframe compression.

Interframe Compression and Video Quality

At a high level, there are two types of compression, intraframe and interframe. Intraframe compression occurs totally within a single frame, with no reference to other frames in the video. The most familiar example of an intraframe compression technology is JPEG, the most pervasive technology used in digital cameras and real-world pictures on the web.

In contrast, interframe compression works between frames, using a system of key and delta frames to eliminate redundancy between frames. Specifically, key frames, also called *I frames* in MPEG-speak, contain the complete frame, compressed solely with intraframe compression.

Delta frames, also called *difference* or B and P frames, only contain pixels that are different from preceding frames (or in some cases, other frames in the sequence). After removing these redundancies, the pixels remaining in the frames are compressed using intraframe techniques.

Here's the key point: with low-motion videos there are lots of interframe redundancies, meaning relatively fewer remaining pixels in each delta frame to compress with intraframe compression. When motion is high, redundancies are much fewer, leaving more pixels to compress with intraframe compression.

If you had unlimited bandwidth, this wouldn't matter, since you could simply increase the data rate of the compressed video stream. However, when compressing video to a fixed data rate, say 300 kbps, you have to apply much more intraframe compression to the high-motion clip to squeeze it down to the same data rate. This extra compression translates to quality loss and is why low-motion clips look better than high-motion clips after compression.

Author's Tip

Data Rate? Bit Rate? Bandwidth?
The term *data rate* typically refers to an audio or video or audio/video file, and most folks use the term *bit rate* interchangeably. So you might compress a file to a data rate of 300 kbps, or a bit rate of 300 kbps. Same thing.

In contrast, the term *bandwidth* generally refers to a device or technology. For example, the theoretical bandwidth of a T1 line is 1.54 mbps.

When Does It Matter?

Most viewers have seen ESPN Motion (*www.espn.com*), which proves that, given sufficient bandwidth, even clips comprised of high-motion sequences can look very good compressed. Of course, ESPN compresses their video at data rates of 400–600 kbps (at 440×330 resolution), which may be more than your network administrators or webmasters allow.

The multiple factors involved in streaming video make it challenging to precisely identify the data rate at which motion will start to degrade video quality. For example, at 500 kbps, video produced at 320×240 resolution will look pristine almost irrespective of motion, while the same video produced at 640×480 resolution will look blocky and degraded.

Still, the chart shown in **Figure 2-2** illustrates the general trend: the lower the data rate, the more you have to care about motion in the video. Generally speaking, at 1 mbps and above (assuming 640×480 resolution), or 500 kbps and above (assuming 320×240 resolution), producing streaming video is very similar to producing for TV, film or DVD. That is, the data rate is sufficient to support significant motion without degrading quality.

At 300 kbps (assuming 320×240 resolution), excessive motion can noticeably degrade quality, and producers should start planning their productions to limit motion. I'm not talking camera lockdown, but simply eliminating extraneous motion, as discussed more fully below. At 100 kbps and below (assuming 320×240 resolution), any motion content can noticeably degrade video quality, and producers should limit camera, subject and other sources of motion to maintain video quality.

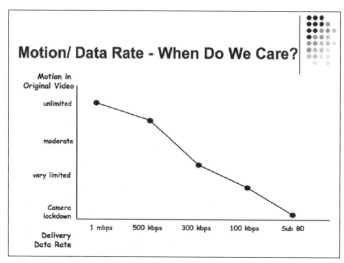

Figure 2-2
The lower the data rate, the more you have to care about motion in the video.

The Importance of Knowing Your Target

This dynamic illustrates why it's so important to understand your target data rate before starting production. More specifically, if your target output parameters are 640×480@1 mbps, you'll shoot and edit completely differently than if it was 320×240@100 kbps.

At a minimum, before starting a project, you should ascertain the:

- Minimum target data rate for distributing the video (e.g., 300 kbps)

- Target resolution (e.g., 400×300)

- Target frame rate (e.g., 30 fps)

- Allocation of data rate between audio and video (e.g., 268 kbps data/32 kbps audio)

What if you'll be distributing the video at multiple output parameters, both low and high? That's the Catch-22.

If you choose the artistic approach, with pans, zooms, slow dissolves, and artistic overlays, your video will look wonderful at higher data rates but potentially awful at lower data rates. If you lock down your camera, use straight cuts and boring still-image backgrounds for your titles, compressed quality will look good at all rates, but the video itself won't win any Oscars.

I can't tell you which road to choose, and it may vary by project. Just understand the implications of each alternative, and explain it to your clients (if any) before getting started.

Limit Extraneous Motion

When producing for lower bit rates where motion is an issue, understand that Flash codecs are egalitarian about motion; they don't care where it comes from, whether it's a shaking camera, a jumping subject, or a motion video behind a title. If motion is there, compressed quality will suffer at lower bit rates. **Figure 2-3** provides an example.

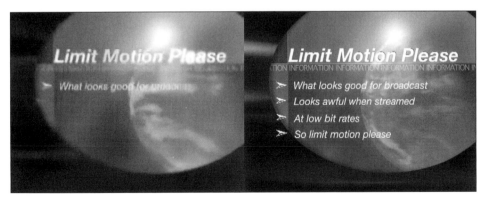

Figure 2-3
Common analog video practices like inserting a moving background behind a title (on the left) will degrade quality. A still image background looks similar and preserves the quality.

The frame on the left shows the title compressed with a spinning globe behind the text, a ubiquitous effect when producing for TV or DVD. The frame on the right uses a single frame from the background video, reducing artistic quality a bit, but vastly improving compressed video quality.

One concept I've found valuable is that of "extraneous" motion. For example, if you're shooting a surgeon in the operating room, the critical motion is her hands working in the incision. All other motion, like slowly zooming to the operating table or shaky handheld footage, is extraneous. Get a tripod, lock the camera into position, and hold that framing.

When you eliminate the extraneous motion, you allow the codec to focus on the motion critical to the video, improving overall compressed quality. Throughout the book, I'll identify techniques that produce extraneous motion, and suggest alternatives that limit motion and produce higher quality. Since I have your attention, let me list some highlights to keep in mind when producing for low data rate streaming:

- Always shoot with a tripod.

- Avoid moving backgrounds, whether crowds, blowing tree branches or water.

- Avoid panning and zooming whenever possible. Either use cuts between multiple cameras or cuts between consecutive shots from a single camera.

- Regarding transitions, typically a straight cut is easiest for codecs to compress at good quality, usually because the encoding tool can insert a key frame at the cut, providing a high-quality start to the next few frames.

- Limit the motion of your onscreen subjects, either by sitting them down in a chair or stool, or even chalking out a box that they shouldn't move out of.

- Otherwise, use very fast (5–15 frame) dissolves, and avoid pushes and other transitions that involve significant interframe motion.

- Similarly, all fade-ins or fade-outs to black (or another color) should be no more than 5–15 seconds.

- Use solid (not moving) backgrounds for titles.

- Limit special-effect usage to a minimum.

Conclusion

In this chapter you learned the streaming-media landscape, specifically how motion impacts streaming quality at lower bit rates. Hopefully, this provided some insight into how shooting for streaming differs from shooting for other traditional distribution media like TV or DVD, and how and when this should affect your production planning and implementation. Now it's time to move to the first step of production, creating your set.

CHAPTER 3

Designing Your Set

Set design has three components: the appearance of the background, how your subjects are dressed and how they are positioned on the set. Without question, set design can have a profound effect on both the perceived and actual quality of your compressed video. That is, choose inappropriate clothing for your subjects, and your video looks amateurish; to add insult to injury, a poor choice like a striped shirt will add an obvious artifact called a *moiré pattern* to the video, degrading visual quality.

In this chapter, I'll describe how to create a simple set for in-house use and how to identify a good background when shooting video on location, say for a case study, interview or testimonial. After reading this chapter, you'll know how to:

- Choose an attractive and highly compressible background for your in-house set
- Choose a set on location that will also promote compressed video quality
- Position your subjects on the set to simplify softening the background with aperture controls, which enhances overall compressibility
- Dress your subjects for compressibility.

Background Choice Is Critical

My first foray into digital video, circa 1994, went like this. I hired a professional crew to film a tutorial on video compression. Their set featured a rosewood desk against a gray fabric background decorated with plants, and graduated lighting accented with spotlights. I wore a snazzy black blazer with little white flecks that looked better than it sounds. On the studio monitors, the video looked awesome.

We broke the set, and about a month later I compressed the video to Indeo 3.2 format. The graduated lighting on the back wall exhibited shifting color bands that crawled in the background like dancing snakes. My coat fared equally poorly, with most flecks gone and those remaining resembling giant dandruff flakes (**Figure 3-1**).

Compressed with the best technology of the day, the video was a 60-minute testimonial to what NOT to do, and the video never saw the light of day. The only return on my substantial investment was a searing lesson that backgrounds and clothing really matter when it comes to compressed video quality. This lesson has saved uncountable projects shot for streaming from the same fate.

Figure 3-1
Note the banding caused by the reflective gray surface and graduated lighting.

About a decade later, I started work on a research report for StreamingMedia.com that involved compressing approximately 42 business, action and entertainment-oriented clips into Flash 8 format. These were general-purpose clips not shot for streaming, so this project provided many additional lessons on which backgrounds compress well and which don't.

Interestingly, I found that some backgrounds showed significant artifacts when compressed at data rates of 1 mbps and above. This led to the scary realization that, while you can fix motion-related problems by throwing additional data rate at the problem, some backgrounds simply aren't fixable.

To supplement this research, I started studying the backgrounds used in streaming videos produced by leading brands and technology companies, as well as broadcast outlets that produced specifically for the web. This research incorporated videos from companies like Microsoft, Real Networks, Proctor and Gamble, Cisco, Hewlett Packard, Accenture, GE, American Express and IBM and Internet-only broadcasters like the Wall Street Journal, BusinessWeek, CNET, Digital Life TV, Forbes.com and several others.

The backgrounds used in these videos quickly broke down into two groups. Most corporations used simple synthetic backgrounds like walls, hanging curtains or painted muslin or canvas backgrounds. Others, particularly for on-location case studies, chose backgrounds in and around the offices of their interviewees. Since the requirements for these two approaches differ, I'll describe them separately.

Choosing and Using Synthetic Backgrounds
This category means any background other than an office or traditional broadcast studio, which usually incorporates backgrounds comprised of walls, curtains and muslin and canvas backdrops. Here are my recommendations.

Keep It Simple

Companies like Microsoft, Deloitte, Accenture and Proctor and Gamble can throw millions at a streaming video studio, but uniformly choose a much simpler approach, a plain curtain or wall like that shown in **Figure 3-2,** from the set of Ziff Davis's Digital Life television program. Clearly, when choosing a set, the goal isn't to show off your company's wealth or design expertise—it's to produce a compressible background. Keeping it simple is rule number 1.

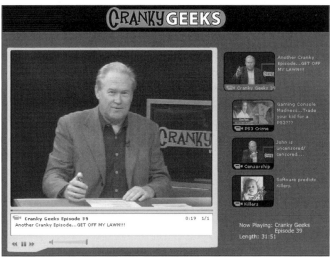

Figure 3-2
John Dvorak in the Cranky Geek's set, with a flat black background, which is simple and effective.

It Had to Be Blue

Here's how the survey videos broke down in terms of color usage:

- Of the 22 videos in this category, nine companies, or 41% (including Deloitte, DL.TV, Microsoft, GE, Proctor and Gamble and Real Networks) chose blue backgrounds.

- Five companies chose white (23%), including Cisco, Intel and Digital Juice. While impossible to be sure, four of the five companies appeared to use chroma key techniques to overlay the video over the background, and only one looked like it was originally shot against white.

- Four companies chose black (18%), including Accenture, Price Waterhouse Coopers, Nucor and Cranky Geeks (Ziff Davis TV).

- Two companies, including American Express and Accenture, chose mottled gray (9%), while CNET used a dark red curtain and Hewlett Packard used a brown curtain.

After much experimentation, flat black has become my "go to" background for optimal compressed quality. It is a stark look, however, and a dark blue compresses nearly as effectively.

I avoid shooting against light, white backgrounds because, like backlighting, it complicates getting good exposure on the face. When you have to shoot against white, move the subject away from the background, light the subject as normal and dim the lights on the background. A white background obviously isn't a problem if you shoot against a chroma-key background and overlay the subject against a white background, but that adds lots of work.

Wall, Curtain or Other Backdrop?

It wasn't possible to determine the physical makeup of the backgrounds used for all videos; some appeared to be chroma keyed, while all black backgrounds were invisible and could have been painted walls or a hanging curtain. Of the rest, five used a hanging muslin sheet or similar background, four used traditional curtains (as in **Figure 3-3**) and four used painted walls.

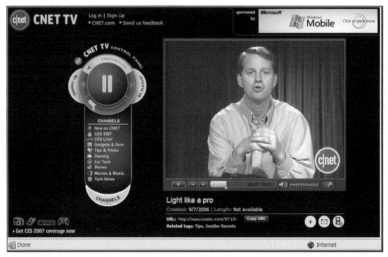

Figure 3-3
CNET's Tom Merritt in a "how-to" video. The curtain in the background is dark red and contrasts nicely with Tom's blue shirt.

Choosing Your Material

Here is a list of considerations with recommendations.

1. *Painted wall vs. portable backdrop?* If you have one fixed set that will be used repeatedly by a limited group of users, as in an Internet TV studio, consider painting the walls of the studio. If you don't have a fixed studio, or your studio will be used by a variety of users, consider a stand-based background with two or three colors to accommodate different clothing, skin and hair color.

2. *Muslin, curtain, canvas or velour?*

   • Canvas backgrounds generally cost more, are stiffer and heavier so require a stand, and need more care, like rolling them up between uses. For these reasons, though, canvas will maintain a more uniform look for a longer term, and if buying for a single location, makes a lot of sense.

- Muslin is less expensive, lighter and can be stored in a bag for easy transport. You can also attach muslin backdrops to fixtures with clamps, potentially eliminating the need for a separate stand. Consider muslin if you have to buy two or three backgrounds on a budget, or if you'll be moving around a lot.

- Curtains are generally the most expensive and least portable options. Consider if using a fixed set that will seldom if ever move.

- Buy velour if you decide to use a black background. It's easy to work with and totally nonreflective, making it very easy to use, but, like canvas, it must be rolled up between uses.

3. *What colors should I buy?* Budget willing, buy two: dark grey and dark blue. These should provide great contrast for virtually all clothing you'll see on the set. If you are budget limited, you probably can get a black velour background for under $50.

4. *Should I get solid or mottled colors?* Get a slightly mottled background, like that shown in **Figure 3-4**, which is nearly identical to the background used by both Accenture and American Express. These look good and tend to hide compression artifacts, which may appear accentuated on completely smooth backgrounds. Avoid fancy or wild patterns, however, and select backgrounds with different shades of the same colors, none with multiple colors.

Figure 3-4
Get a slightly mottled background, but nothing extremely fancy.

5. *What else will I need?*

- A stand to hold the backdrop in place. A stand that's 10' high and 12' wide should cost under $200. Make sure it has a traveling case.

- Clamps. If you plan to permanently mount the backdrop in a studio, consider backdrop-specific clamps that allow you to mount your backdrop without cutting or piercing it. These cost anywhere from $10–$20.

- Gaffers tape. When shooting on location, you'll often have to tape the background to the wall or floor. Gaffers tape is cotton rather than vinyl (like duct tape), so is nonreflective, and won't leave adhesive residue on your backgrounds. You can purchase it in multiple colors to match your background, generally for under $20 for a 60-ft. roll of 3-inch tape.

6. *Where can I learn more and buy?* If you've never purchased this equipment, check out *www.bhphotovideo.com*, which has a complete section on background materials and equipment. Another great site for discounted backgrounds and related materials is *www.amvona.com*, which has extensive buyer comments on most products. Otherwise, Google the terms *muslin canvas video background video* and you'll find plenty of sites selling these materials.

Mistakes to Avoid

The most common mistake is using a background too close in color to a subject's clothing, usually blue on blue. This makes the subject blend into the background when the video is highly compressed. You can avoid this by having different backgrounds available as I suggest above. When you can't change the background, use backlighting (discussed in Chapter 4) to create highlights on the subject's head and shoulders, which improves contrast with the background.

Another common mistake is customizing the background curtain with too much detail, such as the company name, logo and web address. At high compression ratios, this detail can start to look ragged, unnecessarily degrading the appearance of the video. Remember rule number 1—when creating a background for streaming, keep it simple.

Creating Compression-Friendly Real-World Sets

Even after you purchase your movable stands, your CEO may want to shoot in her office, so the surroundings can add an air of authenticity to the message. Although your backgrounds may be portable, sometimes a customer case study, testimonial, or training video looks best when shot in a real-world environment.

Your job then is to produce a compression-friendly background on-site. Here's a list of considerations, many very well demonstrated in **Figure 3-5**, a frame from a Microsoft video on accessibility.

Avoid High-Resolution Detail

First, all objects in the background video should contain relatively low detail. When the background contains too much detail, the codec allocates data rate to maintain that detail, degrading the appearance of the other video, which is generally much more important. Highly detailed backgrounds also tend to shift a lot during playback, which is also undesirable.

For example, in **Figure 3-6**, the background wallpaper had a fine pattern that became highly volatile during compression, shifting around like molten lava, changing colors and generally behaving poorly.

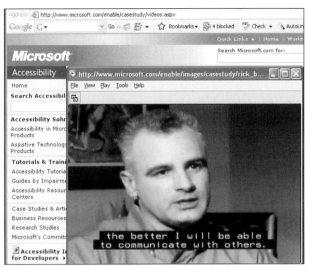

Figure 3-5
Lots of great technique in this video, including a background with minimal detail that's obscured by intentional low lighting.

Figure 3-6
This fine wallpaper pattern turned to shifting lava when compressed below 500 kbps.

Other backgrounds that behave badly include venetian blinds, bookshelves, trees with small leaves and other plants (especially if blown by the wind), brick walls, fabrics with herringbone and similar patterns, or any background with lots of fine objects.

Avoid Well-Lit Open Spaces and Embrace Clutter
Shooting against a white or beige painted wall sounds benign, but has worked poorly for me in several instances. **Figure 3-7** contains a great illustration. Here, tenor Taimo Toomast sang beautifully against a simple tan wall that seemed the perfect background for

high-quality streaming. However, the image shows obvious banding that formed as pixels grouped together and danced on the wall. (Note that I darkened the image slightly in a photo editor to highlight the banding, which was very obvious when playing in color, but less so in a gray-scale still image.)

Banding occurred and became very obvious because there were no objects like pictures or posters to contain the motion. Compare this image to **Figure 3-5**, and you'll note that the Microsoft video had lots of natural boundaries to contain the artifacts in the video, like the two walls, each lit a bit differently, and the chair and painting.

Taimo's background had no boundaries at all, and the compression artifacts ran wild. One corrective approach would have been to drop the lights in the background, which I discuss below. The other would be to place two or three pictures or other objects with minimal detail in the background, which would break up the wall and contain the artifacts.

Figure 3-7
A simple tan wall with graduated lighting turned into a wiggly mess during compression.

Seek Relative Uniformity of Color

Glance back to **Figure 3-5** and you'll note that the color is relatively uniform (looks grey, was crème), with even the painting primarily comprised of browns and whites. This uniformity makes it extremely easy to find clothing that contrasts well with the background and, in this case, the blue shirt worked perfectly.

If there are too many colors in the background, clothing selection and positioning the subject becomes much more challenging. Multicolored backgrounds may look striking, but they can complicate matters significantly.

And Relative Uniformity of Luminance

Luminance is a measure of the brightness of an object. Have another look at **Figure 3-5** and you'll note that the background is relatively uniform in luminance value, with no extreme bright or dark regions. Focus on this aspect of set design while channel surfing through the evening news, and you'll find that most sets share this characteristic, which accomplishes two things.

First, when the luminance value is relatively low, as it is in **Figure 3-5**, you can light the subject well without conflicting with bright spots in the background. Second, consistent luminance values limit the strain on the camera's dynamic range, or the ability to capture scenes with extremes in luminance. Devices with high dynamic range, like expensive film and digital SLR cameras, have a great ability to retain detail when displaying images with very bright and very dark regions.

Devices with low dynamic range, which includes most consumer and prosumer camcorders, can't retain detail when displaying a frame with very dark and very bright regions. This is illustrated in **Figure 3-8** using luminance extremes in clothing rather than background.

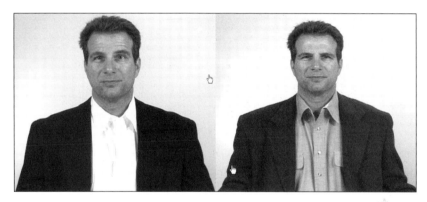

Figure 3-8
The extremes in brightness cause loss of detail in the shirt and jacket on the left.

On the left, I'm wearing a black coat and white shirt, representing very extreme luminance ranges. This range exceeded the dynamic range of my Sony HDR-FX1 camcorder and, as a result, most detail in the coat and shirt is lost.

The frame on the right is identical, except that I'm wearing a tan coat and blue shirt. These colors represent a much smaller range in luminance value, which doesn't strain the camcorder's dynamic range. As a result, you can see the lapels and folds in the coat and collar, buttons and pockets on the shirt.

Looking at your set as a whole—clothing, skin, hair and background—if there are no extremes in luminance, you should be able to retain good detail throughout the image. If luminance extremes exist between any of these elements, you risk losing detail at one or both extremes.

Two other points. First, your eye has a much greater dynamic range than your camcorder. For example, if you were in the room with me while I was wearing the black coat and white shirt in **Figure 3-8**, you would have seen the detail in the shirt and coat. So you really can't trust your eyes to be the judge; even if you can see the detail at both extremes, the camcorder can't.

Second, compression further limits the dynamic range of an image, since compression, by its nature, discards information describing an image, albeit as intelligently as possible. In Chapter 4 I'll describe how to measure the light in the scene using tools like a waveform monitor or zebra stripes. Even without these tools, however, any scene with overly bright and/or dark regions should trigger a concern that the set-up may be stressing the dynamic range of your camcorder and codec.

Darken the Background to Further Limit Detail

OK, have yet another look at **Figure 3-5**. Though the subject is very well lit, the background is noticeably darker, almost as if not lit at all. This has two effects, both beneficial. First, it increases the contrast between the background and subject, making him even more distinctive. Second, it further limits the detail in the background, making it even easier to compress.

This technique proved very popular in the on-location case studies that I viewed on the net, and should be strongly considered by all producers.

Position the Subject as Far as Possible from the Background

Another frequently used technique in on-location case studies and testimonials is to blur the background slightly using aperture controls. This again enhances the contrast between the subject and background, while reducing detail and improving compressed quality.

This is shown to great effect in **Figure 3-9**, which is a frame from one of many great case studies on Hewlett Packard's website (*http://www.hp.com/hpinfo/newsroom/*

Figure 3-9
Place the subject far from the background, and you can blur it using aperture controls, creating a great look and a highly compressible background.

feature_stories/video/). As you can see, the subject is very well lit and in focus, while the seats in the theater behind him are discernable, but blurry. There's sufficient detail to know that the interview takes place in a theater, providing the desired, on-location feel, but the background is blurry and very easy to compress.

The positioning required to achieve this effect varies by camera; essentially, the better the camera, the closer the camera can be to the background. This relates to the "depth of field" capability of the camera, which increases with the size of the camera's CCDs.

Film or broadcast cameras can blur a subject that's four or five feet from the background or another subject, while a consumer camcorder may require much more distance. I discuss how to use the camera's aperture controls to produce this effect in Chapter 5.

The Background Should Be Darker than the Subject's Face

Generally, the subject's face is the most important object in the frame. When the background is extremely bright, it becomes very difficult to make the face light without potentially brightening the background beyond acceptable levels. This is why most producers, including those frames shown in **Figures 3-2, 3-3 and 3-9,** choose a background that enables the subject's face to be the brightest object in the frame.

These are my recommendations for producing a compressible background; now let's look at how to dress for streaming success.

Dressing for Streaming Success

In general, the rules for clothing are very similar to the rules for creating a background, so I'll present them in checklist form.

1. Color contrast is job number 1. The subject's clothing, skin and hair must all contrast with the background or they will blend in upon compression. If any of these elements are similar to the background color, use backlighting to help distinguish the subject from the background (see Chapter 4 for lighting).

2. Dress in solid colors. Stripes, plaids and herringbones degrade severely when compressed. **Figure 3-10,** pulled from a site on the web that will go unnamed, shows a striped shirt that looks totally muddled. Note that the very blurry regions on the right shoulder and left sleeve appear as a blurry, green, red and blue moiré pattern in the actual video.

3. Avoid blacks and whites and other luminance extremes. This is the dynamic range issue again, as illustrated in **Figure 3-8**. Muted grays and dark blues work well, as do browns. When subjects are wearing a suit, advise them to wear a blue shirt underneath, rather than white.

4. Avoid highly saturated reds, greens and blues like the plague.

Figure 3-10
Striped shirts simply don't do well post compression, and should be avoided at all costs.

5.   Other considerations:

- Hair should be neatly combed and/or pulled back. Frizzy, curly hair presents too much detail for codecs to effectively compress and can create artifacts.

- Lose the bling. Large chains, bracelets, earrings and necklaces present unnecessary detail and can become harsh and glittery after compression. They can also reflect light back to the camera, complicating exposure.

- Beware those wearing glasses. When your subject wears glasses, remember to observe whether lights are reflecting in the lenses. If so, often you can avoid or minimize this by lighting the subject from the side.

Theory Is Great, but Test Anyway

If you follow these recommendations to the letter, chances are you'll produce great results. Some problems, however, only become obvious when you compress your video to your target output parameters. Looking back, my biggest mistake with my first tutorial was not testing the background on the set. Of course, since laptop computers barely existed and video capture required the fastest computer in the land, that's probably excusable.

Today, when the most underpowered notebook with a FireWire port can easily capture and quickly encode sample video footage, there's no excuse for not testing your background and clothing design on the set, while you still have time to change it.

Conclusion

In this chapter you learned how to design the ideal synthetic background, and how to choose a highly compressible background when shooting on location. Also covered was how to position your subjects to achieve a soft background, and how to dress for streaming success.

Next chapter we cover lighting and sound, and discuss components that can make or break the overall quality of your streaming video.

CHAPTER 4

Lighting the Set

Without question, lighting is the single most important determinant of streaming quality. Shoot a well-lit scene with a consumer camcorder, or a poorly lit scene with the latest high-def wonder, and the consumer camcorder will win every time. Fortunately, while lighting can be challenging, a little knowledge and some determined effort can go a long way. This chapter provides the former; I'll count on you for the latter.

I'll start with a brief look at the history of lighting, and then describe the optimal procedures for lighting for streaming, including a brief look at the requirements for shooting for chroma key. Along the way, I'll describe how to use the zebra stripes on your camcorder to determine when you've got sufficient lighting on the set.

In this chapter, you will learn:

- The difference between flat and three-point lighting, and when to use each technique

- The difference between hard and soft lighting, and when to use each

- How to use your camcorder and/or video editor to determine whether there is sufficient light on the set

- How to light for chroma key.

Use at Least Three Lights

Most lighting setups are variations on the same three-point lighting scheme; you change the effect by varying intensity, for example, to create shadows or flat lighting, and by using hard or soft lights. Three-point positioning is shown in **Figure 4-1**. On the left is the shot from above, showing the two front lights angled at about 45° in front of our subject, and the back light close to the subject and pointing down on her head and shoulders.

Figure 4-1
The basic three-point lighting set-up: two in front, one in the back.

On the right is the view from the front, showing all three lights positioned above the subject. The two front lights are pointing down at between 15–25°. Since the back light is closer to the subject, it's pointing down at a more severe angle, say 75°.

Obviously, the two front lights provide the main light for the scene and I'll spend lots of time on them below. The primary job of the back light, however, is to help contrast the subject from the background, which is demonstrated in **Figure 4-2.**

The image on the left has no backlighting, and you have a tough time distinguishing the subject's shoulders from the back wall. On the right, you see the lights reflecting off his leather jacket, which is subtle but creates the necessary contrast with the similarly colored back wall. Remember that compression reduces the detail and contrast in the image, which makes backlighting absolutely critical.

Figure 4-2
How backlighting (shown on the right) helps create contrast between the subject and back wall.

Not to preach, or beat a dead horse, but when shooting for streaming, don't ever ignore backlighting; it's probably the most frequent error I see in streaming video. You can choose not to use backlighting in certain circumstances, but always consider its use. Note that back lights are also called *rim lights* or *kickers*.

Keep the following thoughts in mind when selecting and setting up your back light:

- I typically use a hard light for backlighting (described below).
- The light intensity should be between 50–100% of the intensity of the stronger of the two front lights, and I typically use 50%. If you're using 1000-watt fixtures in front, for example, try 500 watts.
- When setting up the back light, make sure that it doesn't shine into the camera or create a light halo.
- Also, be sure that the back light is positioned far enough to the back that it doesn't shine on the subject's forehead.

Use Soft Lights

There are two types of light sources, hard and soft lights. Hard lights are generated by relatively small sources of lights that transmit directly to the subject, and include incandescent and halogen bulbs, and the sun (I know it's pretty big, but it is really far away). Hard lights create a very distinct, well-defined shadow, like that on the left in **Figure 4-3**.

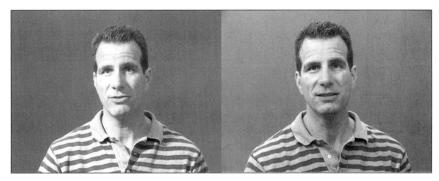

Figure 4-3
Hard lights on the left, soft lights on the right.

The problem with hard lights in the streaming scenario is that they create significant contrast between the lighter and darker regions in the image (like the right and left side of my face) and lots of lines and other detail, which combine to make it tougher for the codec to do its job. Hard lights are also tougher on the subject of the video, and can create that "deer in the headlights" look, and also are generally hotter.

Soft lights are more diffused, and light the scene without creating the same problems. You can buy or create soft lights in many ways, including:

- Buying fluorescent light fixtures, originally offered by Kino Flo incorporated, and now offered by most lighting vendors, including Lowel's excellent Caselite models. Fluorescent lights have the benefit of being much cooler than incandescent or halogen bulbs, but require a much greater area to create the same light intensity.

- You can soften hard lights by installing a "soft box" around the light, reflecting it off an umbrella or reflector, or even a white wall or piece of foam board. I've used Lowel's Rifa-Lite soft box with very good effect as described below.
- You can also soften hard lights by placing a scrim, gel or other diffusion material over the light source.

Have another look at **Figure 4-3**, and note that the left side of my face is darker than the right in both images; the distinction is just starker with hard lighting (on the left). This is the shadowed look I'll cover in the next section, which helps create depth and contouring in the face. For now, understand that you can use soft lights to create both shadowed and flat lighting, though most producers seeking flat lighting will use soft lights.

Overall, I recommend using soft lights over hard when shooting for streaming. As you'll see in the next section, I also recommend flat over shadowed lighting. I just wanted to be clear that they're not the same thing.

Use Flat Rather than Three-Point Lighting

Compare the lighting in **Figure 4-2** and **Figure 4-3**. In the first figure, both sides of the face are lit evenly; in **Figure 4-3**, shadows are evident on the left side of my face. These are the two techniques discussed in this section. Note that while both flat and shadowed lighting use three lights, lighting designed to create shadows is typically called *three-point lighting*, while lighting designed to avoid shadows is called *flat lighting*.

Note that three-point lighting originated as a way to create contrast on grainy black-and-white film and later black-and-white television. Shadows also help create mood, as in film noir pictures with detectives in fedoras with half-lit faces.

It's a killer look for film, but most streaming producers avoid it, as do most news, sports and entertainment producers on TV. Why? In the streaming environment, the shadows and contrast created by three-point lighting are very hard to compress at good quality, especially at low bit rates.

On TV news shows, anchors tend to move too much to sustain three-point lighting, which is challenging to maintain when the subject is turning around or standing up and sitting down. It's very challenging to produce three-point lighting when you have multiple subjects on the set, especially if they're located close together.

Also, three-point lighting requires intense hard lights like incandescent, which are harsh on the eyes and hot. For these reasons, most studios have switched to banks of softer fluorescent lights that light both sides of the face equally, producing overall flat lighting. In fact, in my survey of 13 news-oriented shows that post streaming video to the web, including CNN, CBS, ABC and ESPN, none used three-point lighting. Instead, all moved to entirely flat lighting.

One key reason almost certainly relates back to one of the original purposes of three-point lighting, to create mood. Unless your workplace is a lot more exciting than mine, creating mood probably isn't a goal in your streaming video, particularly for the Q3 earnings announcement or description of a new product offering.

Now there are some exceptions, most notably a series of streaming testimonials offered by Hewlett Packard you can see here:

http://www.hp.com/hpinfo/newsroom/feature_stories/video/

Check out the Digital Entertainment + HP video, in particular. However, they're all extraordinary from a streaming video perspective: 480×360 video at less than 300 kbps (Windows Media, not Flash) with excellent quality and interesting use of three-point lighting. Still, they're product testimonials, so mood lighting is appropriate, and it's mostly used in one-person interviews where conditions can be tightly controlled.

Other factors in the video quality include the large resolution, which provides the pixels necessary to display the contrast created by the shadows; at 240×180 resolution or below, these would look pretty silly. These videos also have a "done by professionals, don't try this at home" feel, and look like they were shot by professional HD camcorders. OK, I'm done drooling.

Overall, if you have video that would benefit from the shadows produced by three-point lighting, go for it, but keep in mind that flat lighting is much easier to produce and harder to mess up. For all other videos, I recommend using flat lighting.

Creating Shadows with Three-Point Lighting

The set-up for three-point lighting is shown in **Figure 4-4**. Generally, when your goal is to create distinct shadows, your three-point lighting set has three types of lights: key, fill and back.

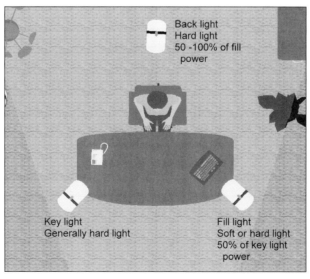

Figure 4-4
Lighting set-up for three-point lighting.

The key light is the strongest light, and generally should be a hard light, to ensure notice-able shadows, or a soft light placed close to the subject. When placing the key light, keep the following considerations in mind:

- Mind the *nose caret*, or the shadow made by the nose. Don't cross the nasola-bial fold, or the crease that runs from your nose to mouth. In **Figure 4-5**, the image on the left is almost directly in front of me, so the shadow is limited to the extreme left side of my face. Moving the light over to about 45° produced the image in the middle, where the nose caret is almost perfectly placed in the fold. On the extreme right, the lighting is too far to my right, and the nose caret extends beyond the fold.

- Also, adjust the height of the light so that the nose caret doesn't cross the lips.

Note that the subject is going to move, so you want to find a good "middle" positioning within that range of motion.

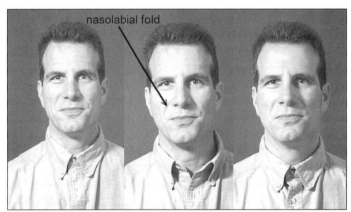

Figure 4-5
Don't cross the nasolabial fold.

The goal of the fill light is to soften the harsh shadows produced by the key light, particular-ly if the key is a hard light. It's positioned opposite the key light and is generally a soft light with about 50% of the power of the key light. If you have two lights of identical power, move the fill light back to weaken the light.

Again, the goal of the back light is to create contrast with the background and it is generally a hard light shined down on the subject at about 75°, at between 50–100% of the key light.

Creating Flat Lighting

There are multiple ways to create flat lighting. For example, many studios use banks of fluorescent lights to light all newscasters on the set equally and evenly.

Using a traditional three-point lighting system, you have two basic alternatives. The first is to use two key lights, as shown in **Figure 4-6**, along with the back light, of course. The second is to use a single soft light, positioned directly above the camera. In a recent shoot, I tried both approaches.

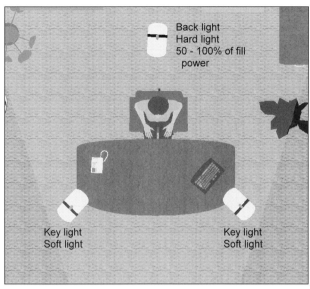

Figure 4-6
Creating flat lighting with two key lights.

Briefly, I was using a Lowel DV Creator 44 kit for the shoot, which includes four different lights. In the dual key setup, I used an Omni-light and Rifa-lite as my two keys. I used a 500-watt bulb in the Omni-light, faced it away from the subject and attached the umbrella to shine the soft light back at the subject. On the other side I used the Rifa-light soft box with a 250-watt lamp positioned much closer to the subject.

This is a fairly common scenario for producers who have traditionally used three-point lighting. Since you don't have two lights of equal power, you simply have to move the lights further or closer to the subject until their face is shadow free.

In the single key light setup, I used the Omni-light and umbrella directly behind the subject, positioned about 25° above the camera. I used a 150-watt clamp light as the back light for both shots, and shot both videos with a Canon XH A1 HDV camcorder in manual mode, with a shutter speed of 60, gain disabled and aperture adjusted as described below to eliminate the zebra pattern.

The results are shown in **Figure 4-7**, with the dual-key video on the left and single-key on the right.

The dual-key approach produced slightly more light to the sides of the face, and a bit less shadow under the chin, and is a touch darker, though I could have fixed that at the shoot by coming down one more f-stop. Overall, the images are very close; if you didn't know what to look for, you probably couldn't tell them apart.

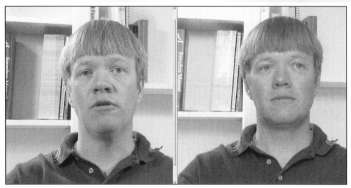

Figure 4-7
Flat light produced by dual keys on the left and single key behind the camera on the right.

During the shoot, the subject noted that the single key was a bit harder on the eyes, but bearable so long as he looked into the camera and not the lights. It did produce a glare over his right shoulder, which would have darkened the face had I been shooting in automatic mode.

On the other hand, the single-key shot is shadow free, eliminating shadows seen in the dual-key approach on the bookshelf and the small shadows from his collar under the neck. While shadows weren't a problem in this shoot, the single-key approach would be much, much simpler in situations where shadows are an issue, particularly when shooting for green screen in close quarters.

Overall, I like the dual-key lighting a bit better, but the single-key approach is worth a try when you only have one key light or when shadows are a problem. I will definitely try it on my next green-screen shoot.

Miscellaneous Deep Thoughts about Lighting

The writer in me just can't let go—there are some additional points that scream to be told. So here they are:

- Watch lighting on TV. I'm not saying that TV styles should dictate your work, but paying attention to lighting between the scores and news can illustrate the art of the possible. Once I noticed that lighting used by ESPN eliminated shadows under the nose and chin, I immediately dropped the height of my lights.

- Mind your color temperatures. This is a chapter all to itself, but the bottom line is: don't mix incandescent (which are yellowish in tint) and fluorescent lights (which are generally bluish). Or sunlight and either of them. Your camera won't know which color to white balance to, and white will appear off tint in one section of the image or the other.

- You can't spend enough time setting up lighting. Usually, you'll know if audio is working or not within minutes, but lighting takes a lot longer to get right. So budget your time accordingly.

- Nobody gets it perfect (and few people other than other videographers ever notice). This is kind of a Chicken Soup for the Videographer's Soul corollary to the previous point. Spend the time to set up the lights, make sure there's sufficient light for the shoot (next section), and learn but don't obsess about the results. You never will be perfect, and in most instances, no one will notice.

Now let's move on to checking exposure on the set to ensure adequate lighting.

Checking Exposure on the Set

The most accurate technique for checking light is to use a standalone waveform monitor, a piece of test equipment that accepts an outbound signal from your camcorder and graphically displays the brightness of the signal. Many users don't have this equipment, so let's address some alternatives.

First, let's set the stage a bit. When shooting for streaming, you should use manual exposure settings; otherwise, your camcorder may boost the gain when you're not looking and introduce noise you could have avoided by adding light or adjusting your manual settings.

As you probably know, the two controls that impact how much light gets into the lens are aperture and shutter speed. Aperture is the diameter of the lens, which is controlled by an "iris" and measured in f-stops. Paradoxically, the smaller the f-stop, the larger the opening and the more light that gets through the lens.

Shutter speed controls how long the shutter stays open for each frame. The longer the shutter stays open, the more light gets to the video, but this also introduces the potential that motion will blur the frame. Faster shutter speeds reduce blurriness, but also limit the amount of light that gets into the video. To limit your variables, in most instances, you'll want to set the shutter speed at around 60 (1/60th of a second), then adjust the aperture until the video is properly exposed.

That said, what does "properly exposed" mean? Basically, you want your scene and subject lit as fully as possible without exceeding the brightness that your camera can capture. **Figure 4-8** shows what I mean, but there's a lot there, so let me explain.

The video on the upper right is Gary, a videographer buddy here in Galax. On the upper left is a video of the LCD viewfinder of the FX1 I used to shoot Gary. On the bottom is a YC Waveform scope in Premiere Pro, showing the brightness levels of the video on the upper right.

On the left of the YC Waveform is a vertical scale from roughly –20 to 120, in IRE, which stands for Institute of Radio Engineers. IRE is a measure of brightness, and the waveform in the scope represents the brightness of the video of Gary on the upper right. Note that while DV camcorders and computer monitors can display brightness in excess of 100 IRE, most TVs can't.

If your video has regions above 100 IRE (or below 7.5 IRE, which is the floor for television sets), these regions get "crushed," which means that the detail becomes lost. At one level, properly exposed means that your video is lit so that no region is over 100 or under 7.5.

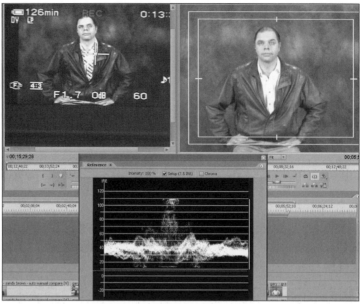

Figure 4-8
A screen from Premiere Pro, showing a video (upper right), a video of that video (upper left), and the YC Waveform scope, which measures brightness in the scene.

It also means that you have a broad spread of exposure so that the brightest regions approach 100 IRE and the darkest regions approach 7.5. For example, in **Figure 4-9**, the brightest region of this video is around 88 IRE, so whites in the video would probably look a bit dull, or lacking in "contrast." If you had a waveform monitor at your shoot, you could either boost lighting or increase the aperture by lowering the f-stop to let more light in. In post, you could fix this by adjusting brightness or contrast, but you'd always prefer to get the lighting right to start with.

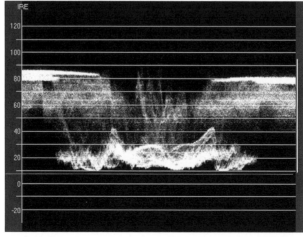

Figure 4-9
A YC Waveform of a video that lacks "contrast" since it doesn't approach 100 IRE at the top.

If you don't have a scope, how can your camera help you assess the brightness of your video? Go back to **Figure 4-8** for a moment. You'll notice in the YC Waveform scope that the brightness of the video goes up to about 110 IRE. If you look carefully at the video on the upper left, you'll notice stripes in Gary's shirt that you don't see on the right. These are "zebra stripes" inserted by the camera to indicate regions that equal or exceed 100 IRE.

From this information, you could reasonably conclude that with the current lighting and f-stop (F1.7 as you can see on the upper left), Gary's shirt is overexposed, so detail in the shirt will get "crushed" and lost. During the shoot, you could adjust to a higher f-stop (and reduce the aperture) to reduce the light on Gary's shirt and eliminate the overexposure. This progression is shown in **Figure 4-10**.

Figure 4-10
Using the Zebra stripes to direct f-stop adjustments.

With an f-stop of 1.7, Gary's shirt is full of zebra stripes. At 2.4, many are gone; at 2.8 almost all are gone. One or two more stops and exposure would be about optimum. On the other hand, notice how Gary's face keeps getting darker and darker as the f-stops increase, perhaps reaching the optimal level in the middle image and almost certainly too dark on the right.

This is why you should advise your subjects to wear clothing darker than their skin tones. When the shirt is too bright, you risk overexposing the shirt to get adequate exposure on the face. Overexposing the shirt isn't a big deal if you only see a little triangle, as in **Figure 4-8** (and with most folks wearing suits and ties), but doesn't look good at all if the shirt loses all detail.

Here are some additional thoughts on setting exposure. First, most cameras allow you to configure the IRE level marked by the zebra stripes, with many switching between 70 IRE, the level of a Caucasian face at optimum brightness, and 100. I prefer working with 100, but you can make your own decision; just remember to check what IRE level your zebra stripes are set for before adjusting your aperture.

Second, it's always better to be a little underexposed than overexposed. Once regions in your video are over 100 IRE, the detail is irrevocably lost. If your video is a bit underexposed, you can simply boost brightness in post.

Third, if you can't afford a standalone YC Waveform, there are several less expensive workarounds. For example, Serious Magic's DV Rack is a software program that contains a suite of audio and video scopes, including the YC Waveform. Before shooting, you can connect your camcorder to your computer via FireWire, and assess your lighting and contrast (*www.seriousmagic.com*).

Another option is to bring a computer with Adobe Premiere Pro or a similar program to the shoot, capture some video and use the YC Waveform to assess your lighting. Most of these programs can capture a live feed from your camcorder, simplifying the task.

Fourth, automatic exposure controls of most camcorders are very sophisticated, and provide a valuable check of your manual settings. After I derive my optimum manual settings, I'll toggle back and forth between auto and manual modes to see how the video compares. If there's a huge difference in lighting or color, it's a sign that I need to review my white balance and exposure settings to ensure the best possible video.

Lighting for Chroma Key

Many producers use chroma-key techniques to place their subjects in virtual sets, a valuable creative technique. Fortunately, now that you know the basics, lighting for chroma key is fairly simple, with just a few key points.

First, light the subject and the background separately. With the background, your goal is to produce even lighting over the expanse of background exposed in the video frame. This makes it easier for the chroma-key filter to do its work, resulting in a cleaner chroma key. To accomplish this, use soft lighting, which is inherently more even than hard lights, and will hide rather than bring out the detail. Most pros use fluorescent lights for this, though I've produced good results by using diffusion filters over halogen lights.

You can use any of the lighting techniques discussed previously on the main subject, taking care that the lighting matches the intended background. When lighting the subject, however, be sure that no shadows from the subject fall on the background, which will make a clean chroma key near impossible.

Generally, in a cramped setting, this means moving close enough to the wall so that the shadow is obscured behind the subject. When working in a larger setting, this means moving the subject far enough away from the background so that shadows fall on the ground. As mentioned, if shadows are a problem, try the single-key approach for lighting your subject, which might make life simpler in either scenario.

That's it. If you're interested in an inexpensive homegrown set-up, check out Keith S. Kolbo's excellent article "Tight Budget Lighting for Chroma Key," *http://www.digitalpostproduction.com/ articles/viewarticle.jsp?id=31427*. John Jackman has two articles on the subject you can find at his website, here: *http://www.johnjackman.com/index.php?id=13*.

Conclusion

In this chapter you learned when to use shadowed and flat lighting and how to set up lights to produce either effect. You also learned how to use a camera's zebra-striping feature to make sure there's enough light on the scene.

In the next chapter, we'll focus on camera work, from choosing the proper framing for the subject to using the optimal camera settings.

CHAPTER 5

Streaming-Related Shooting Skills

Most shot composition and shooting rules of thumb (thumb rules?) were established for film or TV, where the viewing window is much larger than the 320×240 or so used for streaming video. So, while some still apply to streaming, you also need to factor the small viewing windows into some of your decisions.

All that said, this chapter is more for novices than shooting pros, and covers many of the basics, like the rule of thirds, that make video "good video." For this reason, I'll try to highlight the key areas where streaming differs from TV/film to make the chapter more scan-able for pros.

I'll start with a few simple rules on minimizing camera motion, which are critical to high-quality streaming. Then I'll discuss the title safe zone and how it applies (or more accurately, doesn't apply) to streaming video. After that, I'll identify the various shots used in streaming (medium shot, close-up, etc.) and describe how to customize these according to the display resolution of your Flash video.

Next, I'll detail the rule of thirds, which is identical for streaming and other productions, so experienced pros can skip this section. The penultimate section will suggest camera settings to use for optimal streaming quality, and I'll conclude with a description on how to produce a blurry background, which is a great technique for improving the compressibility of your videos.

After reading this chapter, you will know how to:

- Minimize camera motion during shooting
- Choose the framing of shots to match your streaming resolution
- Employ rule-of-thirds positioning in your shots
- Choose and fine tune camera settings for your streaming shoot
- Soften the background via camera aperture controls.

Sound good? Let's get started.

Minimize Motion during Shooting

In case you were sleeping in the class while reading Chapter 2, I'll repeat some of the rec- ommendations I made there with a figure or two. Most important is to eliminate extraneous motion in all your shoots. By far the easiest way to accomplish this is to use a tripod or other stabilizing device, though I'm guessing you do that already.

Number 2 is to limit zooms and pans during shooting. Even a slow zoom or pan updates virtually every pixel in the frame every frame, which doesn't look like much motion to you, but looks like a roller coaster ride to the codec. **Figure 5-1** illustrates this point.

On the left, I'm zooming into the subject and the blockiness is evident. On the right, I've completed the zoom and the image is stable, and the frame looks a lot better.

Figure 5-1
Even slow zooms stress the codec, producing blockiness that disappears once the image stabilizes.

If you need a wide shot to establish the scene, then you want to shift to a medium shot for the bulk of the interview; either use two cameras or cut from the wide shot to the close-up.

Another common mistake is to use moving backgrounds, which also complicate the codec's work with lots of extraneous, non-subject-related motion. You should also avoid animated logos and other moving screen do-dads.

Of course, as discussed more fully in Chapter 2, if you stream at high bit rates—say over 500 kbps or so—you can take the gloves off and increase the motion in the scene. For example, videos at BusinessWeek Online look great despite using a moving background, zooming into the anchors at the start of each segment and deploying an animated logo in the bottom right-hand corner (**Figure 5-2**). And they produce at 400×300 resolution, which is fairly aggressive for Internet-based streaming.

There's no way to easily tell what bit rate BusinessWeek uses, but I'm guessing it's some- where north of 500–600 kbps. If you have that luxury, you can experiment by introducing limited amounts of motion into the scene.

Figure 5-2
High data rate cures all high-motion ills, as seen in this clip from BusinessWeek.com.

While we're here, take another look at the BusinessWeek image. You'll note that it uses flat lighting, as discussed in Chapter 4, as there are no shadows on either anchor's face. In addition, note that both anchors are shown from the waist up with their eyes at about the top third of the screen. More on both of these observations below.

Ignore the Safe Zone

Most television sets eliminate the outer 10–15% of the video file as overscan, so the viewer never sees it. That's why editors like Premiere Pro have options to display the "title-safe zone," which is the inner square in **Figure 5-3**, and "action-safe zone," which is the outer square.

Figure 5-3
The inner square is the title-safe zone, while the outer square is the action-safe zone.

When shooting for television display, the outer edges of the pixels on your camcorder's viewfinder may not appear in the TV, so you have to shoot a bit wider to make sure you don't inadvertently cut out the bass player or the left side of the congressman's aide. Conversely, computer monitors display every pixel, so you can frame more closely.

Just to close the loop, when inserting titles and other graphics in your editor, you typically position them inside the inner box, which is called the title-safe zone. This is 20% from the edge of the video, and represents an area displayed by virtually all television sets. The action-safe zone is 10% from the edge, which is viewable on most but not all television sets.

Framing Your Shots

Even if you've never picked up a video camera, you're probably familiar with terms like close-up, long shot and the like. To most of us, these terms sound general rather than specific.

As with many things, however, these terms actually have precise definitions, and for good reason. When a film director tells the camera person to zoom in for a close-up, he needs the camera to capture the neck and complete head, as opposed to an extreme close-up, which captures only the chin to forehead. This is because in the film world, each shot has a specific use, and when the director wants a close-up, he needs a close-up to achieve that particular effect.

In addition, film and television producers want consistency from shot to shot. For example, when a TV producer tells her camera person to zoom into a medium shot from the left, it should have the same framing as the medium shot she's cutting from on the right; otherwise, the cut looks awkward.

Let's review the shots and their intended use, and then apply them to streaming. I'm assuming that most readers want to present business-oriented shots like training, testimonials, or interviews and will demonstrate the shots most appropriate for these productions, rather than soap operas, dramas or other types of productions.

- **Extreme (or extra) long shot** – generally shows enough of the scene to allow the viewer to understand where the action is taking place.

  Some producers, particularly in sports, break this category into "very long," which might be the standard sideline view of of a football game (or complete stage view of a concert), and "extreme long," which might be a view from the blimp (or a view from the back of the hall in a concert, showing attendees and performers). Since they often vary by type of production, these definitions are less precise than those that follow.

- **Long shot** – shows the entire body of the subject from head to toe, usually used to place the subject in the scene.

- **Medium shot** – generally shows the subject from the waist up, which is great for capturing arm and hand gestures (**Figure 5-4**).

Figure 5-4
A medium shot of host John Dvorak from Cranky Geeks.

- **Medium close-up** – shows the complete head down to the lower chest. This is an intimate shot, great for interviews, case studies and other close interpersonal discussions, but perhaps not for discussing a new expense report policy or the features and benefits of the new widget (**Figure 5-5**).

Figure 5-5
A medium close-up of Angelina Jolie on the Larry King show. Most shots on this show are medium close-ups.

- **Close-up** – shows the complete head down to the upper chest (**Figure 5-6**). This is generally the closest shot you'll see in a business setting, and is useful when the subject is discussing meaningful, personal topics, rather than business-oriented topics.

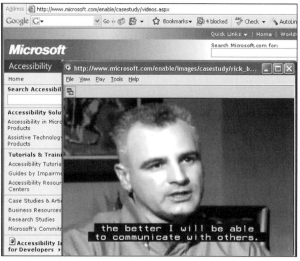

Figure 5-6
A close-up from a Microsoft case study.

- **Big or extreme close-up** – shows chin to forehead in a very intimate shot that really focuses your attention on the subject. In most instances, these attention-getting shots are used to focus the viewer on the emotions of the subject. In **Figure 5-7**, however, the president of PepsiCo is discussing the beneficial

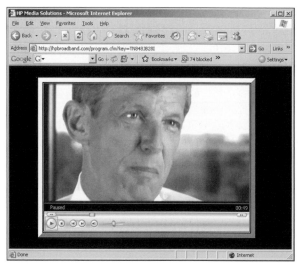

Figure 5-7
An extreme close-up from an HP case study.

effects of a new HP video conferencing system—hardly Oprah-type stuff. Yet the producer chose this extreme close-up and in the context of this video, which you can see at *http://hpbroadband.com/program.cfm?key=TN848JB28I*, this approach works well. Interestingly, at 480×270 resolution, this is a fairly high-resolution video, which doesn't need the extreme close-up to see the executive's face; clearly it was an artistic decision.

These are the general shots at your disposal. Now let's discuss how to use them in streaming productions.

Shot Usage—Sequencing

Most producers start with extreme long shots as "establishing" shots that help the viewer understand the surroundings of the shot. Then they switch to a long or medium shot on the subject, to establish the subject in the scene, then switch to medium close-ups or close-ups for effect.

For example, virtually all videos on BusinessWeek Online start with an extreme long shot of the set, then zoom into medium shots of both anchors. Then, in an interview setting, the producer shifts to a medium close-up or close-up of the multiple subjects. This sequence is near universal in interviews, case studies and most business presentations.

The big question here, of course, is how much this sequence should change when shooting for relatively low-resolution streaming. The surprising answer is not all that much.

Shooting for the Small Screen

When shooting for the small screen, the knee-jerk reaction is to frame as tightly as possible. Sounds great, but the only research available on the subject seems to indicate that viewers prefer the "best" shot over a closer shot. I'll explain.

In "How Low Can You Go? The Effect of Low Resolutions on Shot Types in Mobile TV," authors Hendrick Knoche, John McCarth and M. Angela Sasse studied shot preference for news, sports, music video and claymation videos for low-resolution display, ranging from 120×90 to 240×180 (*http://www.cs.ucl.ac.uk/staff/H.Knoche/publications.htm*).

As you would expect, the authors found that user satisfaction increased with resolution and data rate. On the other hand, when watching news videos, viewers preferred medium shots over medium close-up shots at every viewing resolution. As part of their conclusion, the authors recommended not substituting medium close-ups for medium shots, because the latter shows more "body language" and proved more acceptable to viewers.

In music videos, viewers found medium shots the least preferable and the very long shot most preferable, which the authors stated they could not explain. In the sports videos, which involved soccer matches, the results varied by resolution. At 240×180 resolution, viewer satisfaction peaked for the medium shot, decreasing slightly for long shots, and increasing with very long and extra long shots.

This makes sense, because the extra long shot is the only one that reveals the true fluid dynamics of the game—all others are simply too close. At 240×180 resolution, the participants clearly saw enough detail to meaningfully comprehend what was going on. At all smaller resolutions, viewers were most dissatisfied with the extra long shot, which is also understandable since the resolutions were too small to see the players or the ball.

Also worth considering is that many of ESPN.com's highlights consist of content shot for television display and encoded at 440×330 resolution, at between 400–600 kbps. Obviously, depending upon the sport, these videos contain lots of extra long shots, and since ESPN is far and away the most popular sports site on the net, it appears that few viewers are complaining.

Here's my take. Most sites producing Flash content encode at 320×240 resolution or higher, which is larger than the 240×180 maximum used in the Knoche study. Many sites utilize Flash players that allow viewers to double or zoom the video to full screen. This should be plenty of screen real estate for any type of shot to work effectively.

Accordingly, when making your shot selections, forget about the fact that you're shooting for streaming, and choose the best shot for the effect you're trying to create. Don't use an extreme close-up when the situation cries for a medium shot. Instead, focus your attentions on maximizing the compressed quality of the selected shot by choosing the right background, lighting the scene sufficiently and using the optimal camera settings.

In addition to type of shot, Knoche and his collaborators take a rigorous look at how resolution and data rate impact the perceived quality of streaming video, a topic that we'll revisit in the next chapter. Knoche is a Ph.D student at the University College London studying the quality requirements in mobile multimedia, which isn't a direct match, but is as close as I could find to streaming. The link above is to his page at the university, which contains copies of his various publications and workshops. It's generally dense reading, but both interesting and useful.

Using Rule-of-Thirds Positioning

Let's briefly cover the rule-of-thirds positioning, which is illustrated in **Figure 5-8**. The rule of thirds divides the image into nine pieces like a tic-tac-toe board, with four intersecting points around the center of the frame, called *saddle points*.

Figure 5-8
Two applications of the rule of thirds.

5. Streaming-Related Shooting Skills

When the subject is facing the camera (me, on the left), ignore the saddle points and frame the subject in the center of the image, with eyes at about the top third of the frame. The subject is, in essence, talking to the viewer, and needs to be centered in the frame.

When the subject is speaking to an interviewer, and isn't directly facing the camera, frame them in one of the saddle points, as shown on the right. Always position the viewer in the back of the frame, with the open space (called *look room*) in the direction they are facing. If the subject is moving, you again position them in the back third of the frame, leaving what's called *lead room* in the other two-thirds of the frame.

If you scan the figures deployed so far in this chapter, which are all static shots, you'll notice that most adhere to the rule of thirds. The exceptions are **Figure 5-1**, where I truncated each frame to fit the figure, and **Figure 5-5**. Personally, if I had a camera on Angelina Jolie, the last thing I'd be thinking about is the rule of thirds, so that's perfectly understandable.

Have any doubts? Have a look at the network news, CNN or ESPN over the next few days, and you'll be surprised you never noticed it before. Now that you know how to position and frame the subject, let's move onto the optimal camera settings.

Camera Settings for Optimum Quality

While camera quality certainly contributes to overall video quality, you don't need an awesome camera to produce awesome streaming quality. For example, one of our case studies describes a producer still using the Sony VX1000 camcorder, literally the first 3-CCD DV camcorder available in the States, for many of his shoots (see the case study in Chapter 19).

Whatever camera you use, however, you'll optimize results if you use the proper settings, which is what I'll cover in this section.

Adjust Lighting Controls Manually

I describe how to manually check for and adjust for lighting conditions in Chapter 4. The Cliff Notes version is to disable automatic gain control and set gain to zero, set your shutter speed to 60 (1/60th of a second) and use aperture controls to control exposure.

Tools you can use for this task include zebra stripes on your camcorder or a standalone waveform monitor. You can also capture video to an editor like Final Cut Pro or Premiere Pro and use their waveform monitor scopes to assess brightness and contrast.

Disable Image Stabilization While Shooting from a Tripod

Image stabilization compensates for slight hand shakes during shooting. When shooting from a tripod, these hand shakes don't occur, and cameras can confuse subject motion with small shakes and attempt to compensate, causing the image to shift slightly.

Older camcorders with digital image stabilization may also reduce image resolution slightly with stabilization enabled. For these reasons, whether old camcorder or new, you should disable image stabilization when shooting from a tripod.

Use Manual Focus

I'm a gigantic fan of autofocus and couldn't live without it when shooting most events. However, when shooting interviews, for streaming or otherwise, I almost always shift into manual focus. The reason is simple and relates to the rule-of-thirds positioning, especially when the subject isn't facing the camera as shown on the right in **Figure 5-8**.

Specifically, cameras focus on objects in the middle of the frame. If your subject is in the upper right saddle point, he or she might still be the dominant object in the frame, and focus might be acceptable. If they lean back to reflect upon a question, they're largely out of the picture and the camera will start to hunt for something else to focus on, usually the back wall.

While the camera hunts for something to focus on, the image gets really blurry, which looks unprofessional, and introduces mega interframe changes for the codec to encode, which can cause blockiness and other artifacts.

Remember that zooming doesn't affect camera focus, so as long as the subject and/or camera don't move, you don't lose focus by changing shots. Accordingly, you can zoom into the subject to get the optimal focus, then zoom back out for a long or medium shot without changing the focus. Many camcorders also have a "push autofocus" feature that lets you engage the autofocus mechanism momentarily while in manual focus mode.

Shoot Progressive Video When Available

One of the more technically interesting debates about shooting for streaming is whether shooting in progressive mode will produce better quality than shooting in interlaced mode. My research here is limited, but it shows that while you may achieve a small improvement in quality by shooting in progressive mode, the difference over shooting in interlaced mode won't be earth shaking. That's because most video editing programs have gotten so proficient at deinterlacing that the final output comes very close to actual progressive quality.

If you're new to the entire progressive vs. interlaced discussion, let me explain. As you probably know, most video is interlaced, with each frame comprised of two fields, one containing the odd lines (1,3,5) and the other containing the even lines (2, 4, 6). For NTSC video, which displays roughly 60 fields per second, these fields are actually shot 1/60 of a second apart. In contrast, progressive cameras capture complete frames from top to bottom, about 30 per second in NTSC.

In contrast, Flash is frame based, so when producing Flash video from an interlaced source, your encoding tool has to create one frame from the two fields shot 1/60 of a second apart. This can get ugly without an interpolation method called *deinterlacing* that removes the motion-related artifacts from the video (**Figure 5-9**).

The figure shows a Druze woman spinning a pita over a stove. As you study the top figure, you'll notice little lines of data that look like mini-Venetian blinds, and that the pita has two edges separated by a few pixels in the image.

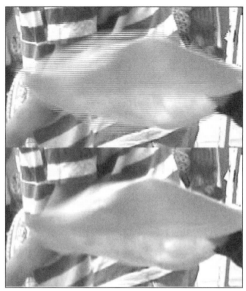

Figure 5-9
Deinterlacing at work. The original frame is on top, the deinterlaced frame on the bottom.

The left edge of the pita is where the video was for one field, the right edge where it was for the other, and the lines show where the two fields don't match up because they were shot at different times. However, in the bottom image, you'll notice that the lines are gone and the entire frame looks smoother. This is deinterlacing at work.

Let's see how this worked in some real-world testing. On the left is video shot with the Canon XL H1 in interlaced mode, but deinterlaced prior to compressing into the Flash video format. In the middle is the XL H1 footage before deinterlacing. On the right is video shot with the JVC GY-HD100 in progressive mode. All videos were encoded into identical parameters using the Flix Pro encoder.

Figure 5-10
Here we see that software deinterlacing (on the left) comes very close to approximating the look of progressive video (on the right).

These results show very little difference between the progressive and interlaced video after deinterlacing; in fact, the monopod I'm spinning looks a bit sharper on the left, even though the middle image reveals a moderate distance between the fields. Again, the software deinterlacing capabilities of encoding tools like Flix Pro are so advanced that they come close to matching that delivered by shooting in progressive.

On the other hand, several producers that I've spoken with on this topic point out that deinterlacing is slow and processor-intensive, and taking it out of the workflow saves time. Others in the know have reported much better results when shooting in progressive mode.

At least part of that, in my view, is that a brand-new progressive-capable camcorder is probably just a better camcorder than the three-year-old interlaced model it replaced, with a better lens and perhaps larger and more sophisticated CCDs (charge-coupled devices that convert the incoming information from the lens into usable data). After all, it's not surprising that a brand-new camcorder delivers better quality than an older camcorder.

No matter, the debate continues. The bottom line, for me, is that if I had a camcorder with progressive capabilities, I would shoot in progressive when shooting for streaming. I wouldn't go out and buy a new camcorder just for that feature, and I certainly wouldn't tell a client (or boss) that buying a new camcorder would produce dramatically better results.

Producing a Soft Background

Have a look at the picture in Figure 5-11. As you can see, the picture is well focused on the face, but out of focus on the seats, which is both aesthetically pleasing and a great technique for improving the compressed quality of your streaming video. Streaming video producers commonly use this technique, and here's how you achieve it.

Figure 5-11
Well focused on the face, but out of focus on the seats. Here's how.

1. First, move the subject as far from the background as possible.

2. Then, move your camcorder as far from the subject as possible and use zoom controls to adjust framing.

3. Third, understand that you can't create this effect in all situations with all camcorders. Essentially, this effect exploits a camera's depth of field, which is the area in the image that is in focus. When it comes to depth of field, shallow is good and long is bad.

   Specifically, a shallow depth of field means that the region in the scene that's in focus is very small, which is the look we're trying to achieve. A long depth of field means that more of the scene is in focus. In **Figure 5-11**, the frame has a relatively shallow depth of field, compared to say, the frame in **Figure 5-2**, which stays in focus throughout the image.

   Unfortunately, depth of field relates almost entirely to the size of the CCDs in your camcorder. In TV and film, producers use car-engine-sized cameras with 2/3" to 1" CCDs that achieve a very shallow depth of field, allowing them to focus on one subject while those two feet to their front or back are blurry.

   I shot **Figure 5-11** with the excellent Canon XH A1 camcorder with 1/3" CCDs, and had to position the subject about 50 feet from the camcorder and about 100 feet from the seats to produce this effect.

   For more on CCD size and depth of field, check out *http://www.mediachance.com/ dvdlab/dof/index.htm.*

4. To produce the shallowest depth of field, the camera's aperture needs to be open as wide as possible.

Indoors, you can support a lower f-stop by reducing the intensity of your lights or moving them further from the subject. Outside, of course, you can turn on your ND filters to reduce light coming into the camera. In addition to the manual mode that I used, note that many cameras have "aperture priority" modes that allow you to dial in the necessary f-stop, and will adjust other parameters, usually shutter speed, to achieve optimal exposure.

Conclusion

We covered lots of ground here, but you'll find value in these lessons in all your shoots, not just those for streaming. In the next chapter, we'll focus on optimizing audio and video quality before encoding, which are invaluable skills when producing Flash video.

CHAPTER 6

Correcting Video and Audio Problems

As hard as we try to get things right during shooting, usually there will be some (hopefully) minor video and audio corrections to make before encoding. This chapter covers the highlights, the common adjustments you'll likely have to make to optimize your encoding results.

If you're an experienced editor, you probably know this material, since these corrections are similar to those you would make for other projects not bound for streaming. On the other hand, if you're relatively new to video production, you may find one or two of these adjustments manna from heaven, a fix for a previously unsolvable problem. I hope so; they've certainly saved many of my projects over the years.

As with many things in streaming, unknown topics that seem intimidating at first (waveform monitor? normalization?) quickly transform into intriguing and then essential tools, with a simple introduction and demonstration. That's what I hope to accomplish here. Specifically, in this chapter, you will learn:

- How to use a waveform monitor to adjust the brightness and contrast of your videos
- How to use color correction to adjust aberrant color and improper white balancing
- How to correct backlit video
- On the audio side, how to remove transient and persistent noises from your audio
- How to use normalization to adjust the volume of your recordings
- How to use compression to boost the legibility of your vocals.

Let's get started.

Introducing the Waveform Monitor

The first thing I do after dragging video to the timeline is to check its values in a waveform monitor. It's become reflexive, almost instinctual, and you'll quickly find it very habit forming. **Figure 6-1** shows Premiere Pro's YC Waveform scope.

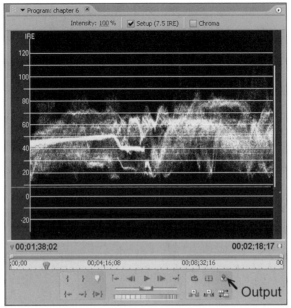

Figure 6-1
The Premiere Pro's waveform monitor.

Briefly, the waveform monitor details the brightness of the pixels in the frame, measured in IRE (for the Institute of Radio Engineers). To be "broadcast legal," the whitest white in the frame can't be higher than 100 IRE, while the darkest dark can't be lower than 7.5 IRE, as signals beyond these levels could interfere with other components of the broadcast stream.

When producing streaming video, the detail will be lost in any whites or blacks that exceed their respective levels. On the other hand, if the brightness values for the image aren't spread across the entire range of legal luminance values, the image lacks "contrast." This is the case in **Figure 6-1**, where the highest signal peaks at about 90 IRE and the lowest at about 15. More on how to fix this in "Adjusting Brightness and Contrast." First, let's learn how to open these scopes in Premiere Pro and Final Cut Pro.

Opening a Waveform Monitor

In Final Cut Pro, choose Tools > Video Scopes and then choose the Waveform monitor in the Layout drop-down list in the Tool Bench. Final Cut Pro opens the waveform scope in a separate window, so you can see both the video and the waveform while making your adjustments.

In Premiere Pro, you can open the YC Waveform scope in the Program Monitor (or more generically, the preview window) by clicking the Output button (the last button to the right in the top row of playback controls beneath the timeline) and choosing YC Waveform. Premiere Pro can show both chroma (color) and luminance values (brightness); hence the YC Waveform designation. I find the color values distracting, so I deselect the Chroma checkbox atop the panel, leaving only the luminance values.

However, when you view the Waveform scope in the Program Monitor, you can't see the video. A better approach is to open a new "Reference Monitor" and then open the scope in that monitor.

Figure 6-2
Opening a Reference Monitor in Premiere Pro.

Here's how to open a separate Reference Monitor and display the YC Waveform:

1. Click Program Monitor's panel menu icon (the little triangle on the top right) and choose New Reference Monitor. Premiere Pro opens a second monitor showing the video on the timeline (**Figure 6-2**).

2. To open the YC Waveform in Premiere Pro, click the Output button (the last button to the right in the playback controls beneath the timeline) and choose YC Waveform.

3. Once open, you can move the Reference Monitor to any location in the interface, either docking the panel or keeping it as a floating window. I usually drop it right below the Program Monitor so I can adjust effects and easily see both the video and selected scope.

Adjusting Brightness and Contrast

Once the waveform scope is open, drag the Brightness and Contrast effect from either program onto the target clip, and adjust the values until the signal is spread from 7.5 to 100.

This is shown in **Figure 6-3**. More specifically, adjust brightness to move the mass of pixels up and down the IRE scale, and adjust Contrast to spread the pixels out or shift them closer together. For example, if you compare **Figure 6-1** to **Figure 6-3**, you'll notice that the latter figure has both brighter pixels and is more spread out, indicating greater contrast.

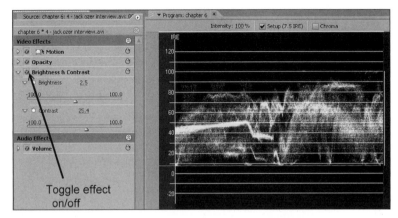

Figure 6-3
Using the Brightness and Contrast filter to expand contrast and brighten the image.

Author's Tip

Viewing Reality

Most of us assume that the brightness and colors of our computer monitor represents reality, the perfect shade, the perfect tone, yet it seldom does. Before starting serious brightness and color correction, calibrate your monitor by adjusting the color and brightness controls found in the Display Properties window (Windows) or System Preferences panel (Macintosh). If you have Photoshop installed on your Windows computer, you likely have a copy of Adobe's calibration utility (called Gamma) in your Control Panel (Windows), while you can use the Calibration utility on your Mac (in the Display panel).

Or you can use third-party tools from companies like ColorVision. If you Google "monitor color calibration" you'll find millions of listings, with the About.com treatment a good place to start. At the very least, after adjusting the brightness and color of a clip, encode a short section and view it on another computer or two. If it looks good on those computers, you can feel more secure about applying the effect to multiple clips.

While the waveform monitor will get you close, fine-tune your image by toggling the effect on and off to gauge the adjustment. In Premiere Pro, you toggle the effect on and off by clicking the little italic *F* next to the filter; with Final Cut Pro you do the same by clicking the checkbox shown in **Figure 6-5**.

It's Not Always Black and White

Most video frames have some pixels that are white and some that are black, in which case the waveform monitor works exceptionally well. However, if there are no black and/or white pixels in the frame, you definitely don't want to increase contrast until the luminance values spread from 7.5 to 100 IRE, since this will distort the image. For example, in a sepia image, there are no whites, so adjusting brightness until you have pixels at 100 IRE will make the video overly bright.

Figure 6-4 shows a visual example of this using Premiere Pro's Levels tool, an alternative to Premiere's Brightness and Contrast effect.

The graph is a histogram that shows the spread of the luminance values in the frame, from black (on the left) to white (on the right). As you can see, there are no pixels at the extreme left or extreme right of the histogram. This could either indicate that there are no extreme blacks or whites in the frame, or that the video lacks contrast.

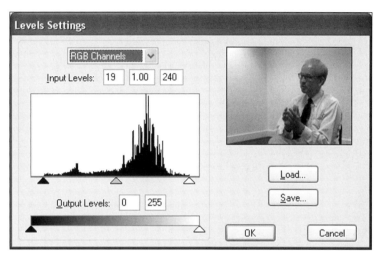

Figure 6-4
Adjusting brightness and contrast with Premiere Pro's Levels effect.

To adjust contrast using this tool, you drag the white triangle on the bottom right of the histogram to the left until it reaches the first pixels, representing the brightest pixels in the frame. Then you drag the black triangle to the right until it reaches the first black pixels.

This process is called *bracketing*, and it tells Premiere Pro to set the lightest pixels in the frame to 100 IRE, and the darkest to 7.5. Again, this works wonderfully if the pixels are actually white and black, but distorts the image if the lightest pixel is actually beige and the darkest navy blue.

One way around this is to shoot some footage at the start of your video that includes a white balance card and some black objects, which guarantees you have both black and

Author's Tip

Applying Effects to Multiple Clips
Once you adjust one clip to perfection, how do you apply that effect to other clips? With Final Cut Pro, you can drag any filter to the Favorites folder in your Effects tab, and then drag it onto any other clip. You can do the same in Premiere Pro by right clicking the applied effect and choosing Save Preset, which places the filter with the current values in the Presets folder in the Effects panel.

Both programs also let you copy and then "Paste Attributes" like filters and other effects. Finally, several of Final Cut Pro's color-related effects have buttons at the top of the Effects panel that let you copy the effect to clips located before and after the clip you're adjusting.

white pixels in the frame. Otherwise, while the waveform is a great tool, you still have to trust your eyeballs.

As I mentioned above, it's good practice to study the waveform monitor for all video included in your project—it's amazing how often you miss video that's lacking in contrast, or less bright than it should be. Adjusting this and exposing the entire range of brightness to the Flash encoder can often make the difference between dull video and footage that seems to jump off the screen.

Color Correcting Your Footage

Let me say this up front. Color correction tools are often clumsy and subjective and far less automatic than you assume they would be in 2007 and beyond. While you can usually *improve* your video substantially in just a few minutes, it can take hours and even days to *perfect* your videos. There are multiple books and DVDs that detail how to color correct your videos, so all I hope to do here is to introduce you to the color-correction tools in Final Cut Pro and Premiere Pro. Let's start with Final Cut Pro.

Final Cut Pro's Color Corrector

Final Cut Pro has several color-correction tools, most notably the Color Corrector and Color Corrector 3-Way. I find the former much more intuitive and equally effective in most instances, so will demonstrate the Color Corrector. I recommend using the 3-way tool only if you can't produce good results with the Color Corrector.

Since the Color Corrector effect has color, brightness and contrast adjustments, you can use it for total image correction, skipping the separate brightness and contrast adjustment described above. Read through the materials on the waveform monitor, however, since I recommend referring to them while making these adjustments.

1. Drag the Color Corrector effect from the Color Correction tab in the Video Filters tab in the Effects panel onto the target clip.

2. After applying the effect, click the Color Corrector tab and then click the Visual button to convert the effect controls to Visual, which should look like **Figure 6-5**.

3. Choose Tools > Video Scopes to open the Scopes panel, then choose the Waveform monitor in the Layout drop-down list in the Tool Bench. If desired, drag the Video Scopes panel to a location under the Canvas (Final Cut Pro's preview window).

4. Adjust brightness and contrast first. Adjust the following controls as necessary to correct brightness and contrast:

   • Whites slider: Use this control to adjust whites to 100 IRE.

   • Mids slider: Use this control to adjust average values in the frame, increasing or decreasing contrast without affecting blacks and whites. Note that the mids slider is a great tool to correct backlighting, where you want to

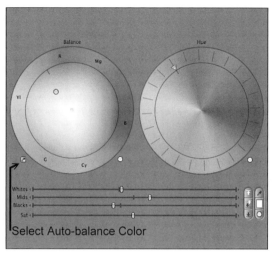

Select Auto-balance Color

Figure 6-5
Final Cut Pro's Color Corrector filter, in Visual mode.

increase the brightness in some areas without adjusting the background. More on this below.

- Blacks slider: Use this control to adjust blacks to 7.5 IRE.

5. Now adjust color. Click the Select Auto-balance eyedropper and click a pixel in the Canvas that should be white. In essence, you're telling FCP "hey, this pixel should be white, color balance the rest of the image accordingly," and that's what will happen. The image I'm adjusting in **Figure 6-5** was tinted blue, the result of shooting outdoors with the white balance inadvertently set to incandescent. As you can see, Final Cut Pro shifted the Balance Control Indicator dot to the upper left, away from blue and cyan.

From there, you can fine-tune the color adjustment by dragging the dot. Specifically, shift it towards or away from center to adjust the intensity of the correction, and otherwise to change the hue.

6. Adjust all other controls as necessary to perfect the image, toggling the effect on and off to assess your results.

I tend to stay away from the Hue control, since the adjustments get off color quickly

Author's Tip

Which Adjustment First?
When adjusting brightness and contrast and also color, which do you adjust first? Most authorities recommend adjusting brightness first, but I generally correct the biggest problem first, be it under- or over-exposure or faulty white balancing. After adjusting this to a reasonable look, I address the other problem.

Of course, none of these adjustments are "one and done" applications, you'll probably have to go back and forth interactively with both color and brightness controls to perfect your video.

(excuse the pun). Try the saturation slider if the colors are generally weak in the image and need pumping up.

Premiere Pro's Auto Color Effect

Premiere Pro also has multiple color-correction effects, including the Auto Color and Fast Color Corrector effects discussed here. Note that the Auto Color effect can correct color, brightness and contrast, so you won't have to separately apply the Brightness and Contrast effect. Again, you should work with waveform monitor open to better gauge the results of your adjustments. Here's how you apply and fine tune the Auto Color effect.

1. Drag the Auto Color effect from the Adjust tab in the Video Effects tab in the Effects panel onto the target clip.

2. Click the Effect Controls panel, and then click the triangle next to the Auto Color effect to expose the controls, then click the triangles next to other controls to expose the sliders (**Figure 6-6**).

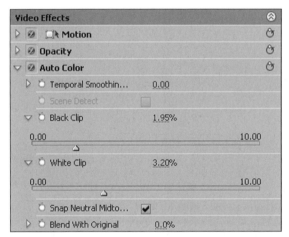

Figure 6-6
Premiere Pro's Auto Color effect.

3. Open a Reference Monitor and change it to waveform view as described above in Adjusting Brightness and Contrast.

4. Once you apply the effect, Premiere Pro adjusts color automatically, with just two adjustments available, both described below.

5. Start by adjusting brightness and contrast. Watching the YC Waveform monitor, adjust the following controls as necessary to correct brightness and contrast:

   • Black Clip slider: Use this control to adjust darker pixels towards 7.5 IRE.

   • White Clip slider: Use this control to adjust lighter pixels towards 100 IRE.

- Click the Snap Neutral Midtones checkbox to adjust midtones. Very often I find this checkbox to be special sauce that really makes this filter work well.

6. The other two controls operate as follows:

   - Temporal smoothing: You set the value in seconds, which impacts how many frames Premiere Pro analyzes to compute its automatic color adjustments. If you notice flicker in the video, adjust this value to one or two seconds; otherwise, use the default value of 0.

   - Blend with Original: This adjusts the percentage of the effect applied to the frames. If the automatic color adjustment computed by Premiere Pro is too stark, you can moderate it by inserting a percentage. At 0% (as in the figure), Premiere Pro applies all of the adjustment to the video; at 100% it applies 0%.

If you can't produce good results with the Auto Color Effect, try the Fast Color Corrector effect, detailed next.

Premiere Pro's Fast Color Corrector Effect

I recommend not using brightness adjustments that are available in this effect, so start by correcting these attributes with the Brightness and Contrast effect as described above, and leave the YC Waveform monitor open.

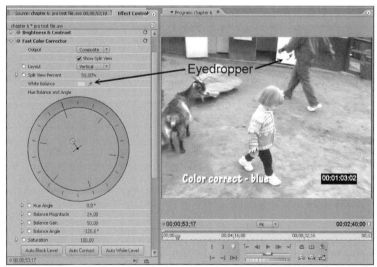

Figure 6-7
Premiere Pro's Fast Color Corrector effect. This clip is from my standard video editor test clip; hence the descriptive text in the frame "Color correct – blue."

1. Drag the Fast Color Corrector clip from the Color Correction tab in the Effects tab in the Effects panel onto the target clip.

2.   Click the Effect Controls panel, and then click the triangle next to the Fast Color Corrector effect to expose the controls, and then click the triangles next to controls within the Effect to expose the sliders (**Figure 6-7)**.

3.   In the Effects panel, click the eyedropper next to the White Balance color chip, and then click a pixel in the Program Monitor that should be white. In essence, you're telling Premiere Pro "hey, this pixel should be white, so color balance the rest of the image accordingly," and that's just what should happen. The image I'm adjusting in **Figure 6-7** was tinted blue, the result of shooting outdoors with white balance set to incandescent. Premiere Pro shifted the color widget dot to the upper left, away from blue and cyan.

Once set, you can manually drag the dot to a new location, or use the digital controls beneath the color wheel to adjust the result. In particular, you'll find the Balance Magnitude adjustment valuable for adjusting the intensity of the correction. Note the Saturation slider, which you can use to boost drab-looking colors.

4.   Note the Show Split View immediately beneath the Fast Color Corrector Effect in the Effect Controls panel. Check this to produce the split before and after view in the frame, which I find very helpful when fine-tuning my color parameters. You can select either a Vertical or Horizontal view from the Layout drop-down list and drag over the Split View Percent to adjust the view even further.

ALERT If you don't uncheck the Show Split View checkbox in the Fast Color Corrector Effect, Premiere Pro will render the split view into the final video, one side corrected, the other side not, which is really hard to explain to a client. So, remember to uncheck it once you've finalized your adjustments.

Fixing Backlit Video

If you shoot enough live video, occasionally you're going to run across a problem with backlit video, like that shown in **Figure 6-8**. In this video, the speaker was originally sitting, and when he stood unexpectedly, the light shining on the wall simply overpowered the otherwise modest lighting in the room. The result was a witness-protection class video.

With Final Cut Pro, you can attempt to brighten the face by applying the Color Corrector effect shown in **Figure 6-5** and adjusting the Mids slider, which should brighten the face without blowing out the whites, in this case the background lights and back wall.

Premiere Pro's Shadow/Highlight tool (**Figure 6-9**) has worked very well for me with the occasional backlit video. You can find it in the Adjust folder in the Video Effects folder in the Effects tab.

Figure 6-8
Backlight issues in this clip caused by bright light shining against the wall. Another clip from my standard video editor test clip.

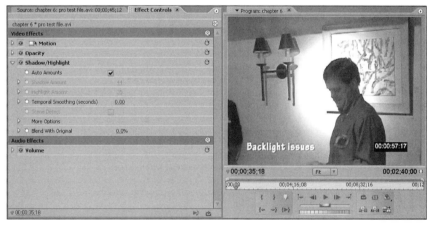

Figure 6-9
Premiere Pro's excellent Shadow/Highlight filter, boosting brightness in the face without blowing out the background.

The first few times you use the filter, I recommend keeping the Auto Amounts checked to work in automatic mode; once you get familiar with the tool, you can uncheck the box and work manually. The Premiere Pro Help file details all manual adjustments; you should check there for details.

These are the typical video adjustments; now let's have a look at audio adjustments.

Fixing Audio-Related Problems

Most streaming video viewers know that producing high-quality video can be challenging at lower bit rates, and they tend to forgive degraded video quality. On the other hand, they also know that high-quality audio is possible at nearly every data rate, so tend to judge poor quality sound more harshly. This makes correcting audio problems critical to viewer satisfaction.

The problems I experience most frequently in my projects are transient pops and clicks, hum or other consistent noises, and also audio without sufficient volume that needs to be amplified. The next few sections will describe how to correct these problems in both Soundtrack Pro and Adobe Audition.

Getting Audio into/out of Your Audio Editor

Both Premiere Pro and Final Cut Pro make it easy to load audio files into their respective audio editors, Audition and Soundtrack Pro. With Premiere Pro, click the audio track, then right click, and then choose Edit in Adobe Audition. With Final Cut Pro, click the audio file, right click and choose Send To > Soundtrack Pro Audio File Project. After making your adjustments, save the audio file in either audio editor, and the video editor automatically updates the audio file within the project.

However, this technique only works for the selected clip, not the entire project. To edit the audio from an entire movie, export the entire audio file, which Final Cut Pro simplifies with a File > Export > For Soundtrack. In Premiere Pro, choose File > Export > Audio.

Once the export is complete, import the audio file into your audio editor, perform your corrections and save the file. Then import the corrected audio file back into your video editor and drag it to a different audio track than the original audio files, lining up the waveform to ensure synchronization. Then mute the original audio tracks by clicking the speaker icons on the left track head of both editors.

Removing Transient Noises in Soundtrack Pro

You don't have to be an expert to see that the audio waveform in **Figure 6-10** needs help. It's audio from an outdoors shoot that needs a volume boost and some clicks removed from the middle and end (these are the waveform spikes that you see). Though hard to see in **Figure 6-10**, there's also persistent hum from the camcorder's microphone. Let's see how much we can improve the quality.

First, let's tackle the clicks, produced by adjusting the ND filter on my camera during recording. By click I mean a very short loud noise, perhaps caused by adjusting a camera control or even kicking your tripod. For longer, more persistent and consistent noises, we'll use a different technique.

I'll start in Soundtrack Pro, which has an automated function for finding and eliminating pops and clicks. Here's how you operate this function, assuming you've already imported the audio file into the program.

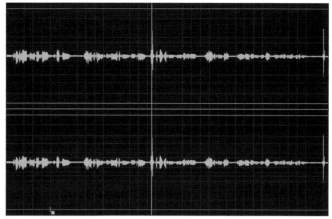

Figure 6-10
A sick audio waveform in Soundtrack Pro. Note the generally low volume and spikes in the middle and end.

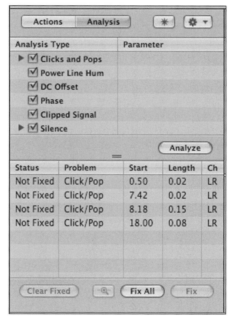

Figure 6-11
Soundtrack Pro's excellent Analysis and Fix function.

1. In the Actions list to the left of the waveform, click Analysis (see **Figure 6-11**). Soundtrack Pro opens several Analysis Type checkboxes for your selection.

2. Click the checkboxes for the problems that you want Soundtrack Pro to search for. In this case, I'm looking for all possible problems.

3. In the middle of the Actions list dialog, click Analyze. Soundtrack Pro analyzes the audio file and highlights all problems found in the audio file.

4. At the bottom of the Problem List, click Fix All to fix all problems.

5. If Soundtrack Pro doesn't sufficiently eliminate the pops, you'll have to finish the job. Though there are a number of other filters you could try, I typically just reduce the volume of the offending noise manually. To accomplish this, zoom into the waveform, select the region containing the pop, and choose Process > Adjust Amplitude. Your goal is to reduce the pop to the level of the audio surrounding it, but not to produce a flat line region that will be just as obvious as the original pop. It might take a couple of tries to get it right; just choose Edit > Undo Amplitude Adjustment, then redo the amplitude adjustment with a different value.

Removing Transient Noises in Adobe Audition

Adobe Audition has a tool called *Repair Transient* whose mission in life is to eliminate pops and clicks while leaving as much of the other audio untouched as possible. It works remarkably well, and is one of Audition's hidden gems. Here's how to apply the effect (**Figure 6-12**).

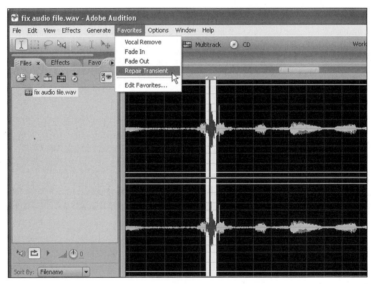

Figure 6-12
Audition's Repair Transient filter is definitely one of my favorites.

1. Use the transport controls beneath the waveform display to zoom into the waveform.

2. Drag your mouse over the waveform, selecting just the offending noise. The more accurate you are here, the better job Audition will do.

3. Choose Favorites > Repair Transient. Audition will remove the offending noise, leaving the background audio. I've had great results with this effect, and I'm sure you will too.

ALERT

When I first started working with Audition, my blood pressure became elevated numerous times because controls were frequently grayed out, seemingly without reason. This includes fairly innocuous controls like Undo ("Wait, I can't undo? What is happening? Do I have to start over? Waaaahhhhh!"). It literally took me weeks of trial and error, but I discovered that if you Pause an audio file during playback (using the button with the sideways equal sign), many controls are grayed. If you click Stop (using the button with the black square), all controls are enabled.

Noise Reduction

The tools discussed above are perfect for random pops and clicks, but don't work for noises like microphone hum, white noise in an office setting or other consistent noises. If you look at the waveform in **Figure 6-12**, you'll notice that flat regions in the waveform are kind of fuzzy; this is the noise that I want to reduce. Though it looks pretty minimal now, once we boost the volume in the audio track below, the flat-line region will become big and bushy, and much more noticeable both visually and when playing back the audio.

Noise reduction works the same in most programs. The first step is to identify the noise for the program, which you accomplish by selecting a region that contains nothing but noise. This is usually called something CSI-ish like a "noise print" or "noise reduction profile." Then you employ the filter to remove the noise from the entire audio file.

It's important to distinguish a "noise gate" from a "noise reduction filter." Say you've got a consistent hum in your audio. *Noise reduction* seeks to remove that hum *throughout* the file, in otherwise silent regions and when there's speech or other sound in the file.

In contrast, a *noise gate* simply mutes regions that are below a certain threshold of sound. In our hum example, a noise gate would mute regions that contain only hum, but would not filter other regions at all, which produces a very artificially-sounding audio file. For persistent noises, noise reduction is vastly superior.

Note also that for some background noises, like 60-Hz hum caused by a ground loop or power line, other filters may work better than noise reduction. For example, Audition has a 60-Hz Hum Notch Filter in the Scientific Filters (Effects > Filters > Scientific Filters (process), while Soundtrack Pro can automatically seek and destroy this hum as part of the auto analysis shown in **Figure 6-11** (Power Line Hum). Accordingly, noise reduction isn't the only arrow in your quiver when it comes to removing background noise from your audio file, though it can be indispensable.

Noise Reduction Overview

Before getting started, let's review the high-level goal for any noise-reduction operation. Simply stated, your goal isn't to remove all the noise, it's to remove as much noise as possible without distorting the remaining audio. Remove too much noise and voices sound mechanical and artificial, and music fuzzy (or worse).

To assist this effort, before applying the filter, both Soundtrack Pro and Audition let you preview both the remaining audio *after* noise reduction, but also the noise the program will eliminate from the audio file.

This is the Noise Only checkbox shown in **Figure 6-13.** When this box is checked and you preview the audio, you hear the noise to be removed. In most instances, if you can hear the speech or music that you want to retain when previewing in this mode, distortion will occur. So typically after applying the effect, I work in Noise Only mode, adjusting the controls until I can't hear any of the audio that I want to retain. Then, I uncheck the box, preview again and check for distortion, and if there is none, apply the filter.

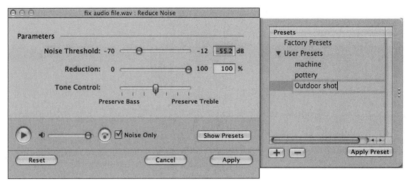

Figure 6-13
Soundtrack Pro's Reduce Noise filter dialog.

Noise Reduction in Soundtrack Pro

Here's how to use the Reduce Noise filter in Soundtrack Pro. Note that Soundtrack Pro applies selected effects to the entire audio file; if this isn't the desired result, click and select the target region after setting the noise print in step 2.

1. Click and drag your pointer over a region in the audio that contains only the background noise. This should select that region.

2. Choose Process > Set Noise Print. This tells Soundtrack Pro that the selected region contains the background noise you're seeking to minimize.

3. Choose Process > Reduce Noise. This opens the dialog shown in **Figure 6-13**.

4. Adjusting the controls is an interactive, subjective process, but here's my workflow:

    •   Click the Noise Only checkbox to the right of the preview slider on the bottom left. This tells Soundtrack Pro to play only the noise that's being removed.

    •   Click the Play triangle to preview the audio.

    •   Adjust Noise Threshold (the level below which is considered noise) and Reduction (amount of reduction applied) until you can't hear any of the audio that you want to retain.

5. Uncheck the Noise Only checkbox, then preview again, checking for distortion. To assist your efforts:

    •   Click the Bypass button (to the right of the volume slider) to toggle the filter on and off during playback.

    •   If necessary, adjust the Tone Control slider to either Preserve Bass or Preserve Treble.

6. When satisfied with the result, click Apply.

    If you're working with multiple clips from the same source (that share the same noise), note that you can save the preset to apply to other clips by clicking the Show Presets button (**Figure 6-13**), which opens the Presets window to the right, then the Plus sign, which inserts the effect into the User Presets folder. To later apply the preset, click the Show Presets button, click the desired preset and then click Apply Preset.

Noise Reduction in Audition

Here's how to use Audition's Noise Reduction filter.

1. Click and drag your pointer over a region in the audio that contains only the background noise.

2. Choose Effects > Restoration > Capture Noise Reduction Profile. This tells Audition that the selected region contains the offending noise.

3. Choose Edit > Select All, which tells Soundtrack Pro to apply noise reduction to the entire audio file. Alternatively, click and drag your cursor over a region in the file to apply the filter just to that region.

4. Choose Effects > Restoration > Noise Reduction (process). This opens the dialog shown in **Figure 6-14**.

5. Adjusting the controls is an interactive, subjective process, but here's my workflow:

    •   Click the Keep Only Noise radio button on the bottom left, which tells Soundtrack Pro to play only the noise that's being removed.

    •   Click the Preview button on the bottom right to preview the audio.

    •   Adjust the Noise Reduction Level slider until you can't hear any of the audio that you want to retain in the preview.

6. Click the Remove Noise radio button, then preview again, checking for distortion. To assist your efforts, click the Bypass checkbox next to the Preview button to toggle the filter on and off during playback.

7. When satisfied with the result, click OK.

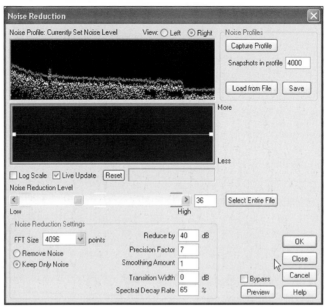

Figure 6-14
Audition's Noise Reduction filter dialog.

If you're working with multiple clips from the same source (that share the same noise), you can save the noise profile to apply to other clips by clicking the Save Button and saving the FFT file. To later apply the noise profile, click the Load from File button and choose the desired profile. Note that this doesn't save the settings that you've applied, just the noise profile.

ALERT If you apply Audition's Noise Reduction effect with the Keep Only Noise checkbox checked, Audition will save only the noise, which is seldom, if ever, the desired result. You'll see a flat line in your waveform monitor, which always causes a fright. No worries, just choose Edit > Undo Noise Reduction (process) and start back at step 4, remembering to click the Remove Noise radio button before applying the filter.

OK, we've removed the transient noises and as much background noise as possible. Now let's boost the volume to acceptable levels.

Understanding Compression and Normalization

Have another look at the waveform in **Figure 6-10;** it's clear that we have to do something about the volume. I'll discuss three options here.

- **Manually adjust the volume.** I could boost the volume by say 10 decibels, which would perk up those waveform peaks, but could cause clipping in the highest volume regions in the audio file, which results in distortion. Those flat peaks you see periodically in the waveform in **Figure 6-15** represent clipping, and usually distortion.

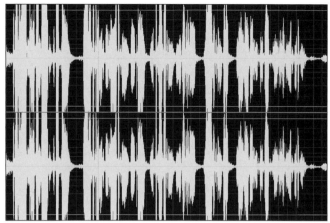

Figure 6-15
Ruh, roh—too much volume boost produced peaking throughout the file, those flat lines you see atop some peaks in the waveform.

- **Normalize the volume.** Normalization boosts the volume of the audio file equally throughout, but never beyond the point that would cause distortion. For example, if you look at **Figure 6-16**, you'll notice that while the volume is higher than **Figure 6-10**, there are no flat lines that represent peaking. Normalization works well, but has one important limitation. Specifically, if you have quiet dialog you need to boost in volume, but other regions (applause, laughing) that are already high in volume, normalization won't significantly boost the dialog, since that might distort the applause. I'll describe how to work around this limitation below.

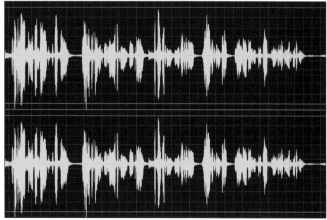

Figure 6-16
Normalization produces higher volume and no peaking or distortion.

- **Compress the audio file.** Where volume adjustments and normalization adjust the volume of the entire audio file uniformly, compression is a technique that boosts the lower levels in the audio file (like soft speech) without boosting the higher levels (like applause or laughing). Though compression is an extremely complicated and technical subject, even a total novice can vastly improve audio quality via easy-to-use presets supplied in Soundtrack Pro and Audition. Note that I didn't show a screenshot of the results of compression because it's hard to discern from **Figure 6-16** visually, though the difference is immediately apparent when previewing the effect.

Overall, when editing files that contain lots of speech, I always apply compression and preview to determine if compression improves the results. If so, I typically maximize the volume of the entire audio file while applying compression to save a step.

If that doesn't improve quality, I undo and try normalizing, saving manual volume adjustment as an infrequently used last resort. I won't discuss increasing audio volume manually, since it's easy to use in both programs; just select the region to boost, then open and apply the appropriate effect (Process > Adjust Amplitude in Soundtrack Pro, Effects > Amplitude > Amplify in Audition).

I'll demonstrate the compressor effect in both Soundtrack Pro and Audition using a vocal preset because that's where most of my experience lies. Note the presets for music, and work with those should your musical recording lack the necessary crispness and volume.

Using Soundtrack Pro's Compressor

Here's how you apply Soundtrack Pro's Compressor effect and adjust audio volume. Note that Soundtrack Pro applies selected effects to the entire audio file; if this isn't the desired result, click and select the target region before starting the process.

1. Choose Process > Effects > Dynamics > Compressor. Soundtrack Pro opens the Compressor effect dialog.

2. Click the Show Presets button.

3. In the Presets panel, click the triangle to open User Presets, then Vocal Compressors.

4. Click to choose Vocal Compression.

5. Click Apply Preset. You should see the controls change in the main Compressor window.

6. Click the Preview button on the bottom left to preview the effect. Toggle the Effect Bypass button (to the right of the volume slider) to assess the benefit of the effect.

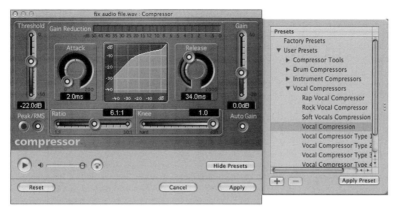

Figure 6-17
Soundtrack Pro's Compressor effect.

7. On the upper right of the Compressor panel, drag the Gain slider up or down as necessary to increase the volume of the clip. Boost until you hear distortion, and then back down a bit. Note the gain in dB. Once you apply the effect, if you see any clipping in the resultant audio file, you'll have to undo and then reapply the effect with lower gain.

8. Click Apply.

Unless you're very skilled with audio, I would not adjust other controls in the compressor panel since they could produce unintended results. If you're not getting the improvement you'd like, click and preview with a different vocal compressor preset.

Using Audition's Compressor

Now let's look at Audition's tool. Note that Audition automatically selects the entire audio file when you choose the Multiband Compressor tool. If you only want to apply the filter to a region in the video file, click and select that region before applying the effect.

1. Choose Effects > Amplitude > Multiband Compressor. Audition opens the Multiband Compressor panel (**Figure 6-18**).

2. Click the Effect Preset drop-down list atop the effect window, and choose Raise Vocals.

3. Click the Preview button on the bottom left to preview the effect. Toggle the Effect Bypass button (to the left of the preview button) to assess the benefit of the effect.

4. On the upper right of the effect panel, drag the Output Gain slider upwards until the loudest portion of your audio file is in yellow figures (but not red, which will cause clipping). Note the gain in dB. Once you apply the effect, if you see any clipping in the resultant audio file, you'll have to undo and then reapply the effect with lower gain.

Understanding Compression and Normalization

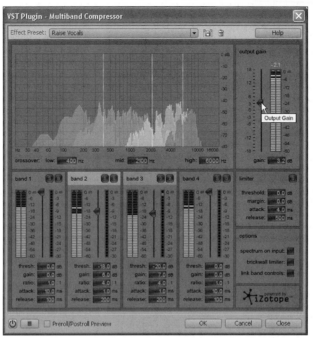

Figure 6-18
Audition's Multiband Compressor.

    5.   Click OK.

Unless you're very skilled with audio, I would not adjust other controls in the compressor panel since they could produce unintended results. If you're not getting the improvement you'd like, click and preview with a different vocal compressor preset.

Perfecting Normalization

Let's switch to the audio file shown in **Figure 6-19** to identify and solve a problem with normalization. Again, normalization boosts the entire audio file by the same decibel level to the maximum level available without producing distortion. For example, if you applied a normalization filter to the entire audio file shown in **Figure 6-19**, it probably wouldn't increase audio volume at all, since the highest regions of the audio file are already close to clipping.

What to do? Click and drag to select the region containing the lower-volume audio that you'd like to amplify, and apply the filter to that region only. This will boost that audio to the maximum without causing clipping.

In use, normalization is very simple to apply; you choose how loud to make the audio, in either decibels or percentage format **(Figure 6-20)**, and pull the proverbial trigger.

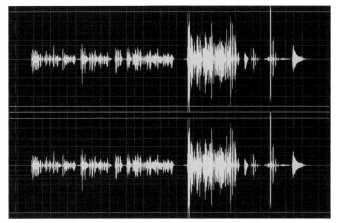

Figure 6-19
Normalization won't help this file because it can't boost the quiet regions without distorting the loud regions.

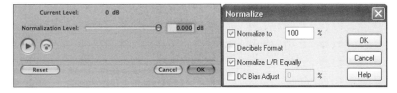

Figure 6-20
Setting the normalization level to 0 dB (on the left, Soundtrack Pro) or 100% (on the right, Audition) boosts audio as much as possible without distortion.

I usually normalize to 100%, though some authorities, most notably Jay Rose, author of *Producing Great Sound for Digital Video* (CMP Books, 2003), recommend normalizing to –2 dB. Play the audio file after normalizing and if you hear any distortion (or see any clipping), undo and adjust the normalization level downwards.

You can find Soundtrack Pro's normalize function by choosing Process > Normalize, or choose Effects > Amplitude > Normalize (process) for Audition. Remember to highlight a section beforehand if you don't want the entire file normalized.

Recommended Audio Workflow
Always remove transient noises first and then apply noise reduction (if necessary), then compression and finally normalization if the volume isn't where it needs to be. Note that the compressor and normalization filters will boost any background noises remaining after your first application of the noise-removal filter, just as they boost all other audio in the file.

Don't be afraid to reapply the noise reduction at this stage, but preview carefully to ensure that you don't distort the audio remaining in the file. Remember that a little noise sounds much more natural than the mechanical, robotic voices produced by the overapplication of noise reduction.

Conclusion

In this chapter you learned how to perfect video appearance and audio quality. In the next chapter you'll learn about preparing your video for compression, including how to choose your target output parameters and scale, deinterlace and otherwise process your video for maximum quality.

CHAPTER 7

Preparing for Compression

You've created the set, shot the video and now you're ready to encode. But first you have the thankless task of choosing the output parameters for your Flash video, like resolution, frame rate and data rate. I say thankless because it's the type of decision that someone will always disagree with.

For example, if your video is huge and visually perfect, your finance types will complain that you're spending too much on bandwidth. If you lower the bit rate, viewers will either complain that the image is too small (though visually perfect) or visually degraded (though very large). Oh, well, it's lonely at the top and all that. There obviously is no right answer but I will try to identify factors to consider before choosing your final output parameters.

Once you make your output decision, you have to somehow get your pristine DV or even HD video down to the target resolution and deinterlaced, if necessary. Do you do that in your editor or your encoding tool? I'll discuss factors to consider in making that decision as well, and conclude with a quick look at the potential benefits of noise filtering before encoding.

Specifically, in this chapter you will learn:

- Factors to consider when choosing output parameters like resolution, data rate and frame rate
- How to allocate bit rate between audio and video
- How (and why) to produce square-pixel output
- Different workflows for producing video to these targets
- What deinterlacing is and how to apply it
- A little bit about noise reduction filtering.

Let's begin.

What We Know about Flash Output Parameters

Despite the encouraging section head, let me start with what I don't know. Specifically, sitting here in my home office in Galax, Virginia on this fine sunny day, I have no idea which output parameters you should use for your streaming content. This will vary by budget, content type, target audience and a host of other factors. What's right for ESPN or DL.tv is probably not right for you, but it is worth considering, along with a number of other related factors.

So let's start with what we do know, and build from there. Many of these observations are fairly basic, if not trivial, and some are discussed in other chapters, but all of them impact the decisions we're making in this chapter, so I include them as background.

Technology and Market Fundamentals

Let's start with some observations about streaming technology and the streaming marketplace.

Small Videos Offer Higher Quality but the Progression Isn't Linear

A video produced at 640×480 resolution has four times more pixels than one produced at 320×240. If you presume a similar frame rate, say 30 fps, does this mean that the larger video needs a data rate of 4× the smaller video to achieve the same quality?

Intuitively, you would say yes, but have a gander at **Figure 7-1.** On the left is a video encoded at 320×240×30 fps at a data rate of 260 kbps (video only). On the right is a video encoded at 640×480×30 fps at a data rate of 468 kbps (video only). Note that to produce the figure, I scaled the larger video down to 320×240, rather than scaling the smaller image up.

Figure 7-1
Comparing videos encoded at different resolutions and data rates.

If you do the math, you'll find that the video on the left allocates about .1128 bits/pixel, while the video on the right allocates about half that, at .0508. Yet visually, on this very challenging frame where the skateboarder is landing a jump, the frames look about the same.

Why? I'm not sure, but it seems that all codecs get more efficient when working with larger images. The key takeaway is that you don't have to boost bandwidth linearly to maintain quality as you boost the resolution of your videos. A 4× jump in resolution will not require a concomitant 4× boost in bandwidth to maintain quality.

Halving the Frame Rate Doesn't Double the Quality

Back in the early days of CD-ROM video, it was common to produce at 15 fps. Intuitively, since this halved the number of frames encoded in the stream and thereby doubled the bits per pixel, it should also double the quality. Back then, it seemed to work.

However, with streaming codecs, it doesn't seem to work. Not only does the video look more choppy, the per-frame quality remains about the same. Witness **Figure 7-2**.

Figure 7-2
Video encoded at 15 fps on the left, and 30 fps on the right.

Here, I encoded the same skateboard video to 640×480×300 kbps, at 15 fps on the left and 30 fps on the right. Logic would tell you that the video on the left should be sharper, but the text and observer are actually sharper on the right.

These experiments are backed by real-world data, as none of the Flash sites I contacted used less than 30 fps. Since the Windows Media player provides frame-rate data, I checked a number of random Internet sites, including Accenture and CBS, and found that all produced at 30 fps.

So, halving the frame rate to double the quality makes lots of sense, but doesn't seem to work (and isn't being used by others). So, encode at 30 fps.

High-Motion Videos Need Higher Bit Rates for Equivalent Quality

I'm guessing that you didn't fall out of your chair in surprise when you read this section head, but it's a fact you need to consider. This is why ESPN publishes at 440×330 resolution at data rates up to 600 kbps, while Digital Life TV, a show comprised of static talking heads kept lively by rotating through three camera views, produces at up to 640×480 at 600 kbps.

If your video has high motion content, you either need a smaller window or higher data rate than talking head or similar video.

Broadband Is Faster and More Pervasive

While this varies by target audience, in general, broadband penetration continues to grow and speeds are increasing. Many sites targeting mass markets are boosting data rates to levels that seemed unreachable or unreasonable even a few months ago.

Many, many sites are now publishing at 600 kbps and higher, and I actually found a clip on *www.cbs.com* that was produced at 741 kbps (480×360×30 fps). Granted, it was a 30-second clip where a few seconds of buffering could almost guarantee smooth playback, but still that data rate is amazingly high.

Blip.tv, a YouTube-like site, publishes at 512 kbps, while Vidiac, which runs several user-submitted video sites and licenses technology to others, encodes at 528 kbps.

Obviously, this extra data rate costs bandwidth dollars. However, these are the sites to which your video is compared. If you don't start to "push the envelope," it will quickly look like you're "behind the curve." So "think outside the box" and consider boosting your data rate (that enough clichés for you)?

Pigs Get Fat, Hogs Get Slaughtered

On the other hand, if you choose too high a data rate, and distribute via the Flash Media Server, your low-bandwidth viewers may never be able to watch your video playing smoothly, since it doesn't get cached locally. This is definitely not acceptable for mission-critical video.

In addition to server cost, local caching is one reason that most large video sites distribute Flash video via progressive download, since it ensures smooth playback, albeit perhaps at the cost of a slight wait. So don't forget to factor in your delivery method when choosing a data rate.

It's OK to Be Short and Fat

If you're Danny DeVito or Flash video, so long as you're distributed via progressive download. Specifically, if your video is relatively short, say less than 2 minutes, you can encode at a very high data rate, prebuffer a good chunk of video before you start playing, and then race to the finish, hoping the video finishes before the buffer runs out, stopping playback. This is likely the theory CBS uses to display a 30-second preview at 741 kbps.

If you're streaming a 40-minute show, like DL.tv, however, you have to assume that a good portion of your viewers will want to watch all the way through when they click Play on your web page. To meet their needs, you have to be more conservative, and more closely match your target with the actual streaming bandwidth of your viewers.

Size-Related Observations

Now let's look at what we know about video resolution.

If You're Not Getting Bigger, You're Getting Smaller

When I first started producing streaming video, 320×240 was considered "quarter screen" video because the typical desktop ran at 640×480 resolution. In contrast, today I'm writing this chapter on my PowerPC G5 operating at 1920×1200 resolution on my gorgeous Apple

Cinema display. It's a lot bigger than the 13" monitor I used back in 1995, and the 320×240 window has dropped from quarter screen to precisely 1/32.

The minimum resolution for any of my computers is about 1280×1024, into which you can fit 17 320×240 windows, and every one of them would look positively tiny. So if you're not increasing your video resolution, it's getting smaller as your viewers move to increasingly larger resolutions.

Bigger Isn't Always Better

Here, I'm referring to the results of a number of studies relating to Mobile TV, specifically comparing the "video quality acceptability" of video displayed at a number of resolutions, from a low of 120×90 to a high of 320×240. The studies, mostly performed by students and faculty of University College London, analyzed four different media types: news, sports, music videos and animations.

The studies are available as an article named "Can Small Be Beautiful? Assessing Image Resolution Requirements for Mobile TV" and a presentation titled "Quality of Experience in Mobile TV." You can find links to both on the home page of coauthor Hendrik Knoche, at *http://www.cs.ucl.ac.uk/staff/H.Knoche/publications.htm*. While these studies aren't directly on point, they're close enough to deliver some interesting value.

Specifically, at extremely low bit rates where larger screen videos were clearly degraded, many viewers preferred the smaller screens. However, once the data rate crossed a threshold that eliminated the worst of the artifacts, viewers almost unanimously preferred the larger screen, irrespective of content.

The main exception related to news, where many viewers preferred a smaller screen that presented text more clearly, and facial expressions without artifacts.

What do I take from this? Viewers prefer high-quality video in a small screen over degraded-quality video in a big-screen. On the other hand, viewers also prefer big-screen over small-screen video when the quality is equivalent.

More on this later in the section called "What Viewers Want."

Flash Scales (Comparatively) Poorly

I know, I know, gazillions of YouTube viewers can't be wrong. Still, while other technologies like Windows Media and RealVideo can scale using hardware on your graphics board, Flash can't. This has two serious implications.

First, it means that scaling with Flash is more CPU intensive, because the host CPU does all the work. In addition, graphics chips have sophisticated scaling and deinterlacing features that optimize the quality of the scaled video, which are impossible to implement in software using the Flash Player.

The net/net? While scaling is essentially "free" with the other technologies, meaning no quality loss and no performance hit, scaling Flash video consumes more CPU resources and doesn't look as good.

So if your strategy to improve video size was to produce at relatively low resolution and scale during playback, evaluate the strategy in light of these factors, especially if you're pursuing viewers on older computers. In addition, if you plan on offering a scaling feature in your Flash Player, make it an option, not the default viewing mechanism.

What Viewers Want

Now let's consider a couple of realities about what viewers like and dislike about streaming video, again drawing from the University College London studies.

Enough Is Enough, More Is Too Much

The studies performed by Knoche, et al., are nearly uniform in one respect, as illustrated in **Figure 7-3**, which is a screen from a workshop given by Knoche with M. Angela Sasse, his first supervisor at the University.

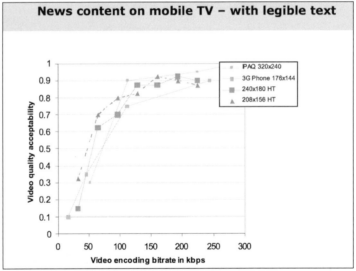

Figure 7-3
How additional bandwidth increases viewer satisfaction.

Briefly, the slide assesses viewer satisfaction relating to news content containing legible text on mobile TV, as displayed on a number of devices. The left axis is video quality acceptability, while the bottom axis is the encoding bit rate.

As you can see, viewer satisfaction increases sharply at all viewing resolutions as bit rate jumps from 0 to 100 kbps, but then the rate slows dramatically, especially for the 320×240 video displayed on the iPAQ, where tripling the data rate increases quality acceptability by about 10%. For the 240×180 and 208×156 videos, viewer satisfaction actually decreased with additional data rate.

In financial terms, your initial investments in bandwidth enjoy a high rate of return, but once quality is "acceptable," the rate of return drops, and even goes negative. How do you find the acceptable point? Let's jump to the next section.

What Viewers Love to Hate

In their article "Can Small Be Beautiful," Knoche and his coauthors asked their participants to specify what made the video they were watching unacceptable. With news videos, almost 100 of 128 viewers commented about text detail, which according to the article included the news ticker, headlines, clock, logos and captions. Of relevance to this discussion, facial and general detail drew about 30 comments each, as did audio fidelity.

This tells me two things. First, when planning your shoots, eliminate as much detail as possible, since these stress the codec, display artifacts readily and are a significant source of complaints. Second, when choosing a data rate, be sure it's high enough to avoid visibly degrading text or your subject's faces or other details. If you can't eliminate these at your selected data rates, then either drop your resolution or boost your data rate.

We're getting close to decision time; now let's have a look at resources to consider when choosing your encoding parameters.

Finding the Guideposts
Encoding Presets Are Usually Way Too Conservative

All Flash encoding tools include presets that you can easily use to encode your videos. When you're just starting out, these are a great way to quickly and easily encode your files, no muss, no fuss.

On the other hand, they're also very, very conservative, and are designed to make your video look good at all costs. Unfortunately, since you're paying the bandwidth costs, blindly using presets may not be a good financial decision.

For example, Sorenson Squeeze's 768-kbps preset, shown in **Figure 7-4**, uses a video data rate of 615 kbps and a frame size of 320×240. At a lower data rate, ESPN is producing at 440×330, while Digital Live TV produces at 640×480.

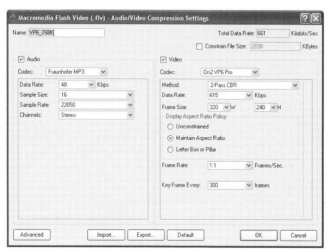

Figure 7-4
Some presets in Sorenson Squeeze are very conservative.

Use Windows Media as a Guide

One of the best ways to choose encoding parameters is to find a site with similar content and see what they're doing. One frustrating characteristic of the Flash Player is that, unlike Windows Media Player, it doesn't identify the resolution or data rate of the FLV file it's playing.

You can determine the resolution by taking a screen grab of the Flash video and measuring the height and width in your still-image editor, but there is no easy solution for data rate. In these instances, while not exactly apples to apples, you can find a site that's using Windows Media video and see what resolution and data rate they're using.

In terms of quality at a given data rate, Windows Media and Flash (with the VP6 codec) are reasonably close, and Windows Media, while used less and less, is certainly easier to find than RealVideo files, which also display their data rate and resolution. Note that you can't draw the same conclusions from QuickTime files, which are generally encoded to much higher data rates than Windows Media, Real or Flash.

Once you find a Windows Media file on a site that looks interesting, start playing the file. If the file plays in Media Player, choose File > Properties to see the Properties window shown in **Figure 7-5**. To see playback statistics, including the frame rate of the video, choose View > Statistics, and click the Advanced tab of the Statistics screen.

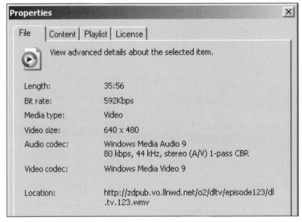

Figure 7-5
Windows Media files display their data rate in the Properties window.

If the video is embedded into a web page, right click the video and choose Properties or Statistics to view these screens.

Note that while the visual quality of Flash video is similar to Windows Media, the quality of the MP3 audio-codec used by Flash can't compare to what the Windows Media and Real audio codecs deliver. Accordingly, let's have a quick look at the audio side of things and then I'll summarize and make some recommendations.

On Flash-Related Audio

Once you identify your target data rate, you have to allocate that bandwidth between video and audio. Here are some observations to consider.

Viewers Accept Degraded Video, but Not Degraded Audio

Most Internet viewers accept minor visual degradation as the price of streaming; it's wonderfully convenient, but the picture is generally small and not quite as clear or crisp as TV or DVD. However, since most early streaming audio was powered by excellent audio codecs from Real and Microsoft, savvy Internet viewers have come to expect clear, artifact-free audio.

This means that you have to allocate sufficient audio bandwidth to produce such audio, which is an issue because . . .

Flash Audio Sux

Sad, but true, at least when it comes to quality. Clearly, MP3 was wildly successful as an independent compression technology without ties to big bad Microsoft, or mighty Real Networks, but comparative quality is quite low compared to the audio codecs produced by either company.

This means that you'll typically have to allocate more of your bit rate to audio when encoding into Flash format than you might with Windows Media or Real.

Music Is Harder to Compress than Speech

This is the "duh!" equivalent of higher motion video is harder to compress than talking head video, but I wanted to get it out on the table. If you're encoding speech, often you can produce very clear quality at 32 kbps, even with MP3 audio.

On the other hand, with music you may have to go much higher. For example, Blip.tv encodes at 96 kbps, while Vidiac.com encodes at 128 kbps.

Of course, there's music, and then there's music. If you have a polite 15-second riff leading into a 20-minute, all-speech sales presentation, it's probably not worth encoding at 128 kbps, especially if the average listener will probably use $15 speakers by her computer.

On the other hand, if you're presenting a music video where audio quality is paramount, you have to allocate the necessary bandwidth to do it right. This usually means 96 kbps or higher.

OK, you're convinced that you need to choose a large screen size, with high-quality audio. Now the questions become "what screen size?" and "how do I get my video to that screen size?" To answer the first, we have to get into one of the most complex areas I'll cover in the book.

However, once you understand this, you'll be able to produce video of any size, from any source, without distorting the aspect ratio in any way. It's a wonderful skill set to have, so let's jump into what I call "that whole square pixel thing."

That Whole Square-Pixel Thing

There's a fundamental difference between how computers display video and how NTSC and PAL televisions display video. In this section, I'll describe what the differences are and why you care, addressing source videos in the following order:

• NTSC standard definition (SD) 4:3 video

• NTSC SD 16:9 video

• NTSC HDV video

• PAL SD 4:3, 16:9 and HDV.

The PAL discussion will rely partially upon theories explained in the NTSC discussion, so even if you're from across the pond, you should read up on NTSC first.

Again, this is challenging, highly theoretical stuff, but you have to understand it to produce video that looks right, and to recognize when it isn't. Let's start with a couple of basic definitions.

Resolution, Pixel Aspect Ratio and Display Aspect Ratio

Start with a look at **Figure 7-6**, the Properties screen from Premiere Pro analyzing an NTSC DV video file named *ae scale.avi*. As you can see, the Image Size, or resolution as I'll call it, is 720×480. To be painfully clear, this means that if you analyzed the video file itself, you would find 720 horizontal pixels and 480 vertical pixels.

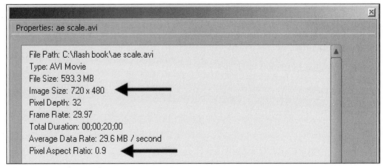

Figure 7-6
Premiere Pro's Properties screen tells us that DV video has a pixel aspect ratio of 0.9.

Notice the pixel aspect ratio shown on the bottom of the figure, which you can see is 0.9. In essence, this directs the television set or software player that plays this file to show 0.9 horizontal pixels for each actual horizontal pixel, or about 90%. On the other hand, when displaying Flash video, computers typically display in so-called "square pixel" format, which means that each horizontal pixel displays at 1.0 (or 100%) of its full resolution.

Intuitively, you know that if a TV squeezes the image to 90% of its original resolution and the computer doesn't, one of the displays has to be wrong. In this case, it's the computer display. Specifically, if you display the DV file at its full 720×480 resolution on the computer, the picture would look about 10% wider than it should be. You can observe this in **Figure 7-7**.

Figure 7-7
A DV frame displayed on a computer (left) and same frame on a television set. Notice how it's skinnier on the right.

On the left is a DV frame of my friend Lisa displayed on a computer screen. The image on the right is that same frame displayed on a TV and, as you can see, Lisa's face is noticeably narrower on the right. That's because the television set knew to shrink the video to its pixel aspect ratio of .9, while the computer didn't.

Display Aspect Ratio

OK, so now you know about video resolution and *pixel* aspect ratio. So what is *display* aspect ratio? Simply, it's the aspect ratio of the video displayed either on TV or in streaming video. Interestingly, the display aspect ratio of all older (non-widescreen) television sets is 4:3 (NTSC and PAL, by the way), which means four horizontal pixels for every three vertical pixels.

If you do the math, our 720×480 DV frame doesn't have a display aspect ratio of 4:3; it's about 4.5:3, which is wider. Multiply the 4.5 by the pixel aspect ratio of .9 and you get 4.05, which is close enough for the consumer electronics industry. Again, the bottom line is that televisions squeeze the horizontal pixels of a digital video file by .9 before display; otherwise, they would look too wide.

What does this mean for streaming video? Basically, if you display NTSC video pixel for pixel, it looks too wide, which distorts display, as you can see on the left in **Figure 7-7**. To compensate for the .9 aspect ratio of NTSC 4:3 video, you have to scale the video into a 4:3 display resolution like 640×480, 480×360, 440×330, 400×300 or 320×240. That's why these resolutions have become so popular.

And, to be absolutely sure that the video has the correct display aspect ratio, you have to output using a pixel aspect ratio of 1, which is called *square pixels*. Though most of the time choosing square-pixel output is very clear in the encoding interface, unfortunately sometimes it's not, as we'll see below. Then you have to experiment until you get it right.

Let me be clear; when using 4:3 DV source video, you can render Flash video files that don't have a display aspect ratio of 4:3, and it's actually very simple to do if you set your project up right. However, for novices seeking a quick and correct answer, outputting in 4:3 DV video to any 4:3 resolution like 640×480 or 320×240 is usually the safest solution.

Now let's have a quick look at NTSC DV video shot in 16:9 widescreen mode.

Standard Definition 16:9 Video

Figure 7-8 shows Premiere Pro's Properties screen for a DV video shot in widescreen mode, which is also called 16:9 mode, or Anamorphic, particularly in Final Cut Pro. You'll note that the image size is still the same 720×480, but that the pixel aspect ratio is 1.2, which directs the display device to stretch each horizontal pixel to a width of 1.2 pixels during display.

Let's do the math and see how applying a pixel aspect ratio of 1.2 to a 720×480 file produces a display aspect ratio of 16:9. If you multiply the 720 horizontal pixels by 1.2 you get 864. Divide that by 16 and you get 54. Multiply that by 9 (for the 16:9 ratio) and you get 486, which is close enough to the true 480 pixels to display correctly.

What output resolution should you use to output your widescreen Flash video files? Again, you can use any resolution that you'd like, but the simplest approach is to output a file with a 16:9 display aspect ratio like 480×270, or 640×360, again making sure to output square pixels.

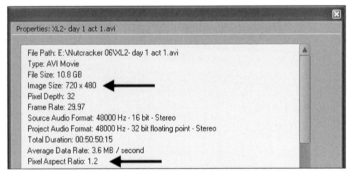

Figure 7-8
Premiere Pro Properties screen showing a DV file shot in widescreen mode.

For example, **Figure 7-9** shows a frame of a widescreen video of Stevie Barr, banjo player for a local band called No Speed Limit. I shot this in widescreen mode and output the Flash video file at a resolution of 480×270, which is a display aspect ratio of 16:9, and square pixels, and the Flash video file looks perfect.

The simple rule of thumb is to produce your Flash video at a resolution that matches the display aspect ratio of the original video, making sure to select square pixels. Let's see how that works with HDV video.

Figure 7-9
Stevie Barr of the No Speed Limit band, output in 480×270 resolution for 16:9 widescreen display.

HDV Video

Figure 7-10 shows Premiere Pro's Properties screen for HDV video. The actual resolution (image size) in pixels is 1440×1080, and the pixel aspect ratio is 1.333. Working from what we've learned to this point, this means that you stretch each horizontal pixel by 1.333 to display it correctly.

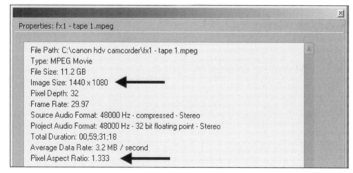

Figure 7-10
Premiere Pro's Properties screen for HDV video.

If you multiply the horizontal pixels (1440) times the pixel aspect ratio (1.333) you get 1919.52, which you can round up to 1920, making the final display resolution 1920×1080.

What's the display aspect ratio? 1920 divided by 16 equals 120, which when multiplied by 9 equals 1080. So, as you already knew, HDV has a display aspect ratio of 16:9.

In this regard, working with HDV video is just like working with widescreen DV; following the simple rule of thumb, the easiest way to produce video with a correct display aspect ratio is to output to a 16:9 resolution, like the 480×270 resolution in **Figure 7-9**. Truth be told, **Figure 7-9** was actually produced from HDV video, but the result would have been the same if shot in widescreen DV.

With this as background, let's switch over to PAL.

Working with PAL

Figure 7-11 shows the now-familiar Premiere Pro Properties screen analyzing a PAL video. As you can see, the video has a resolution of 720×575 and a pixel aspect ratio of 1.076. This means that, instead of squeezing video during display, like NTSC DV 4:3 video, PAL expands it.

What's the final post-scaling display resolution? If you multiply the horizontal resolution of 720 by 1.067, you get 768, for a final display resolution of 768×576. What's the display aspect ratio?

It's 4:3, just like NTSC. Want proof? Divide 768 by four, and you get 192. Multiply that by three to get 576.

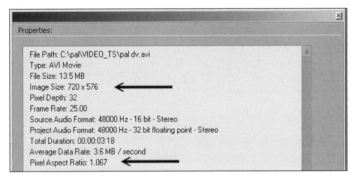

Figure 7-11
Premiere Pro's Properties screen for PAL SD DV 4:3.

Intuitively, this makes sense, since all PAL TVs have display aspect ratios of 4×3 or 16×9, just like NTSC. What does this mean for Flash videos? Essentially, the same rules that apply to NTSC video apply to Flash. That is, when working with 4:3 source materials, like normal SD DV, output your video files in a 4:3 resolution like 320×240.

When working with 16:9 source, whether widescreen DV, HDV or other PAL-based high-definition format, output in a 16:9 resolution. In all cases, output square pixels.

Now that you know how to identify the right output resolution, let's put it all together.

Summary and Recommendations

To summarize, you've got lots of reasons to go big with your video; as screen resolutions increase, you have to boost your video resolution to make the same impact, and you know that it won't take a linear rise in bandwidth to accomplish. While you can scale Flash video to larger resolutions, it won't look great or work well on older computers, so scaling is better presented as an option rather than the standard mode of viewing.

Though this may not be specific to your target viewers, in general, bandwidth is increasing and many consumer publishers like ESPN, YouTube and others are leveraging this to produce bigger screen videos at very good quality.

When formulating your final parameters, consider the amount of motion in the video, its duration and your delivery technique, remembering that you have to be more conservative with your data rate when delivering via a streaming server. Whatever data rate you choose, remember that once you cross a threshold that makes video quality "good enough," the return on your investment for additional bandwidth drops considerably.

Basically, you can approach the decision in one of two ways. I'll discuss each in turn.

Assign a Data Rate, Find the Resolution

Here, your analysis of your target audience, economics and all other relevant factors dictates a certain data rate. To identify the appropriate resolution, take the following steps:

1. Find a representative clip about 5–10 minutes long.

2. Allocate audio first. If your content has music, start at 128 kbps; if speech, start at 64 kbps. Encode at these bit rates and listen to the compressed file. If quality is acceptable, drop the data rate to the next level until quality is unacceptable due to obvious degradation. Then find the minimum bit rate above that level,that sounds artifact free. That's your audio bit rate.

3. Subtract the audio bit rate from your total allocation, leaving your video bit rate. Now you'll try to find the largest resolution with acceptable quality. Start by encoding the video at 320×240 (or 320×180 for 16:9) resolution and 30. I'll expand on this in the next chapter, but try both one-pass constant bit rate (CBR) and two-pass variable bit rate (VBR)

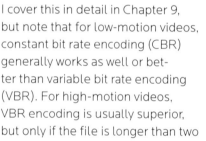

Author's Tip

I cover this in detail in Chapter 9, but note that for low-motion videos, constant bit rate encoding (CBR) generally works as well or better than variable bit rate encoding (VBR). For high-motion videos, VBR encoding is usually superior, but only if the file is longer than two minutes or so. When performing these analyses, you can typically choose the technique that will work better for your content, or, to be totally thorough, you can try both.

Note that Sorenson Squeeze is the perfect tool for this type of analysis, since it can take one source file and encode to a number of different data rates and/or resolutions. In contrast, Flix Pro can encode multiple files to the same parameters, but not one file to multiple parameters.

encoding. Note that the file needs to be at least two minutes long for VBR to really work.

Assess quality after each encoding run, paying particular attention to obvious artifacts in text, logos, faces or similar areas, which were the primary issues identified by the viewers in the Knoche, et al., studies. If these are not degraded, encode at increasingly higher resolutions, boosting horizontal resolution by 40 pixels and vertical resolution by 30 pixels (or 32 and 18 if widescreen).

Find a resolution where quality is clearly unacceptable, and then find the minimum bit rate above that resolution that is acceptable. That's your video bit rate.

Note that if video quality isn't acceptable at the lowest resolutions, you need either to tone down the motion in your videos to make the files more easily compressible, or ask for a higher bit rate. If 40 is the new 30, then 320×240 is the new 160×120, certifiably postage-stamp video. Like they say, if you can't go big, you shouldn't go at all.

Assign a Window, Find a Data Rate

The reverse scenario, of course, is when marketing says, "We need a 640×480 window, no matter how much bandwidth it takes." Here, to find that bandwidth, pursue the following analysis.

1. Find a representative clip about 5–10 minutes long.

2. Allocate audio first. If your content has music, start at 128 kbps; if speech, start at 64 kbps. Encode at these bit rates and listen to the compressed file. If quality is acceptable, drop the data rate to the next level until quality is unacceptable due to obvious degradation. Then find the minimum bit rate above that level that sounds relatively artifact free. That's your audio bit rate.

3. Now let's find the necessary video data rate. Start with a video-only data rate that's clearly sufficient; say 400 kbps for 320×240 (320×180 for 16:9), 600 kbps for 440×330 (480×270) and 800 kbps for 640×480 (640×360). Encode using both one-pass constant bit rate (CBR) and two-pass variable bit rate (VBR) encoding at the starting data rate, and then view the encoded file, paying particular attention to obvious artifacts in text, logos, faces or similar areas, which were the primary issues identified by the viewers in the Knoche, et al., studies.

If the file isn't acceptable, bump the data rate up by about 25 kbps, re-encode and re-analyze until you find a video data rate that produces acceptable quality. If the file produced by the first encoding is acceptable, do the reverse, except drop the data rate by approximately 25 kbps each encoding run. After you find a file that's clearly unacceptable, view the files encoded at the sequentially higher data rates and identify the first that shows minimal artifacts in the key areas. That's your video bit rate.

After completing this analysis, you should be able to finalize most basic encoding parameters. So you know where you're going; let's figure out how to get there.

Scaling to Your Target Resolution—Where and When?

Most video producers edit their videos in a traditional editor like Adobe Premiere Pro or Final Cut Pro, then either directly output to Flash using an internal Flash Encoding Module (Premiere Pro) or via a third-party plug-in like Flix Exporter (Final Cut Pro).

Alternatively, you can export what I call an "intermediate" file that you can input into a third-party encoder like On2 Flix Pro or Sorenson Squeeze. In many cases, particularly when producing FLV files with an alpha channel (since you have to change the format anyway), you may want to scale down to your target resolution when producing the intermediate file.

Accordingly, the next section will cover how to produce FLV files directly and intermediate files in Premiere Pro and Final Cut Pro. Since some producers will perform these tasks in Adobe After Effects, I've covered that as well.

I'll start with Premiere Pro since we've been working with its Properties screens, then move to Final Cut Pro and then Adobe After Effects. Note that, in Chapter 9, I detail the complete workflows for these options for all three programs; here I describe how to create the optimal project preset and show only those screens that relate to output resolution.

Producing the Correct Output Resolution in Premiere Pro

By far the easiest way to produce Flash Video with the proper display aspect ratio in all editors, including Premiere Pro, is to create the project using the desired output resolution and pixel aspect ratio, which will always be square. This technique lets you produce video of any arbitrary resolution, from any source, whether HDV, HD or DV. Since you're outputting at the same resolution you're designing in, you also get the most accurate preview of how the ultimate video will look.

Creating a Customer Project Preset in Premiere Pro

Let's set up the scenario. I shot some interviews with the No Speed Limit band in HDV, but the band wanted to explore outputting in multiple resolutions, including 4:3, 16:9 and 300×300. So, I'm starting with widescreen HDV and need to produce a variety of output resolutions. To get to 4:3 in Premiere Pro, here's what I would do:

1. Run Premiere and click New Project when the Splash Screen appears.

2. Click the Custom Settings tab. In this screen:

   - Change Editing Mode to Desktop

   - Set Frame Size as desired (I'm using 440×330, but it could be any frame size

   - Set the Pixel Aspect Ratio to Square Pixels (1.0)

   - Set Fields to No Fields (Progressive Scan)

   - Leave all other fields at their defaults.

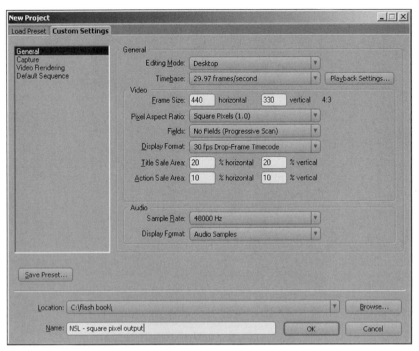

Figure 7-12
Creating custom project settings in Premiere Pro.

3. If desired, click the Save Preset button on the lower left-hand side of the window, and name and save the preset. It will forever thereafter appear as a preset you can select as normal when starting a new project.

4. Name and save the project as normal.

Again, once you've set up the project properly, you can input video from any source, and Premiere Pro automatically handles the aspect ratios correctly. For example, in **Figure 7-13**, I'm working on the interview with Josh Pickett, the lead guitar player, as he explains how the band came to play at Virginia Governor Tim Kaine's inauguration.

This footage is from the same HDV tape as the Stevie Barr interview shown in **Figure 7-9**, but it looks like 4:3 resolution video in Premiere's Program Monitor. You can see on the left in the Effects Controls panel that I've scaled the video to 39% of its original resolution, which gives me plenty of room to zoom in for a medium close up and perfect rule-of-thirds positioning (can't do much about the light pole, however . . . sigh).

Again, in Chapter 9, I detail, step by step, how to produce intermediate files in QuickTime format for encoding in a third-party Flash encoder and how to encode directly to Flash format from Premiere Pro. I'll describe in each case how to maintain the appropriate display aspect ratio. In this chapter, I'll jump right to the critical screen or screens to identify the proper settings.

Figure 7-13
Editing the 16:9 footage in a 4:3 window provides a great preview.

Outputting an Intermediate QuickTime File in Premiere Pro

To output an intermediate file to encode to Flash in another encoding tool, you would export an uncompressed QuickTime file using the parameters shown in **Figure 7-14**. Again, your goal is to output using the same resolution and aspect ratio as your project file, particularly the square pixel aspect ratio.

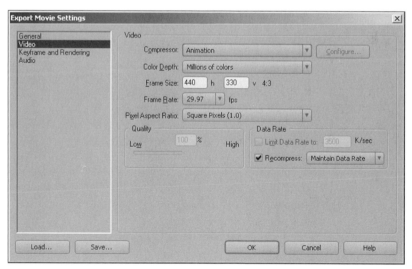

Figure 7-14
Premiere Pro output settings for an intermediate file to input into a third-party encoder.

Outputting Via the Flash Encoding Module in Premiere Pro

To output a Flash video file directly from Premiere Pro, you work through the Export Settings window of the Flash Encoding Module shown in **Figure 7-15**. It's definitely tiny in the figure, but if you look at the bottom left-hand corner, you'll see the text "Source: 440 w × 330 h." This lets you know that I'm working in a project file of that resolution (see **Figure 7-12**).

In the Basic Parameters window on the right, I input 440×330 as my Frame Width and Height, and the tiny text on the bottom right of the preview window reflects that, reading "Output: 330 w × 330 h."

All is in harmony; say "hhhhmmmm." Though the source video has a pixel aspect ratio of 1.33, Premiere outputs the appropriate square-pixel resolution at any output resolution, because that's what I specified in the project file.

Figure 7-15
Flash output settings in the Adobe Media Encoder. Note the Deinterlacing checkbox in the upper left (which often doesn't work).

Author's Tip

In **Figure 7-15**, if you click the Options button in the Video Codec section you open the Flash Video Encoding Settings screen, which has a control for resizing your video. Note that you don't have to re-size video in this window to produce your video; the resolution controls shown in **Figure 7-15** govern.

If you do resize, and the resolution doesn't match that input in **Figure 7-15**, you'll distort the display aspect ratio in the Flash video file.

However, if I typed in 16:9 resolution like 480×270 in the Basic Parameters window, Premiere Pro would preserve the aspect ratio of the video by inserting letterboxes on both sides of the video.

Here are some final summary points on aspect-related issues in Premiere Pro:

- Premiere Pro can't *change* project settings once they're set, but you can import a project into a project, and Premiere Pro will apply the new proj-ect settings to any sequences created in the old project. This can be really helpful if you produced for SD DVD using an SD DV preset, but now want to output Flash video. Specifically, you can set up your Flash project to the desired output parameters as discussed above, and then import your SD project into the Flash project. You'll probably have to resize the videos in the sequences, but you're not starting at square 1. Alternatively, you can render a final file from the SD project, create a new project for streaming, and then input the final output file from your HD project.

- In general, the display aspect ratio of your project (4:3 or 16:9) will practically dictate the display aspect ratio of your Flash video. That is, if you selected the standard preset for 4:3 SD DV, it's simple to output a 320×240 file with the proper display aspect ratio. However, if you try to produce a 16:9 Flash video file from that same project, say at 480×270, the file would have black letterboxes on the sides. Similarly, if you tried to produce 4:3 video from a 16:9 project, you'd see letterboxing on the top and bottom. While there may be a workaround, it's definitely easier to simply create a new project file using the target output parameters.

- Accordingly, so long as your output resolution matches the display aspect ratio of your project, you don't absolutely need a custom project. On the other hand, if your target output resolution is not 4:3 or 16:9, creating a custom project set for your target output resolution is definitely the way to go.

Enough about Premiere Pro; let's have a quick look at Final Cut Pro.

Producing the Correct Output Resolution in Final Cut Pro

In this section, I'll describe how to maintain the correct display aspect ratio in Final Cut Pro, and show you the key screens and settings to make it happen when producing intermediate files and Flash files with On2's Flix Exporter. In Chapter 9, I'll detail the entire workflow for both operations.

In a nutshell, Final Cut Pro works pretty much the same way as Premiere Pro. Specifically, for those who didn't read that section:

- The easiest approach for creating aspect-ratio correct Flash video is to create and use a Sequence Preset with the target output settings for your Flash video file, irrespective of whether you're producing an intermediate QuickTime file or Flash file. With this technique, you can input any source video, pan and zoom within and render video with the correct display aspect ratio.

- That said, you can easily output 4:3 resolution video from 4:3 sequences—for example, outputting a 400×300 file from an SD DV sequence. Ditto for 16:9 video from widescreen (er, Anamorphic in FCP-speak) projects, like 480×270 files from an HDV or widescreen DV project.

Creating Sequence Presets in Final Cut Pro

Let's work through the procedure of creating a Sequence Preset, then open a sequence and apply the preset. Follow the bouncing ball.

1. Click Final Cut Pro and choose Audio/Video Settings. Final Cut Pro opens that window.

2. Select the Sequence Presets tab.

3. Click any preset and click the Duplicate button. This creates a duplicate preset you can customize and name (see **Figure 7-16**).

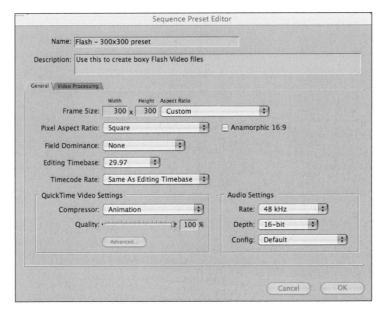

Figure 7-16
Creating a sequence preset in Final Cut Pro.

4. In this window:

    *   Customize the Name and Description. Be as witty and pithy as possible (hey, you're working on a Mac!).

    *   Insert the target resolution. Note that it does not have to match 4:3, 16:9 or any other display aspect ratio, though you may have to Choose Custom in the Aspect Ratio list box to input nonstandard settings.

    *   In the Pixel Aspect Ratio list box, choose Square.

    *   Do not check the Anamorphic 16:9, under any circumstances (even if you're working on HDV video or are outputting 16:9 resolution files).

- In the Field Dominance list box, choose None.

- In the Compressor list box, choose Animation. This is the codec you'll use to render your intermediate files.

- Leave the audio settings as shown.

5. Click OK to close the Sequence Preset Editor window and return to the Sequence Presets tab of the Audio/Video Settings window.

6. The new Preset should show up in the Presets window. If desired, you can click the area to the immediate left of the new preset, and Final Cut Pro will apply the preset to all new sequences.

To change existing sequences, right click the sequence in the Browser window and choose Settings, which will open the Sequence Settings window (**Figure 7-17**).

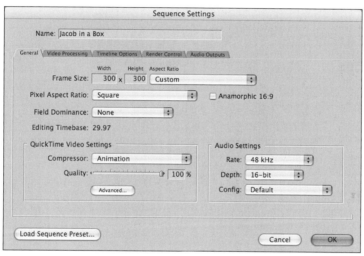

Figure 7-17
You can also change preset settings in the Sequence Settings window.

Author's Tip

QuickTime's Animation codec has become the codec of choice for producing intermediate files for encoding elsewhere. I discuss how to use it to preserve alpha channel information after chroma keying in Chapter 9 (hint—you need to configure it for millions of colors+).

I ran a quick test against the Apple Intermediate codec, and the Animation codec was twice the size, but the colors were noticeably brighter. Note that when Adobe creates FLV files in Adobe After Effects and Adobe Premiere Pro, the programs first create intermediate files in QuickTime format using the TGA codec using Millions+ colors. If you're unhappy with the Animation codec, you might want to give the TGA format a try.

There you can input the desired settings manually, or import the sequence preset you just created by clicking the Load Sequence Preset button on the lower left.

Once you finalize your project settings, you can import footage from any source and Final Cut Pro will automatically manage the aspect ratios for you. For example, **Figure 7-18** shows No Speed Limit's bass player Jacob Eller. Though it's an HDV video file with a display aspect ratio of 16:9, the aspect ratio within the 300×300 window is correct.

Figure 7-18
Editing an HDV file in a 300×300 window in Final Cut Pro. I finally got rid of that light pole!

Outputting an Intermediate QuickTime File in Final Cut Pro

One of the cool things about creating a sequence preset is that you've already set your encoding parameters, so you don't need to review them when you're ready to export. Just choose File > Export > QuickTime Movie, then name and save the file without even looking at the export parameters.

If you haven't created a preset, you'll have to output using the QuickTime Conversion option, which I detail in Chapter 9. The key resolution-related controls are in the Export Size Settings window shown in **Figure 7-19.** In this window:

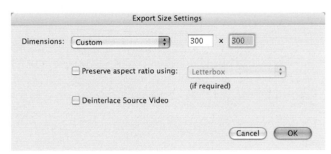

Figure 7-19
Exporting to the proper resolution and aspect ratio in Final Cut Pro.

- Choose the target resolution in the Dimensions list box, or choose Custom, and manually enter file height and width.

- Do not click the Deinterlace Source Video project; this will have no effect (see note below).

- Assuming that your goal is full-frame (no letterboxing or cropping), aspect-ratio correct video, do not check the Preserve Aspect Ratio checkbox.

  - If you created a custom preset, or inserted an output resolution that matches the display aspect ratio of the sequence (like 320×240 for SD DV, or 480×270 for HDV), you shouldn't have to click the Preserve Aspect Ratio checkbox.

  - When outputting a resolution that doesn't match the display aspect ratio of the sequence, if you don't check the checkbox, Final Cut Pro will produce the file at that resolution, which will generally distort the aspect ratio of the intermediate file. If you click the Preserve Aspect Ratio checkbox, you can choose to have Final Cut Pro preserve the aspect ratio via letterboxing or cropping, or choose scaling, which will again distort the video.

Author's Tip

I discuss deinterlacing in detail below. For now, in my tests, deinterlacing solely in the QuickTime output panel shown in **Figure 7-19** did not deinterlace the file. To produce optimal results in Final Cut Pro, you should apply the program's Deinterlace filter when producing intermediate files via the QuickTime export routine. You can find it in the Video subfolder in the Effects tab.

Outputting Via Flix Exporter in Final Cut Pro

OK, now let's output an FLV file directly using Flix Exporter. Once again, I'll detail this entire workflow in Chapter 9, but show the "money" screen in **Figure 7-20**, specifically the Width and Height parameters and the Use host dimensions checkbox.

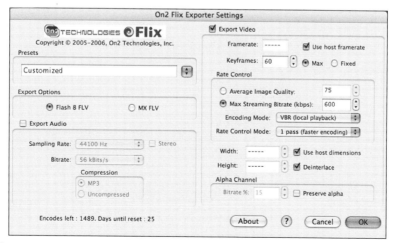

Figure 7-20
Exporting with Flix Exporter in Final Cut Pro.

Here's how to use these controls:

- If you've created a custom sequence setting that matches your target output resolution, click Use host dimensions. This is the easiest case.

- If you're scaling down to a resolution that matches the display aspect ratio of your sequence (like 320×240 for SD DV, or 480×270 for HDV), uncheck the Use host dimensions checkbox and type the target Width and Height. Flix Exporter will scale to that target.

- If the target doesn't match the display aspect ratio of the sequence, Flix Exporter will squeeze the video into the selected resolution, most likely distorting the appearance of the compressed video.

- Note that checking the Deinterlace checkbox does deinterlace the video without applying Final Cut Pro's own deinterlace filter (unlike QuickTime's deinterlace checkbox shown in **Figure 7-19**).

Producing the Correct Output Resolution in After Effects

After Effects is a great tool for compositing, animation and many other special effects. This section describes how to maintain the correct display aspect ratio in After Effects, and shows the key screens and settings to maintain that aspect ratio when producing intermediate files and Flash files with After Effect's Flash Encoding module and On2's Flix Exporter. In Chapter 9, I'll detail the entire workflow for all three operations.

In a nutshell, After Effects works similarly to Premiere Pro and Final Cut Pro. Specifically:

- If your goal is to produce aspect-ratio correct video without a letterbox or cropping, the easiest approach is to create and use a custom composition setting that matches the target resolution of your Flash video file, irrespective of whether you're producing an intermediate QuickTime file or Flash video file. With this technique, you can input any source video, pan and zoom within the video and produce video with the correct display aspect ratio.

- That said, you can easily output 4:3 resolution video from 4:3 compositions—for example, outputting a 400×300 file from an SD DV project. Ditto for 16:9 video from widescreen projects, like 480×270 files from an HDV or widescreen DV project.

Creating Custom Composition Settings in After Effects

Let's start by learning how to create a custom composition setting. After creating a new composition, do the following:

1. Click the composition in the Project panel and choose Composition Settings. After Effects opens the Composition Settings window (**Figure 7-21**).

2. If desired, type the Composition Name.

3. Type the desired Width and Height in the respective boxes.

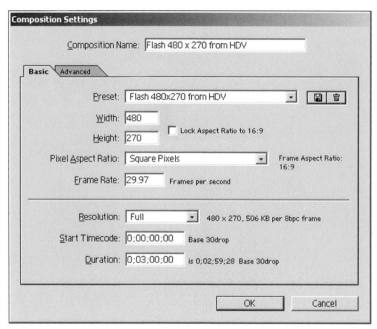

Figure 7-21
Creating a composition preset in After Effects.

4.   From the Pixel Aspect Ratio drop-down list, choose Square Pixels.

5.   Complete the other parameters as necessary for your project.

6.   When the preset is complete, click the small diskette to the right of the Preset drop-down list. This will open a window that allows you to name and save the preset. In future projects you'll be able to select it from the drop-down list, rather than creating it from scratch.

Once you finalize your composition settings, you can import footage of any pixel or display aspect ratio and After Effects will automatically manage the aspect ratios for you.

Outputting an Intermediate QuickTime File in After Effects
If you're outputting a QuickTime intermediate file, click File > Export > QuickTime Movie, and you'll see the same QuickTime export controls you'll see in Final Cut Pro, or QuickTime Player.

Again, the most important screen is the Export Size Settings screen shown in **Figure 7-22**.

In this window:

•   Choose the target resolution in the Dimensions list box, or choose Custom, and manually enter file height and width. In this case, because I was using a 480×270 preset, the dimensions appeared automatically in the fields.

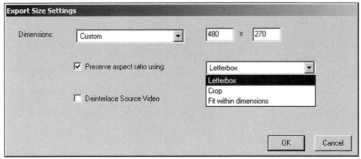

Figure 7-22
Outputting an HDV file into a 480×270 Window in After Effects.

- After Effects should deinterlace automatically each time you render to a frame-based format, whether QuickTime or Flash video. Since After Effects essentially hands off a deinterlaced file to the encoding utility, you don't have to choose deinterlacing in that utility.

- Assuming that your goal is full-frame (no letterboxing or cropping), aspect-ratio correct Flash video, do not check the Preserve Aspect Ratio checkbox.

  - If you created a custom preset, or inserted an output resolution that matches the display aspect ratio of the composition (like 320×240 for SD DV, or 480×270 for HDV), you shouldn't have to click the Preserve Aspect Ratio checkbox.

  - When outputting a resolution that doesn't match the display aspect ratio of the composition, and don't check the checkbox, After Effects will distort the aspect ratio of the intermediate file. If you click the Preserve Aspect Ratio checkbox, you can choose to have After Effects preserve the aspect ratio via letterboxing or cropping, or choose scaling, which will again distort the video.

Outputting Via the Flash Encoding Module in After Effects

This is the Flash Encoding module that After Effects inherited from the Flash 8 Video Encoder after the merger with Macromedia. To access the module, click File > Export > Flash Video, which takes you to the Flash Video Encoding Settings screen, which, after you click the Show Advanced Settings button, will take you to **Figure 7-23**.

Here's how to use these controls:

- If you've created a custom composition preset that matches your target, you can leave the Resize video checkbox unchecked. After Effects will hand the module a deinterlaced, 480×270 sequence that it will encode at that resolution.

- If you're scaling down to the same display aspect ratio as a standard project file (like 320×240 for SD DV, or 480×270 for HDV), check the Resize video checkbox and enter the target resolution. Note that I've never seen the Maintain aspect

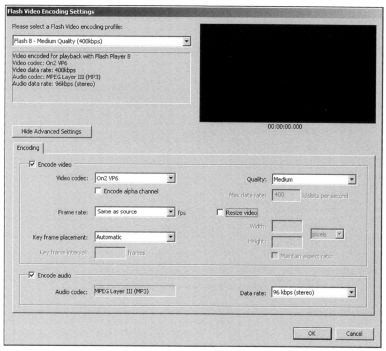

Figure 7-23
Exporting with the Flash Encoding module in After Effects.

ratio checkbox become active when outputting from either Premiere Pro or After Effects; if you enter a resolution that doesn't match the display aspect ratio of your project, After Effects will simply compress to that resolution, distorting your video file.

Outputting Via Flix Exporter in After Effects

To access Flix Exporter, choose File > On Technologies Flash Video – FLV, and you'll get to the screen shown in **Figure 7-24**, which, not surprisingly, looks a lot like **Figure 7-20**. Again, I'll detail all encoding decisions in Chapter 9, and here focus on the Width and Height parameters and associated controls.

Here's how to use these controls:

- If you've created a custom composition preset that matches your target, click Use host dimensions.

- If you're scaling down to the same display aspect ratio as a standard project file (like 320×240 for SD DV, or 480×270 for HDV), uncheck the Use host dimensions checkbox and type the target Width and Height. Flix Exporter will scale to that target. If the target doesn't match the display aspect ratio of the source footage, Flix Exporter will squeeze the video into the selected resolution, distorting the appearance of the compressed video.

Producing the Correct Output Resolution in After Effects   105

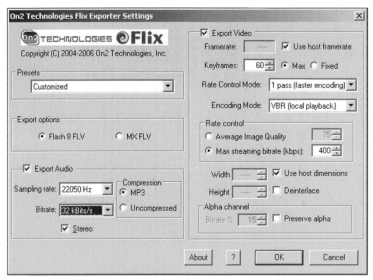

Figure 7-24
Exporting with Flix Exporter in After Effects.

- Checking the Deinterlace checkbox has no effect, since After Effects is deinterlacing the video before handing it over to the plug-in.

OK, almost home. Now that we've seen how to scale to the proper resolution, let's address deinterlacing, which I've danced around the entire chapter, and also have a quick look at noise reduction filtering.

Preprocessing Your Video

Winding down this beast of all chapters, in this section I'll cover two final details in perfecting your video. The first is deinterlacing, the second noise filtering.

Deinterlacing

As you probably know, most video is interlaced, with each frame comprised of two fields, one containing the odd lines (1,3,5) and the other containing the even lines (2,4,6). For NTSC video, which displays roughly 60 fields per second, these fields are actually shot 1/60 of a second apart.

In contrast, Flash is frame based, so when producing Flash video from an interlaced source, your encoding tool has to create one frame from the two fields shot 1/60 of a second apart. This can get ugly with high motion video, since a lot happens in that 1/60th of a second and the fields don't precisely match up. That's why, when producing Flash video, you should always deinterlace your source videos to remove the motion-related artifacts (**Figure 7-25**). Deinterlacing is a technique that intelligently combines the two fields to reduce or eliminate interlacing artifacts.

Figure 7-25
Final Cut Pro without deinterlacing filter on the left, with it on the right.

When I noted above that Final Cut Pro didn't perform well without the deinterlacing effect applied, I meant that simply clicking the checkbox in the QuickTime export controls had no effect, as you can see in **Figure 7-25** on the left. The text and observer guy look blurry, because there's basically two images of each, one from each field. On the right, I applied Final Cut Pro's deinterlace filter, and the problem went away.

All editing and encoding tools have deinterlacing filters, which you should always apply when encoding interlaced source videos. Once you get the dials and levers set correctly, they all work well, but sometimes it takes a while to find all the controls.

We've seen the deinterlace controls for most applications already; when detailing encoding procedures in Chapter 9, I'll include enabling deinterlacing as a separate step to make the workflow as clear as possible.

Noise Reduction

Most encoding tools offer some kind of noise reduction designed to reduce the artifacts created by noise in the video. Their effectiveness always depends upon the content of the clip.

In general, if your clips are high quality and relatively noise free, don't bother to even try noise reduction; you'll simply blur the video with little benefit. If your clips are very noisy, noise reduction is worth a try, but experiment on shorter sections before applying to the entire clip.

Noise reduction sounds trivial, but it's really not, as the tool must determine what's true noise (e.g., graininess) and what's true motion (the cute blond winking at me). The best noise-reduction filter I've ever worked with is a tool called AlgoSuite from Algolith (*www.algolith.com*). It's expensive and slow, but if you've got a serious noise problem in some footage that you absolutely need cleaned up, it's definitely worth the time and money.

Conclusion

Whew, I'm exhausted, and I'm sure you are too. We covered lots of ground in this chapter, finding the optimal display resolution, frame rate and audio/video data rate, then making sure that you output at the right display aspect ratio. A final look at deinterlacing and noise reduction should allow you to totally perfect your footage.

Next chapter, I'll discuss how to produce alpha channel video with a variety of tools. Then, in Chapter 9 I'll pull it all together with detailed workflows for producing FLV files from a number of popular editing and encoding applications.

CHAPTER 8

Producing Alpha Channel Video

Flash 8 introduced the ability to utilize FLV files with an alpha channel in Flash projects and key out the background in real time during playback. The only caveat (as detailed in Chapter 15) is that real-time keying is processor intensive on the viewing station, which can slow playback on lower-end computers.

To successfully create real-world (as opposed to animated) video with an alpha channel, you'll have to shoot against a blue or green screen. I won't describe that process in this book, though I touch on lighting for such video in Chapter 4. Instead, I'll focus on the workflow for creating FLV files with an alpha channel, which has two stages:

- Using a chroma key or similar effect in an editor or encoding tool to eliminate, key out or chroma key the background (all the same thing, of course, just different terms for it)

- Producing the actual FLV with alpha channel.

Your workflow will vary based upon your editing application and preferred encoding tool. With some programs, like Adobe After Effects, you'll have up to three options, which are:

- Applying the chroma-key effect and outputting an intermediate QuickTime file for encoding to FLV format with an alpha channel in a separate Flash encoding tool like Sorenson Squeeze or On2 Flix Pro

- Applying the chroma-key effect and outputting to Flash format using the internal Flash encoder based upon the Flash 8 Video Encoder, which offers only single-pass, constant bit rate encoding (CBR)

- Applying the chroma-key effect and creating the FLV file with alpha channel using On2 Technologies Flix Exporter, which supports one and two pass, and CBR and variable bit rate encoding (VBR).

Premiere Pro offers the first two options, but not the third, while Final Cut Pro offers the first and third, but not the second. With other tools, like On2's Flix Pro encoder, you can apply a chroma-key filter and encode in a single step.

This chapter starts with a general description of how to apply a chroma-key effect, and then describes how to produce an intermediate QuickTime file with alpha channel for encoding into FLV format with an alpha channel in another encoder.

After that, I'll identify the two mandatory options for creating an FLV file with alpha channel, and finish with an application-specific tour of some key editing and encoding tools. Overall, in this chapter, you will learn:

- The available workflows for most common editing and encoding applications

- How to use chroma key or similar filters to key out the backgrounds in Adobe After Effects, Adobe Premiere Pro, Apple Final Cut and On2 Flix Pro

- How to create a QuickTime intermediate video with an alpha channel in Adobe After Effects and Premiere Pro and Apple Final Cut Pro that you can import into a Flash encoding program to produce into an FLV file with an alpha channel

- How to render an FLV video with an alpha channel in Adobe After Effects, Adobe Premiere Pro, the Adobe Flash Media Encoder, On2 Flix Pro and Flix Exporter and Sorenson Squeeze.

Author's Tip

Both Sorenson (*www.sorensonmedia.com*) and On2 (*www.on2.com*) offer free trial versions of the encoding tools discussed in this chapter. If you'd like to follow along with some of the encoding workflows demonstrated below, consider downloading these now.

If you're charged with setting up the chroma-key shoot and need information on choosing a background, you might find an article I wrote for EventDV called "Compositing 101" helpful; you can find it on the web at: *http://www.eventdv.net/Articles/ReadArticle.aspx?ArticleID=8596*.

Note that Chapter 9 details the rendering and encoding workflows for all tools discussed in this chapter. For this reason, I'll only address those controls necessary to produce an FLV file with an alpha channel or intermediate QuickTime file with alpha channel.

Perfecting the Chroma Key

Whatever workflow you select, the first production step is applying the filter or effect that keys out the background. Optimally, your goal is to totally eliminate the blue or green screen background while completely preserving the foreground image, and smoothing the edge between the subject and the background you've eliminated. This will result in a high-quality image displayed over the Flash video background with no residue from the background or jagged edges.

Note that the ultimate quality of the chroma key depends upon two basic factors: how well you've shot the video, and the quality of the chroma-key program that you're using. If the video is unevenly lit, shot with too little light or using a consumer-grade camcorder, you may not be able to produce a high-quality result. In addition, not all software chroma-key tools are created equal, and some provide a much better quality than others.

Most video editors offer multiple chroma-keying tools that work more or less similarly. In this chapter, I'll demonstrate the procedure using screens from several different chroma-keys tools to provide a broad look at their operation and capabilities. By way of background, in all examples, I'll work with a clip titled *jan green screen.avi*, which is a clip of me shot against a green screen.

To start in the editor, you would typically drag the chroma key clip to the top timeline track in your video editor. In **Figure 8-1**, I've inserted a white matte on track Video 1, and inserted *jan green screen.avi* to Video 2. That's because the white matte will help me set the chroma-key controls in Premiere Pro; once I've applied the filters and finalized my parameters, I'll delete the white matte, drag the green-screen file down to Video 1 and render the file.

Like most editors, Premiere Pro has multiple keying filters like Color Key and Green Screen Key. Over the years, I've used the Chroma Key filter to good effect, which is why I started there, but if you can't get good results with this filter, try the others.

Have a quick look at the controls in **Figure 8-1**. Like most keying tools, the first step is to click the eyedropper and choose a spot in the background that represents the color that you're seeking to eliminate. I typically

Author's Tip

At the time of this writing, Premiere Pro could not create an FLV file with alpha channel or even an intermediate QuickTime file with alpha channel, due to a bug in version 2.01. Adobe is aware of the problem and plans to address it in an interim release, which hopefully will be available when you read this book.

If not, you can apply chroma-key filters in Premiere Pro and render in After Effects. You just import the Premiere Pro project into After Effects, drag the sequence down into a composition and render the composition as described below. Note, however, that if you have After Effects, it's usually a better tool for chroma keying than Premiere Pro anyway, so you might as well do all the work in After Effects and skip Premiere Pro for this activity.

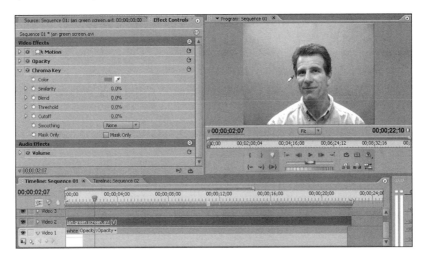

Figure 8-1
Applying the Chroma Key filter in Premiere Pro.

choose a spot in the middle, which hopefully will represent an average value. With Premiere Pro, if you press the Ctrl key before you click the eyedropper, Premiere will average the value of the pixel chosen using a 5×5 grid surrounding the pixel, which provides a better average value.

After selecting the background color with the eyedropper, you adjust Similarity, or the equivalent tool, to expand the range of colors eliminated. Generally, you expand the range until the background disappears, or until you start eroding the foreground subject. Other controls vary by editor and effect. Experiment with all controls until you completely eliminate the background without eroding the subject.

Smoothing the edges between your subject and the background is critical to quality; Premiere offers a Smoothing list box that I always set to High, the strongest setting. Most other tools offer a slider, which smoothes the edge but can get blurry when you apply too strong a value.

To help judge the effectiveness of your keying, zoom into the preview screen and examine all the edges between the subject and the background, which is where many problems appear. Many programs let you toggle the background between black, white and the checkerboard shown in **Figure 8-2**, which is Final Cut Pro.

Also helpful is the mask view (click Matte view in Final Cut Pro, which is shown in **Figure 8-2**). This reverses the effect display, and shows where the filter is keying out portions of the subject. These are the dark areas you see in my profile in the figure, which obviously indicate that you need to fine tune your settings.

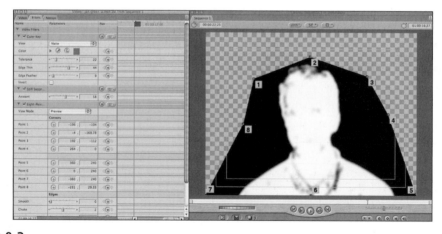

Figure 8-2
To perfect the chroma key, zoom in to examine the edges, and click into mask view. Those dark spots throughout the image are definite problem areas.

Two other keying-related tools are worthy of note. First is a *garbage matte*, which lets you draw a 4-, 8- or 16-point shape around your subject and eliminates any of the background outside those points. In **Figure 8-2**, I've drawn an 8-point garbage matte around my head, and anything outside the black figure will automatically be excluded from the image. This is especially useful when you're having problems obtaining a clean key around the outer edge.

The other tool I've applied in Final Cut Pro is Spill Suppression, which eliminates some of the color fringing that often appears around the edges of the subject in the chroma-key video. This can also make the difference between good and great quality.

Before rendering, scan through the entire file to make sure the chroma-key effect works cleanly throughout. Oftentimes, if a subject leans forward or otherwise catches the light differently in some frames, you may have to adjust the values of the chroma-key filter on those frames to cleanly eliminate the background. While all editors allow you to set key frames to make such an adjustment, On2 Flix Pro doesn't, which can hurt quality in real-world videos.

If you've applied a garbage matte, you also want to make sure that you didn't inadvertently cut off an arm or other limb when the subject moves. In this video, for example, I reach up to point to a lighting fixture with my left arm, which would definitely go beyond the garbage matte shown in **Figure 8-2**.

Finally, before rendering, it's also good practice to drag your video a bit to one side to assess whether the chroma-key clip is impacting the background. For example, in **Figure 8-3**, a screen shot from After Effects, the strip of white to my right shows the area of the background that's not beneath the green-screen clip.

Author's Tip

I know you find this discussion fascinating, but what you're really wondering is what is the proper spelling of chroma key? After all, we've seen it spelled chroma key and Chroma Key in this chapter, and you've probably seen chromakey, chroma-key and perhaps even ChromaKey. Well, it's like this. If you enter the term chromakey into *www.dictionary.com*, you'll see it listed as either chroma key (in dictionary.com) and chromakey (in the Crystal Reference Encyclopedia). So, I'm assuming both of these are right.

For the record, I've adopted the dictionary.com spelling throughout the book. However, if Adobe, Apple or On2 decide to call their filter "Chroma Key" I'll refer to the filter with that spelling, so you'll be able to find the filter without confusion.

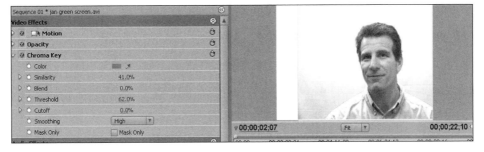

Figure 8-3
Dragging the clip to one side reveals whether the chroma-key effect is darkening the background.

The rest of the background is grayish white, indicating that the chroma-key clip is darkening the background, which would produce a blurry mess in our alpha channel Flash video. Though it's easy to see here, sometimes you won't notice this effect until you drag the clip to one side.

Overall, understand that applying a chroma-key effect is an interactive, potentially time-consuming exercise; try a little of this and a little of that, check and double check the results, and you'll be sure to produce the highest possible quality.

Creating QuickTime Movies with an Alpha Channel

After applying the chroma-key effect in your video editor, you can output a QuickTime file with the alpha channel related information and render your FLV file in another encoder. If creating such an intermediate file, use the QuickTime animation codec, with a color depth of Millions of Colors+. Note that using any other color depth will not work, since the alpha channel information won't pass through to the encoder.

Though the interfaces differ and workflows differ, all editors expose the encoding controls shown in **Figure 8-4.** Output your QuickTime file using these settings, and On2 Flix Pro and Sorenson Squeeze will recognize the alpha channel information and preserve the transparency in the final FLV.

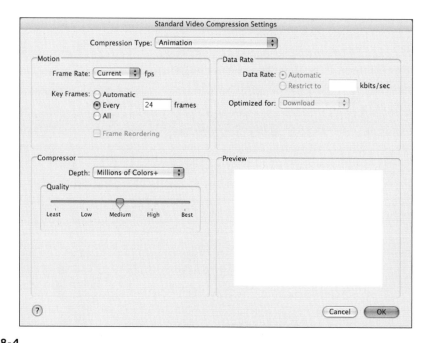

Figure 8-4
To preserve alpha channel information from the chroma-key effect, compress using QuickTime's Animation codec to these settings.

When creating this intermediate file, you should also scale your video down to your final output resolution and deinterlace your video. Again, all editors present this differently; **Figure 8-5** shows the controls from Final Cut Pro.

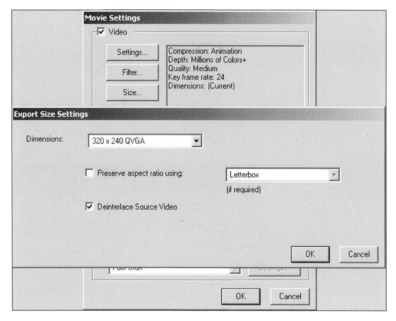

Figure 8-5
Scaling during output from your editor saves lots of disk space.

What about audio? When producing an intermediate file for later encoding, you should simply pass through the uncompressed audio and compress to final MP3 format while encoding to Flash.

Creating the FLV File with Alpha Channel

Sometimes you'll create the FLV file with alpha channel in a third-party editor using the intermediate file you just created; other times you'll create it directly in your editor. Either way, there are two high-level requirements for creating an FLV file with an alpha channel, which are:

- You must encode using On2's VP6 codec
- You must engage the Encode alpha channel switch present in all Flash encoding programs.

Figure 8-6, a shot of the custom encoding screen from Adobe's Flash 8 Video Encoder, illustrates both of these conditions.

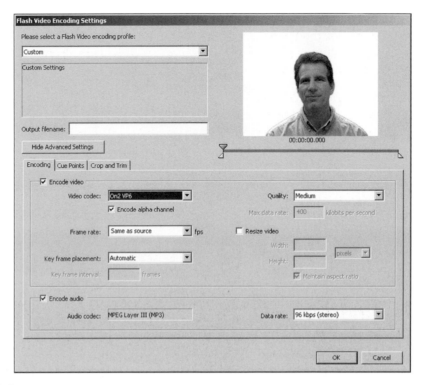

Figure 8-6
To encode an FLV file with alpha channel, you must use On2's VP6 codec and engage the appropriate alpha channel control, here the Encode alpha channel checkbox.

As you'll see below, all Flash encoders let you choose either the VP6 or Sorenson Spark codec, and you must choose the former. All also have checkboxes or similar controls that enable encoding with alpha channel. With this as background, let's start looking at the individual applications.

Application-Specific Details

With the previous sections as prologue, I'll run through the capabilities of each application that can perform a chroma-key operation in politically correct alphabetical order. I won't detail the chroma-key operations of each program; for a more detailed discussion, see the previous sections.

Adobe After Effects

As mentioned at the start of this chapter, Adobe After Effects has three alpha channel-related output options: producing an intermediate QuickTime file for encoding elsewhere, producing an FLV with alpha channel using the Flash Encoding module, or producing an FLV with alpha channel using On2's Flix Exporter. After describing After Effect's chroma-key capabilities, I'll illustrate the key screens in all three output alternatives. Once again, you can find the detailed workflow in Chapter 9.

Chroma Keying in After Effects

The Keylight plug-in from The Foundry and Framestore CFC is the best chroma-key plug-in I've ever used; it comes standard with the professional version of After Effects, or you can buy it for around $400 if you have the standard edition.

The filter is shown in **Figure 8-3**. Generally, once you choose the screen color with the eye-dropper (remember to use the Ctrl key to average the values), the plug-in does the rest. The only downside is a slight tendency to darken the background, which you can see by dragging the image a bit to the right and resolve by adjusting Screen Gain.

If you don't have this plug-in, After Effects has a traditional Color Key filter that works well, which you can supplement with a Spill Suppressor. Unlike Final Cut Pro's spill suppression tool, with After Effects you need to choose a color to suppress with the eyedropper.

Since you've probably already keyed out the background, you can't click there, so the easiest technique is to select the color chip next to the Key Color, as shown in **Figure 8-7**. Also shown in the figure is a four-point mask inserted to serve as a garbage matte.

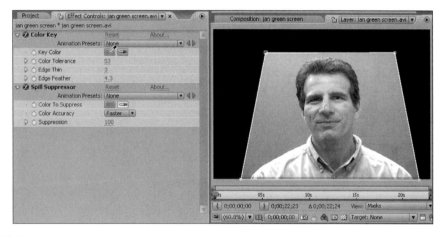

Figure 8-7
Keying in After Effects.

Outputting an FLV File with Alpha Channel with the Flash Encoding Module

After you've applied and tested your chroma-key effect, After Effects can directly output an FLV file with alpha channel using its Flash Encoding module, which only offers one pass, CBR encoding. If you decide to go this route, make sure to check the Encode alpha channel in the Flash Video Encoding Settings screen shown in **Figure 8-6**.

Outputting an FLV File with Alpha Channel with Flix Exporter

After you've applied and tested your chroma-key effect, After Effects can output an FLV file with alpha channel via the Flix Exporter, assuming you're purchased this third-party tool. To access the tool, choose File > Export > On2 Technologies Flash Video - FLV. After Effects opens the On2 Technologies Flix Exporter Settings window (**Figure 8-8**).

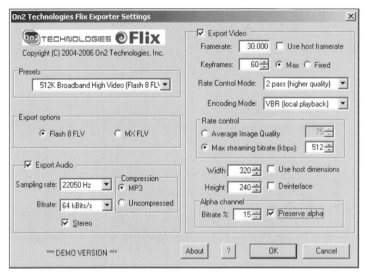

Figure 8-8
Encoding an FLV Video file with On2's Flix Exporter.

1. To export an FLV file with alpha channel:

    •   In the Export options area, check the Flash 8 FLV checkbox

    •   In the Alpha channel area, click the Preserve alpha checkbox and set the desired Bitrate % (the default is OK).

2. Click OK to close the dialog and name and save your file as normal.

Author's Tip

Alpha Channel Bitrate %

In both Flix Pro and Flix Exporter, On2 lets you set the Bitrate percentage for the alpha channel (**Figure 8-8**), as does Sorenson Squeeze (**Figure 8-14**). On2's default is 15%, while Sorenson allocates 25%.

Neither of these made sense to me, since alpha channel information, though a full 8 bits, must be easier to compress than the random pixels that make up a real-world image. So I encoded the same green-screen file with an allocation of 1% and 25% in Sorenson Squeeze, with the results shown in **Figure 8-9**.

The two images are nearly identical, as was the real-time video playback, though the file with the bit rate of 1% was about 15% smaller. I asked Sorenson about their allocation, and they reported that, in their tests, feathered edges looked best at 25% allocation.

(continued)

Alpha bitrate - 25%

Alpha bitrate - 1%

Figure 8-9
Assessing the benefit of a 25% allocation to alpha bit rate. Not much difference, eh?

Obviously, if the data-rate alpha channel allocation doesn't affect quality, it makes sense to make it as low as possible to preserve bits for the real-world videos. I recommend that you run some tests on your alpha channel videos and keep dropping the allocation until you see a qualitative difference.

Outputting an MOV File with Alpha Channel
Your third option with After Effects is to output an MOV file in the required parameters for encoding to FLV with an alpha channel in other Flash encoding programs like On2 Flix Pro or Sorenson Squeeze. The procedure is simple; once you reach the Standard Video Compression Settings screen shown in **Figure 8-4,** conform your settings to those found in that screen, taking care to use the Animation Compression Type with Millions of Colors+ as the color depth.

Adobe Premiere Pro
After applying the chroma-key effect in Premiere Pro, you can either produce an intermediate MOV file for encoding elsewhere or render an FLV with alpha channel using the Flash Encoding Module. Flix Pro Exporter is not an option. After describing Premiere Pro's chroma-key capabilities, I'll describe both output alternatives.

Author's Tip

The procedures described in this section should work, and likely will by the time you read this book, but didn't work for me while I was writing. Specifically, Premiere Pro never output a file with alpha channel that worked properly with Flash, whether I encoded directly to FLV format or produced an intermediate QuickTime file (which worked perfectly with the other tools).

I've asked for Adobe's input and wasn't able to get this resolved before the book went to printing. Please check for updated information on *www.flashvideobook.com*.

Chroma Keying in Premiere Pro

I produce the best results with Premiere Pro using the Chroma Key filter that's shown in **Figure 8-1**. Premiere Pro also offers a Sixteen-Point Garbage Matte, but no spill suppression. Note that After Effects, even without the Keylight filter, performs a cleaner key than Premiere Pro, so I would definitely use After Effects if possible, rather than Premiere Pro.

Outputting an FLV File with Alpha Channel with the Flash Encoding Module

After you've applied and tested your chroma-key effect, After Effects can directly output an FLV file with alpha channel via the Flash Encoding module, which only offers one pass, CBR encoding. If you decide to go this route, make sure to check the Encode alpha channel in the Flash Video Encoding Settings screen shown in **Figure 8-6**.

Outputting an MOV File with Alpha Channel

Premiere Pro can also output an MOV file for encoding to FLV with an alpha channel in other Flash encoding. The money screen here is in the Export Movie Settings screen you can access by choosing File > Export > Movie and clicking the Settings button (**Figure 8-10**). After choosing QuickTime as the File Type in the General tab, switch over to the Video tab, where you'll see the now-familiar settings for the Apple Animation codec.

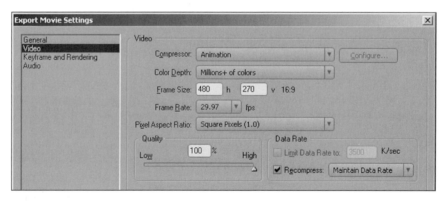

Figure 8-10
Setting video parameters in Premiere Pro's Export Movie Settings dialog.

Final Cut Pro

After applying the chroma-key effect in Final Cut Pro, you can either produce an intermediate MOV file for encoding elsewhere or render an FLV with alpha channel using On2's Flix Exporter. After describing Final Cut Pro's chroma-key capabilities, I'll describe both output alternatives.

Chroma Keying in Final Cut Pro

I produce the best results with Final Cut Pro using the Color Key filter, though Apple's flagship video editor also offers Chroma Keyer and Blue and Green Screen effects. In addition to Blue and Green Spill Suppressor effects, Final Cut also offers an Eight-Point Garbage Matte, both shown in **Figure 8-2**.

Other keying-related filters include Color Smoothing Filters for both 4:1:1 and 4:2:2 source videos, which are designed to improve keying quality but showed little effect in my tests.

Outputting an FLV File with Alpha Channel with Flix Exporter

After applying and testing your chroma-key effect, Final Cut Pro can output an FLV file with alpha channel via the Flix Exporter as shown in **Figure 8.8.** Note that you access these controls via QuickTime Conversion by choosing File > Export > Using QuickTime Conversion, and choosing On2 Flash Video – FLV (**Figure 8-11**).

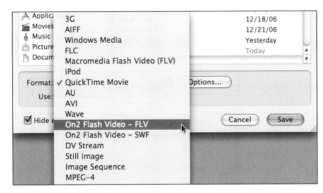

Figure 8-11
In Final Cut Pro, Flix Exporter is an option in the QuickTime Conversion settings.

Click the Options button to see the Flix Exporter settings, and make sure you've checked the Flash 8 FLV checkbox and the Preserve alpha checkbox.

Outputting an MOV File with Alpha Channel

Final Cut Pro can also output an MOV file with the required parameters for encoding to FLV with an alpha channel in other Flash encoding programs like On2 Flix Pro or Sorenson Squeeze. Using the regular QuickTime Conversion workflow, make sure you conform your settings in the Standard Video Compression Settings dialog to those shown in **Figure 8-4**.

On2 Flix Pro

On2 Flix Pro offers basic chroma-key functionality and, of course, can encode the resulting video into an FLV with alpha channel. The program is ideal for animations with totally uniform backgrounds and well-executed real-world green-screen and blue-screen shoots that don't have much variation in lighting and other conditions.

However, the lack of key frames, garbage mattes and other features may defeat a clean key with some real-world shoots. In these instances, you'll produce better results by chroma keying in a different application, exporting a QuickTime file using the Animation codec with Millions+ colors.

Chroma Keying in On2 Flix Pro

To chroma key in Flix Pro, load the source file as normal and then follow these steps:

1. On the bottom right of the File tab, click Video Editor. Flix Pro opens the Editor (**Figure 8-12**).

2. Click the eyedropper and select a representative region in the background.

3. Adjust the basic keying parameters using the Chroma and Luma tolerance controls.

4. Adjust the edge quality using the Edge Thin, Edge Blur and Halo Reducer controls.

5. Check Key First to ensure that keying is applied before any other filters.

6. In the Filter options section on the top right, click the Deinterlace checkbox.

7. Click the Close button to return to the main encoding interface.

Figure 8-12
Flix Pro's Chroma Key controls in the Editor window.

Outputting an FLV File with Alpha Channel with Flix Pro

With Flix Pro, you can start by choosing a Flash 8 FLV Video Preset, or click the Flash 8 FLV checkbox on the right, which selects the On2 codec, **Figure 8-13**.

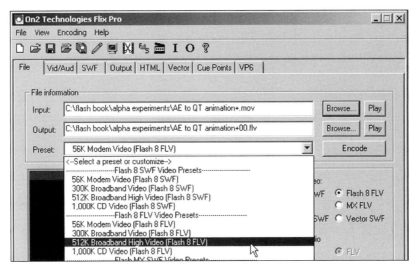

Figure 8-13
Start with Flix Pro by choosing a Flash 8 FLV preset.

Then click the Vid/Aud tab to reveal the compression settings. In the middle center of the window, you'll see a section titled Alpha Channel Settings. Click the Alpha checkbox, and set the desired Bitrate %. Otherwise, set your encoding parameters as desired, and choose Encoding > Encode to start encoding.

Encoding in Sorenson Squeeze

Sorenson Squeeze is a pure encoder that supports alpha channel output, but has no chroma-key capabilities. Accordingly, to produce an FLV file with alpha channel in Squeeze, you have to start with a file like the Intermediate QuickTime file we've discussed throughout the chapter.

To create the FLV file with alpha channel, you have to meet the now familiar requirements—you must encode with the VP6 codec and you have to enable the Compress Alpha Channel switch.

Figure 8-14 shows Squeeze's Macromedia Flash Video (.flv) Audio/Video Compression Settings window. You may have to click the Advanced button in the bottom left corner to expose all encoding controls.

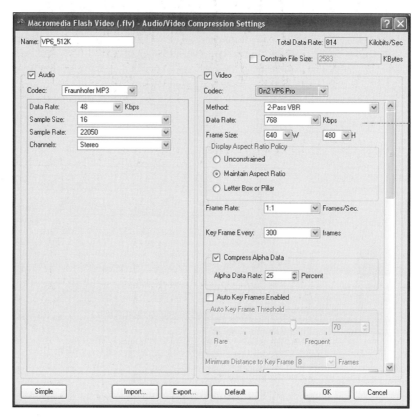

Figure 8-14
Here's where you set Flash encoding parameters in Sorenson Squeeze.

Once you get there, make sure you've selected a VP6 codec, check the Compress Alpha Data checkbox and assign the desired Percent to the Alpha Data Rate. Set other settings as desired, and encode as normal.

Deploying FLV Files with an Alpha Channel

Once you've created the FLV file with alpha channel, deploying the file is simple. So long as you use a Flash 8 or higher component to play the video file, the background will automatically disappear, and all layers beneath the video will automatically show through.

Conclusion

In this chapter, we learned how to apply a chroma-key effect in a number of software programs, and to either produce an intermediate QuickTime file with that alpha channel information or the FLV file itself. We also covered the requirements and controls for producing an FLV file with alpha channel.

Next chapter you'll learn the strengths and weaknesses of the various Flash video-encoding tools and the encoding workflow.

CHAPTER 9

Encoding Your Video

You should come into this chapter with all critical decisions, like resolution, audio and video bit rate and frame rate set in stone (see Chapter 7). If producing Flash video with an alpha channel, you should have already keyed out the background (see Chapter 8).

Still, you have some fairly weighty decisions to make. Which codec will you use, Spark or VP6, and will you encode using constant bit rate encoding (CBR) or variable bit rate encoding (VBR) techniques?

Where will you encode the video? In your editor (if possible) or a third-party encoder? Is there a substantial qualitative difference between the tools? If the latter, what type of intermediate file format will you use between editor and encoder, and when will you deinterlace and scale to target resolution?

Finally, what are the specific steps to produce your intermediate or final files? These are the issues I'll address in this last video production chapter, before handing you off to Stefan Richter with pristine FLV files in hand, ready to learn how to create SWFs with lovely skins, and progressively download or stream them to your waiting viewers.

Specifically, in this chapter you will learn:

- Which editing preset to use in Adobe Premiere Pro, Adobe After Effects and Apple Final Cut Pro to facilitate streaming production

- Whether to use the Spark or VP6 Flash codec

- Whether to encode using CBR or VBR techniques

- Whether to encode in your video editor or using a third-party encoder

- The respective quality produced by Flix Pro and Sorenson Squeeze, the preeminent third-party Flash encoders

- The workflows for producing intermediate files, including which codecs to use for output and when to deinterlace and scale

- The workflows for compressing to FLV format in six, count 'em, six, different programs.

It's a doozy of a chapter, which pulls together much of what we learned over the last two, so let's get started.

High-Level Editing Workflow

Every time you edit video that you'll use to produce streaming Flash video, you have to choose an editing preset. I covered this a bit in Chapter 7, but wanted to summarize and centralize my thinking on the subject.

If you're editing solely for streaming output, I recommend that you create a custom preset for your target output parameters, which I describe how to do in After Effects, Premiere Pro and Final Cut Pro in Chapter 7. That way, if you're producing video at 480×270 resolution, as I will in this chapter, you're working in a 480×270 window. In my view, this provides the most accurate preview of your final video, lets you easily pan and zoom within your video to perfect frame composition and avoids most aspect-ratio issues when you finally render.

Note that you can use standard DV, HDV or other presets so long as the resolution of your streaming file has the same display aspect ratio of your preset. For example, Final Cut Pro and Premiere Pro can easily output aspect-ratio-correct 320×240 videos from a 4:3 DV project, or 480×270 videos from an HDV project.

However, if you are attempting to produce nonstandard output, like 300×300 from any source, or 320×240 video from an HDV source, a custom preset specifying that output resolution is your best tool to avoid letterboxing, aspect-ratio distortion or both.

The situation is more complicated if you're repurposing video footage originally produced for another medium, like TV or DVD. Here, you've got a perfectly finished file using the ideal preset for that output, and simply want to render some streaming video. Again, so long as the Flash video file you're producing has the same display aspect ratio as the source project, you should be fine. If you're going nonstandard, I recommend that you change the preset.

Again, as noted in Chapter 7, though you can't change a preset in Premiere Pro, you can import your original project, say produced using a 16:9 DV preset, into another project with a custom preset, say 480×270 output. Any sequence produced in the old project that you open in the new project will use the new project settings. With After Effects and Final Cut Pro, you can just change the composition or sequence settings directly.

My Project

In this chapter, I will produce a 480×270 Flash video file from HDV source video using After Effects, Premiere Pro and Final Cut Pro. I created a custom preset or the equivalent in all three programs, but will address how to produce that video if using a standard HDV preset in all programs.

My source footage is from a concert performed by local band No Speed Limit on New Year's Eve, 2006. It was a two-camera shoot, both HDV (the Sony HDR-FX1 and Canon XL A1), and was a big deal for several reasons, most notably the fact that the Rex Theatre in Galax had finally worked the kinks out of its new sound system and had installed new stage lights.

In addition, the concert promoter rented tuxes for the boys in the band, and a lovely formal outfit for Amber, the lead singer, so it was the first time that I could shoot them *sans* ripped blue jeans and camouflage shirts. Finally, after three attempts, lighting, sound capabilities and attire all came together to enable the ideal demo DVD to send to concert promoters.

As mentioned, I've decided on 480×270 resolution, and also a frame rate of 29.97 fps, video data rate of 400 kbps and audio data rate of 96 kbps. I've got some encoding and workflow decisions to make before I press the proverbial encode button, most notably variable vs. constant bit rate encoding, which I'll work through in this chapter, and then start processing.

Which Codec, Spark or VP6?

This is an easy one. Unless you absolutely have to use Spark, say for compatibility with a locked-down installed base of Flash Players in a corporate or government installation, use VP6. The quality is much, much better.

VBR or CBR?

Briefly, constant bit rate encoding techniques compress all scenes in your video to the same bit rate. This means that low-motion scenes, which are easy to compress, and high-motion scenes, which are much harder to compress, get the same bit-rate allocation.

When using a relatively low bit rate, low-motion sequences will probably look good, but quality could suffer in the high-motion sequences. However, CBR techniques are fast and produce a consistent bandwidth over the duration of the file, making it easier to stream.

In contrast, variable bit rate encoding techniques adjust the data rate to match scene encoding complexity, applying higher data rates to high-motion video, and lower data rates to low-motion video. Even when the total average bandwidth is the same as CBR, VBR can produce better overall quality because wasted bandwidth is shifted from low-motion sequences to high-motion sequences.

VBR usually requires two passes, one to analyze the video, the other to compress the file, which obviously slows encoding. The bandwidth of VBR streams also varies over the duration of the video, increasing with high-motion sequences and reducing with low-motion footage. This makes VBR encoded sequences tougher to stream smoothly over bandwidth-constricted connections.

What the Market Tells Us

The evidence here is fairly consistent; most producers use VBR, though there are some interesting outliers. Here's what I've heard from various producers:

- ESPN uses two-pass VBR for all high-action video, but uses CBR for time-sensitive encoding or video with low motion content

- DL.TV uses VBR for all codecs, including Flash

- Vidiac, an Atlanta-based provider of video content hosting and management technology, uses CBR because VBR takes four times longer "while delivering little additional quality." Vidiac also noted that the data spikes in VBR streams also produced some "playback inconsistencies," which also weighed into their decision.

Hmmmm. If you're streaming from a Flash Media Server, those playback inconsistencies have to be a concern.

What My Research Tells Us

In 2006, I produced two research reports for StreamingMedia.com, including "Flash Codecs, 2006, Choosing and Using the Optimal Flash Codec." It's a fascinating read, I might say, perfect for insomniacs, and still for sale on the site. And, if you order now . . .

OK, I'm back in author mode. As part of the report, I analyzed which encoders and encoding techniques produced the best quality using a 6-minute test file that contained 42 different scenes with varying complexity, from talking heads to the high-motion skateboarder you've seen floating around this book. One particularly relevant finding was this:

- "Since the Macromedia Flash Encoder produced CBR files, and Flix Pro and Squeeze VBR files, our benchmark tests also measured CBR vs. VBR quality. In general:

    - CBR encoding produces higher-quality, low-motion (business-oriented) files.

    - As the motion in the content increases, CBR quality drops, and VBR becomes superior."

Basically, for low-motion, talking-head video, CBR proved more effective than VBR, which makes sense, because there are no high- and low-motion scenes to juggle the data over; they are all low motion. You can't rob from the rich and give to the poor if everyone is equally rich.

Also worth considering in this equation is that CBR encoding, via the Flash 8 Video Encoder or export capabilities in Premiere Pro or After Effects, are essentially free, while you'll have to shell out $150 or more for VBR encoding.

Accordingly, if your videos are primarily low-motion footage, say news announcements or interviews, CBR will likely produce higher-quality files faster and cheaper. If you're encoding high-motion footage, VBR is definitely the way to go. Once you opt for VBR, you should choose two-pass encoding, which enables the encoder to analyze the entire video file and allocate bandwidth most efficiently.

My concert footage is a mix of high and low motion, so I'm opting for two-pass VBR and will implement that in every encoding session.

VBR-related Encoding Options

When you opt for VBR encoding, you choose a target data rate, and the encoder usually exposes some VBR-specific encoding options that you may find useful. **Figure 9-1** shows these encoding controls from the Sorenson Squeeze Encoder.

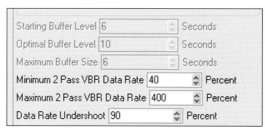

Figure 9-1
VBR-specific controls in the Sorenson Squeeze encoder.

These controls perform as follows.

Minimum Two-Pass VBR Data Rate

This sets the minimum data rate the encoder will apply to low-motion sequences. If you were encoding at 400 kbps, at the current setting of 40%, the encoder would go no lower than 160 kbps for any sequence in the video.

Adjust this percentage upwards if the low-motion content in your video looks degraded after compression, and the encoder will increase the allocation to those low-motion sequences. While this could degrade the quality of the higher-motion sequences, most viewers expect high-motion sequences to be a bit degraded, but react poorly when talking heads show artifacts.

Maximum Two-Pass VBR Data Rate

This sets the maximum data rate the encoder will apply to high-motion sequences. At 400%, the encoder will spike the video data rate up to 1600 kbps, which is pretty whopping over any kind of connection.

If you're streaming highly variable content from a Flash Media Server, these data spikes could make it challenging for some viewers to achieve smooth playback. Obviously, with progressive download, this matters less, since the viewer will ultimately achieve smooth playback from a local cache.

VBR Variability

This setting determines how much the data rate will vary in the VBR file. In the Squeeze and Flix Pro encoders, a setting of 0% means no variability, while 100% means a "highly variable" bit rate. Both use a default of 70%.

Author's Tip

The Law of Diminishing Returns

We're about to take a look at advanced encoding options like key-frame setting, sharpness and others. This may sound funny from a guy writing a book about compression, but with a few exceptions noted below, I typically don't mess with these controls and leave them at their default values. Why?

In my experience, this kind of tinkering can take forever (tinker, compress, compare; re-tinker, compress, compare) and in many instances the lessons you learn are hard to apply to other clips. More importantly, most of the time, the quality improvement, if any, is usually small and hard to see without side-by-side comparisons that your viewers won't ever see.

If you choose the best background, light the scene well, shoot with proper parameters, scale to the right aspect ratio, deinterlace and choose the best encoding technique, you're probably at 98% of the quality potential. You could spend hours chasing the other 2% or not. Conversely, if you messed up anywhere along the workflow, and are submitting degraded-quality video to the encoder, messing with the settings probably won't buy you any additional quality.

Bottom line, unless you see a problem that you can definitely tie to an encoding parameter, like degraded low-motion footage in a VBR file, you probably should just accept the defaults.

How this control interacts with the two previous controls is unexplained and uncertain, which is confusing, since they obviously can conflict. In my tests, I've always used the default setting for variability and adjusted my min/max data rate with the two controls above.

Data Rate Undershoot

Both Flix Pro and Sorenson Squeeze offer this control, which according to their mutual help file lowers the output data rate to ensure that "there are bits in the buffer to improve difficult sections." At the current setting of 90%, the encoder would produce 90% of the target data rate of 400 kbps, or 360 kbps. I prefer to set my data rate using the main data-rate control, so typically leave this at the default value of 100%.

For my concert footage, I'm thinking that 400 kbps of video should be plenty, so I'll leave the VBR controls at their default and hope for the best. I'll examine all close-ups in the final footage to make sure that these low-motion clips retain good quality and, if necessary, boost the minimum Two-Pass VBR data rate. I probably wouldn't mess with VBR Variability or Data Rate Undershoot under any circumstances.

Advanced Encoding Controls

Most encoding tools, particularly third-party tools like Flix Pro and Sorenson Squeeze, offer a selection of advanced encoding controls, some that we've discussed before, some that we haven't. Here, I'll describe the common ones so you'll be familiar with them when we get into the encoding workflows themselves.

Key-Frame Settings

In Chapter 2, I described interframe compression as:

> [I]nter-frame compression works between frames, using a system of key and delta frames to eliminate redundancy between frames. Specifically, key frames, also called I frames in MPEG speak, contain the complete frame, compressed solely with intraframe compression.
>
> Delta frames, also called *difference* or B and P frames, only contain pixels that are different from the immediately preceding frame (or in some cases, other frames in the sequence). After removing these redundancies, the pixels remaining in the frames are compressed using intraframe techniques.

As you would guess, key frames are generally larger than delta frames since they contain a complete frame's worth of information. The key-frame interval for most Flash encoders is 60, so when encoding at 30 fps, this means a key frame every 2 seconds.

Here are some interesting factoids about key frames:

- When playing back a video file, if you use the video slider or other controls to seek within a video file, the player must first jump to a key frame, then reconstruct frames forward to the selected frame. More frequent key frames therefore enhance interactivity, though at 60, your video files should be plenty accessible.

- Key frames are most valuable on the first frame of a scene change, since they immediately reset to the new video. When an encoding tool (like Sorenson Squeeze) has an option like "Auto Key Frames," you should always enable it.

- More frequent key frames help maintain the quality of high-motion footage, since they keep updating to the new footage. On the other hand, since key frames are larger than delta frames, more frequent key frames means smaller and therefore lower-quality delta frames (at the same target bit rate).

With my concert footage, I definitely want to make sure auto key frames is enabled, and will likely leave the other settings at their default. After encoding, I'll play the Flash video clip and pay close attention to the quality of the video when the camera angles change. If the video is fuzzy and takes a second to clear, I know that key frames were not assigned to those scene changes, and I'll either check the settings of my encoder, or, if this option isn't available in the encoder, change encoders.

Deinterlacing

As I described in Chapter 7, if you're working with interlaced input, sooner or later you need to deinterlace. If you're producing an intermediate file in your editor, you can choose to deinterlace then; if you don't, you have to deinterlace in your encoding tool.

To reverse the auto key frame situation, Squeeze automatically deinterlaces interlaced source footage, while Flix Pro makes you set a switch, a requirement which has burned me more than once when I forgot to set it. Deinterlacing was not an option with the Flash 8 Video Encoder, though it is with CS3.

Note that while you can't deinterlace with the Flash 8 Video Encoder, you can deinterlace when producing FLV files with the Flash Encoding module upon which it is based in Premiere Pro and After Effects.

For my project, I will deinterlace either when encoding from the editor or creating the intermediate file for the third-party encoder.

Other Parameters

Other common parameters worth noting include:

- **Drop frames to maintain data rate** – This option does what it says, dropping frames during encoding to meet the target data rate, with a potential decrease in playback smoothness, particularly in hard-to-compress sequences. If you're distributing via a Flash Streaming Server, maintaining data rate is critical, so if this option is available, select it. On the other hand, if distributing via progressive download (like my concert footage) so long as the overall file size doesn't spike by more than 5–10%, it's probably better to opt for smoothness over strict adherence to data rate.

- **Encoding speed** – Some encoders let you choose between Best, Good and Fastest (Squeeze) or Good and Best (Flix Pro). For draft work, the fastest encoding settings are fine, but for final files, choosing the slower option can often noticeably improve quality.

- **Quality settings** – If an encoder offers quality settings (like 75%) instead of a bit rate, I always go with the bit-rate control. If quality is available in addition to a bit-rate setting, I always set it at the highest available setting. I'll be the first to admit that this makes no sense in many instances, as when you're producing video with the QuickTime animation codec (which is essentially a raw, uncompressed codec) but that's my general rule, and I'm sticking to it.

- **Buffering** – My coauthor Stefan Richter tells me that the Flash Media Server controls all relevant buffering mechanisms between the server and remote viewer. Some programs, most notably Flix Pro, allow you to adjust buffer settings within the compressed FLV file itself. I didn't experiment with these, and can add no value beyond pointing you to the help file, and advising you not to mess with these unless you really know what you are doing.

Output and Encoding Workflows

Let's spend a moment and discuss editing and encoding workflows, specifically addressing issues like:

- How do you decide whether to encode in your video editor or a third-party tool?

- If encoding in a third-party tool, which format should you output to, and when should you scale and deinterlace?

Where to Encode

As mentioned above, the Adobe Flash Media Encoder, both standalone, and as a plug-in to Premiere Pro and After Effects, can only use CBR techniques to encode to FLV format, which reduces its effectiveness with high-motion videos. Accordingly, when encoding high-motion videos, consider a third-party tool, whether a separate encoder or Flix Exporter for After Effects (and Final Cut Pro), which is a plug-in On2 sells that does produce VBR and CBR files.

In addition, consider a third-party encoder when:

- Producing multiple files, where batch encoding capabilities enabled by Flix Pro and Sorenson Squeeze really come in handy. Note that:
  - Flix Pro can only output FLV files, where Squeeze can output multiple formats.
  - Flix Pro's batch capabilities can output multiple source files to one encoding setting, but not one file to multiple encoding settings. If you're creating multiple-bit-rate alternatives to deliver via the Flash Media Server, Squeeze can do it and Flix Pro can't.

More on Flix Pro vs. Sorenson Squeeze

Since we're comparing Flix Pro and Squeeze, I thought I would throw in some quality-related data from a Sorenson Squeeze 4.5 review that I wrote for *StreamingMedia Magazine*.

Of course, for many producers, quality is the most important buying criteria, and here's where it gets really close. Again, Squeeze's clips seem a bit more highly saturated and vivid, which really helps in many scenes. Even producers happy with Flix should download and try Squeeze, just to see how perhaps adding a bit of color saturation in their editors might improve overall appearance. Squeeze also seemed to preserve fine detail better than Flix Pro, though occasionally produced more visible aliasing.

In two of three scenes shot against a compression-unfriendly background, generally an open, light-colored, reflective wall, Squeeze showed more compression artifacts than Flix Pro, though in the other clip the situation was reversed. If producers encoding with Flix Pro bumped saturation a bit in their editors, and Squeeze producers utilized a compression-friendly background, you couldn't tell the difference between the two quality-wise without a scorecard.

One grumble is that Squeeze doesn't accurately hit encoding targets when encoding to Flash format, often being as much as 10–15% off. This proved irritating to me because it took several tries to produce a file with the same bit rate as the Flix file, but may not be relevant for many producers. However, be sure to check file size when encoding to Flash format with Sorenson Squeeze, just to make sure you're in the ball park.

Bottom line, if you're producing in multiple streaming formats, or producing the same file to multiple encoding parameters, Squeeze is the clear winner, while Flix wins out if you need to key out a chroma-key background while encoding. Otherwise, it's pretty much of a draw.

Couldn't have said it better myself.

Outputting Intermediate Files

If you've decided on the third-party route, you have to output an intermediate file from your video editor to input into the encoding tool. Here, the questions are which format should you output in, and when should you scale and deinterlace? Let's get the easy ones out of the way first. Specifically:

- If you created a custom preset for your video file, say at 480×270, your best option is to produce an intermediate file at that resolution and deinterlace during the process. Use the QuickTime Animation codec with bit depth set at millions.

- If you're producing alpha channel video, your only option is to output an intermediate file, and you should scale to final resolution and deinterlace during rendering. Again, use the QuickTime animation codec, using Millions+ as a bit depth. Chapter 9 details how to use the chroma-key effects in Premiere Pro, Final Cut Pro and After Effects. In this chapter, I'll review the entire rendering workflow.

- If you're working in HDV or other high-definition format, and scaling to a lower resolution for distribution, I would scale, deinterlace and output a QuickTime file from my editor (QuickTime Animation codec with bit depth at millions). I haven't done a lot of work with Squeeze or Flix Pro with HDV video, but results have been erratic.

The other situation is that you're working in standard DV or other SD preset. Your choices here are:

- Outputting a file in DV (or other SD format) and scaling and deinterlacing in the encoding program, or

- Scaling and deinterlacing during output from your editor.

The key point here is that DV is a codec, and rendering back to DV may involve another layer of compression. Specifically, if all you do is capture and trim your video, then output back to DV, the editor probably won't re-encode the video during rendering; it will simply produce another file with the original frames intact. If this describes the extent of your editing, you can consider outputting a DV file and scaling and deinterlacing in your encoding tool.

At the other extreme, if you color corrected and brightened your video and added titles, transitions and effects, your editor will have to re-encode most frames back to DV to render the DV file. Since each layer of compression produces additional artifacts, however minor, the best practice in this instance would be to output a QuickTime file using the Animation codec at your target resolution, and deinterlace in the process.

My Decisions and Targets

Table 9-1 shows the ultimate target file parameters and selected encoding settings for my FLV output. This will provide a handy reference for me when I produce FLV files using these multiple tools, and will outline for you the types of decisions that you need to make before you start encoding.

I've even included a handy, dandy, empty column you can use for your own encoding settings, creatively titled "Your Target Settings," at no extra charge. Please use and enjoy.

Table 9-1
Output parameters for FLV file.

Parameter	Target Settings	Your Target Settings
Resolution	480×270	
Frame rate	29.97 (choose use source when available)	
Codec	VP6 Pro	
Video bit rate	400 kbps	
Audio bit rate	96 kbps MP3	
Audio parameters	44 Hz/16-bit/stereo	
Encoding technique	Two-pass VBR	
VBR options	Default	
Key frame	Auto insert if available/ Default interval	
Deinterlace	Yes – in editor, not encoding program	
Alpha channel	No (yes if alpha channel footage)	
Drop frame to maintain data rate	No (but I will check overall data rate to verify that it's close)	
Encoding speed	Best (slowest)	

Table 9-2 shows the targets for the intermediate file I'll create in this chapter.

Table 9-2
Output parameters for intermediate file.

Parameter	Target Settings	
Resolution	480×270	
Codec	QuickTime Animation	
Key frames	All	
Bit depth	Millions (millions+ if alpha channel)	
Audio bit rate	Uncompressed, 44/16-bit/ stereo if available	
Aspect ratio (if available)	Square pixel	Square pixel
Deinterlace	Yes	
Quality	Highest	
Alpha channel	No (yes if alpha channel footage)	
Encoding speed	Best (slowest)	

I'll try to match these targets against the specific controls exposed by all the editing and encoding programs described below, but invariably there will be some differences. Controls will also look different on editors and encoding tools not covered here. Between the information in the table and the background discussion provided here and in Chapters 7 and 8, I'm sure you'll be able to figure out the right settings.

Application-Specific Details

With these targets set, let's implement them in a number of applications, starting with Adobe After Effects.

Adobe After Effects

After Effects is best suited for short, intense bits of highly creative, ultratechnical editing, particularly alpha channel and animation work, and doesn't offer the multicam capability necessary to complete this concert project. Still, since this chapter is meant to tie workflows from previous chapters together, I'll complete the exercise as if I had produced the concert in After Effects.

Adobe After Effects has three relevant output options: producing an intermediate MOV file for encoding elsewhere, producing an FLV using the Flash Encoding module, or producing an FLV using On2's Flix Exporter. Some preparatory notes:

- As noted above, the Flash Encoding module included with After Effects can only produce CBR, not VBR, while the Flix Exporter can produce VBR and CBR. I would not ordinarily use this CBR-only option for this concert footage, but I will demonstrate the workflow.

- I describe how to create a composition preset for After Effects in Chapter 7. In this chapter, I will work from the preset shown in **Figure 9-2**.

- After Effects automatically deinterlaces when producing frame-based output like Flash video or QuickTime, so I won't enable any deinterlace settings in any of the encoding modules. You should do the same, but as always, examine your footage carefully to make sure that the program is deinterlacing for you, as well.

- If you work through After Effects Render Queue, make sure Field Render is set to Off in the Render Settings window to ensure AE doesn't interlace during encoding.

Outputting an FLV File in After Effects with the Flash Encoder Module

To use the Flash 8 Video Encoder module, follow these steps:

1. Click File > Export > FLV Video (FLV). After Effects opens the Flash Video Encoding Settings.

2. Choose the Flash 8 – Medium Quality (400 kbps) profile from the encoding profile list box.

3. Click Show Advanced Settings to expose all encoding options (**Figure 9-3**).

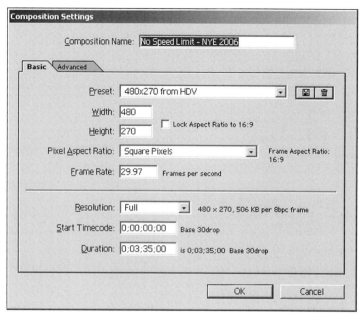

Figure 9-2
Here's the After Effect Composition Settings used for this project.

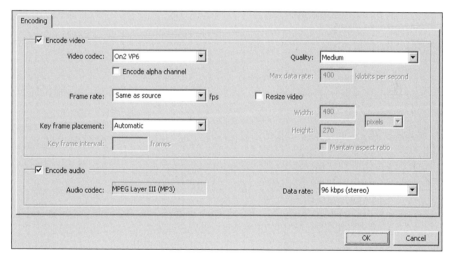

Figure 9-3
Adobe's Flash Video Encoding Settings.

4. In this screen:

   • **Video codec** – Select On2 VP6 (should be selected already).

   • **Encode alpha channel** – It's not an issue for this footage, but when encoding footage with an alpha channel, check the Encode alpha channel checkbox.

- **Frame rate** – My target is 29.97, so I'll leave Same as source. Otherwise, click the list box and choose the desired rate.

- **Key-frame placement** – See the complete discussion in the Flash Video Encoder section below. Bottom line is that the Automatic setting inserts a key frame every 2 seconds, and that there is no auto-insert upon scene-change capability. Again, this is acceptable for draft work, but not if you have a lot of scene changes.

- **Quality** – My focus is data rate, which is 400 kbps according to the grayed-out box, which is my target for video (and the default preset). To adjust this, click the drop-down list, choose Custom and insert the desired data rate. Note that this is video data rate only.

- **Resize video**

  - The Flash Encoding module automatically picked up the composition resolution, which is my target of 480×270. No change needed here.

  - To change resolution, click the Resize video checkbox and insert your target resolution. If your target resolution doesn't share the same display aspect ratio as your composition, your video may appear stretched or otherwise distorted (see discussion in Chapter 7).

- **Encode audio** – Check this checkbox, and choose the target data rate.

5. Click OK to close this dialog, then name the file and store it in the desired location as normal.

Outputting an FLV File in After Effects with Flix Exporter

After Effects can also output an FLV file via the Flix Exporter. Here's how to use this tool:

1. Click File > Export > On2 Technologies Flash Video – FLV. After Effects opens the On2 Technologies Flix Exporter Settings window (**Figure 9-4**).

2. In this window, you can either select a preset or set all settings manually; I'll do the latter:

   - **Export options** – Click the Flash 8 FLV checkbox.

   - **Export audio** – Check this checkbox to include audio, and also the MP3 compression checkbox, as Uncompressed is too bulky for web video. Choose the target Sampling Rate and Bitrate, and check the Stereo checkbox if desired.

   - **Export video** – Click this checkbox.

   - **Frame rate**

     - If your target frame rate is the same as your source footage, as is the case for my concert footage, click the Use host frame rate checkbox.

     - If different, uncheck this box and type the desired frame rate in the box.

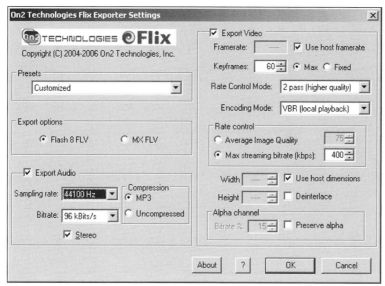

Figure 9-4
Using On2's Flix Exporter from After Effects.

- **Key frames** – On2 Flix Exporter will auto-insert key frames at scene changes. Unless you have some dramatic reason to change this, I would leave this setting at the default of 60 with Max checked.

- **Rate control mode** – Choose 2 pass (higher quality).

- **Encoding mode** – Choose VBR (local playback).

  - Again, VBR is appropriate for my concert video because it has a mix of high- and low-motion content and will be viewed via progressive download. If you're streaming, be sure to monitor streaming quality to make sure that data rate spikes don't interrupt the viewing experience.

- **Rate control** – Click the Max streaming bit rate (kbps) checkbox, and insert your target.

- **Width and Height**

  - Click Use host dimensions if your composition preset matches your target output resolution (which it does here).

  - To change output resolution, uncheck the Use host dimensions checkbox and type your targets in the Height and Width fields. If your target resolution doesn't share the same display aspect ratio as your composition, your video may appear stretched or otherwise distorted (see discussion in Chapter 7).

- **Deinterlace** – Should have no effect when rendering from After Effects. Do not select, but check your rendered file to be sure.

Author's Tip

Flix Exporter is convenient, but doesn't offer all the encoding options accessible in Flix Pro, particularly the variable bit rate controls. For ultimate fine tuning of these or other parameters, you'll need either Flix Pro or Sorenson Squeeze.

- **Alpha channel** – It's not an issue for this footage, but when encoding footage with an alpha channel, check the Preserve alpha checkbox. Accept the default Bitrate % or modify as desired (I discuss the Bitrate % allocation in Chapter 8).

3. Click OK to close this window, then name the file and store it in the desired location as normal.

Outputting an Intermediate QuickTime File in After Effects

After Effects can also output an intermediate QuickTime file for encoding to FLV in other Flash encoding programs like On2 Flix Pro or Sorenson Squeeze. Here's how:

1. Click File > Export > QuickTime Movie. After Effects opens the Movie Settings window.

2. Click the Settings button. The Standard Video Compression Settings screen shown in **Figure 9-5** will open.

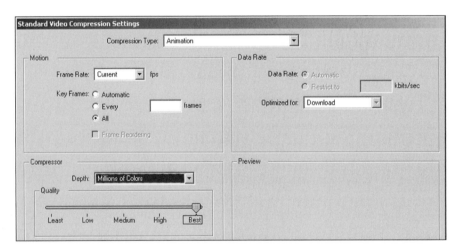

Figure 9-5
Customizing intermediate file compression settings in After Effects.

3. In this window:

- **Compression type** – Choose Animation in the list box.

- **Frame rate** – Choose Current if the same as your composition, or choose another target in the list box.

- **Key frames** – Click the All checkbox.

- **Compressor depth**

    – When producing alpha channel video, choose Millions of Colors+ (not shown).

- Otherwise, choose Millions of Colors.

- **Quality** – Drag the slider to Best.

- Leave all other controls at their defaults.

4. Click OK to close the dialog and return to the Movie Settings window.

5. Click the Size button to open the Export Size Settings window (**Figure 9-6**). In this window:

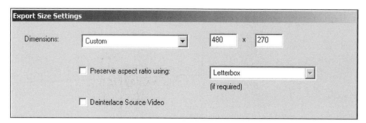

Figure 9-6
Choosing the target output resolution for the intermediate file in After Effects.

- **Dimensions** – If you created a custom composition setting as I did here, the Dimensions should match your target output resolution.

  - To change this, choose the desired resolution in the Dimensions drop-down list or choose Custom and type your target width and height in the respective fields.

  - Assuming that your goal is full-frame (no letterboxing), aspect-ratio-correct Flash video, do not check the Preserve Aspect Ratio checkbox. If you created a custom preset, or inserted an output resolution that matches the display aspect ratio of the project preset (like 320×240 for SD DV, or 480×270 for HDV), you shouldn't have to click the Preserve Aspect Ratio checkbox. If you didn't, click the checkbox and choose your poison: letterboxing, cropping or scaling (see discussion in Chapter 7).

  - Deinterlace Source Video: After Effects should hand the QuickTime encoder deinterlaced footage, so you should not have to check this checkbox.

6. Click OK to close this window and return to the Movie Settings window.

7. Make sure that the Sound checkbox is checked, and click the Sound Settings button. After Effects opens the Sound Settings window (**Figure 9-7**). Conform your settings to those shown in the window and click OK to close the window.

8. Accept all other defaults in the Movie Settings window, and then click OK to close that window; name and store the file in the desired location as normal.

Figure 9-7
Passing through uncompressed sound when creating our intermediate file in After Effects.

Adobe Premiere Pro

Premiere Pro is an ideal tool for producing our multicam concert, and offers two options for producing our Flash video file. Specifically, you can either produce an intermediate MOV file for encoding elsewhere or render an FLV using the Flash Encoding module. Some introductory thoughts:

- As noted above, the Flash Encoding module included with Premiere Pro can only produce CBR, not VBR. I would not ordinarily use this option for this concert footage, but I will demonstrate the workflow.

- I describe how to create a custom project preset for Premiere Pro in Chapter 7. In this chapter, I will work from the preset shown in **Figure 9-8**.

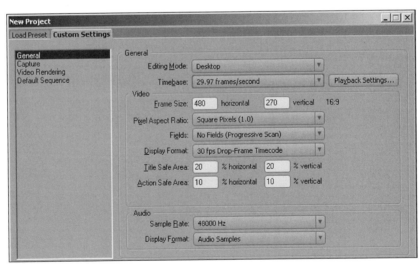

Figure 9-8
Here's the Premiere Pro project preset I'm working from.

- Premiere Pro's deinterlacing capabilities are somewhat confusing, because there are multiple controls in different places, and some seem to work intermittently. However, there are two things I absolutely know about the process:

- First, the one absolutely sure way to deinterlace is to right click every clip on the timeline, and choose Field Options to open the menu shown in **Figure 9-9**. Then, click the Always Deinterlace checkbox. That's right—you have to do this for every clip on the timeline.

Figure 9-9
The sure-fire way to deinterlace in Premiere Pro.

- Second, the Deinterlace button in the Export Settings window of the Adobe Media Encoder (**Figure 9-10**) doesn't always work, but if the video in the preview window is not deinterlaced, it won't be in the final file. You may not like the result, but at least you can see it coming.
- On the other hand, the deinterlace control on the QuickTime output parameters does work, so if you're creating a QuickTime intermediate file, you don't have to deinterlace each clip separately via the Field Options window.

With these thoughts behind us, let's start outputting! First, the FLV file, then the intermediate QuickTime file.

Outputting an FLV File in Premiere Pro with the Flash Encoding Module

Premiere Pro can directly output an FLV file using the Flash Encoding module, with the limitations described multiple times above. To create an FLV file with the Flash Encoding module, follow these steps:

1. Click File > Export > Adobe Media Encoder. Premiere Pro opens the Export Settings window (**Figure 9-10**). There's Amber Collins wearing a black suit against a black background, which looks wonderfully elegant, but was an absolute bear to shoot.

2. **Format** – In the Format list box, choose Macromedia Flash Video (FLV).

3. **Basic Parameters** – In the Basic Parameters area, type the target Frame Width and Frame Height. If you created a custom preset at your target encoding parameters, the Source resolution on the lower left of the preview window should match the Output resolution on the lower right.

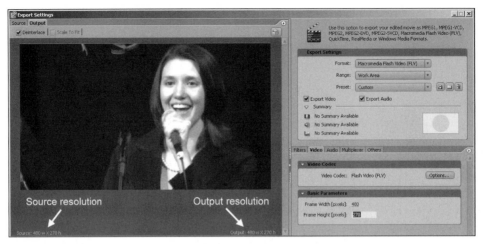

Figure 9-10
The Export Settings window of the Adobe Media Encoder. Note the Deinterlace checkbox on the top left, which works erratically (or not at all) for me.

- If the resolution you input here doesn't match the display aspect ratio of the source project, your Flash video will likely have a distorted display aspect ratio.

- If you click the Options button in the Video Codec section (the next step) you open the Flash Video Encoding Settings screen, which has a control for resizing your video. Note that you don't have to resize the video in this second window to produce your video, just those shown in **Figure 9-10**.

4. Click the Options button in the Video codec area. Premiere Pro opens the Flash Video Encoding Settings.

5. Click the Show Advanced Settings button to view all encoding parameters. Though you got there a different way, you're looking at the same parameters discussed in steps 2–4 of the section above titled "Outputting an FLV File in After Effects With The Flash Encoding Module" (**Figure 9-3**). Apply the settings the same way as described there, except note that output resolution is controlled by the Frame Width and Height input in **Figure 9-10**, not in this screen.

6. Click OK to close the Flash Video Encoding Settings Window, and then OK again to Close the Export Settings window. Name and save your file as normal.

Outputting an Intermediate QuickTime File with Premiere Pro
Premiere Pro can output an intermediate MOV file for encoding to FLV in other Flash encoding programs like On2 Flix Pro or Sorenson Squeeze. Here's how:

1. Click File > Export > Movie. Premiere Pro opens the Export Movie dialog.

2. On the lower right, click Settings. Premiere Pro opens the Export Movie Settings dialog.

3.   Click the General tab on the left. In this window:

    •   Select QuickTime in the File Type list box.

    •   Set other options as desired.

4.   Click the Video tab on the left (**Figure 9-11**). In this window:

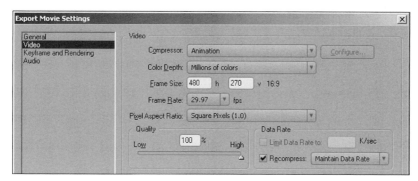

Figure 9-11
Setting key video parameters in Premiere Pro's Export Movie Settings dialog.

    •   **Compressor** – Choose Animation in the Compressor list box.

    •   **Color depth** – Choose Millions of colors unless encoding with an alpha channel, in which case choose Millions+ of colors.

    •   **Frame size** – Type your target height and width in the respective boxes. If working with a custom preset that matches your target resolution, or if you choose an output resolution that matches the display resolution of your project, Premiere Pro should output aspect-ratio-correct video without letterboxing or cropping. Otherwise, your display aspect ratio may be distorted.

    •   **Frame rate** – Choose the desired frame rate.

    •   **Pixel Aspect Ratio** – Always choose Square Pixels.

    •   Conform other settings to those shown in the figure.

5.   Click the Keyframe and Rendering tab on the left (**Figure 9-12**). In this window:

    •   **Bit depth** – Check the Use Project Setting for Bit Depth.

    •   Check the Deinterlace Video Footage checkbox. Unlike the Deinterlacing control in the Adobe Media Encoder, this control actually works, so you should not have to manually deinterlace every clip on the Timeline via the Field Options window (**Figure 9-9**).

    •   Leave all other options at their defaults.

6.   Click the Audio tab on the left. In this window:

    •   Select Uncompressed in the Compressor list box.

    •   Select other parameters as desired.

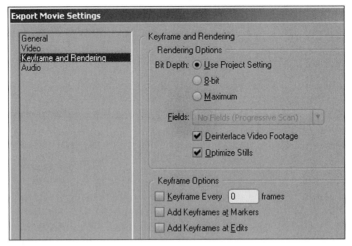

Figure 9-12
Keyframe and Rendering options. Hey, this deinterlace control actually works!

7. Click OK to close the dialog, then name and save the file as normal.

Final Cut Pro

Final Cut Pro is also a wonderful tool for producing my multicamera concert and can output an intermediate file in QuickTime format or export direct to FLV via On2's Flix Exporter. I describe how to produce a custom Sequence Preset for Final Cut Pro in Chapter 7, and I'll use the preset shown in **Figure 9-13** for my concert.

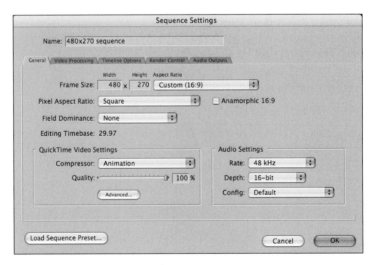

Figure 9-13
Here's the preset I'll use in Final Cut Pro for my concert video.

As I noted in Chapter 7, deinterlacing using the QuickTime export controls has no effect; you have to apply Final Cut Pro's deinterlacing filter, which is in the video subfolder in the Effects tab. You obviously have to apply that to every clip in the video. On the other hand, if you click the deinterlace control while exporting direct to FLV using the Flix Pro Exporter, On2's module does deinterlace.

Let's have a look at the workflows.

Outputting an FLV File from Final Cut Pro with Flix Exporter

As you would guess, exporting from Final Cut Pro using Flix Exporter is very much like exporting from After Effects, so after showing you how to access On2's export module, I'll refer back to the After Effect's description. I know it's inconvenient, but think of the trees we'll save!

Here's how to use this tool:

1. Click File > Export > Using QuickTime Conversion. Final Cut Pro opens the QuickTime Save dialog.

2. Click the Format list box, and choose On2 Flash Video – FLV (**Figure 9-14**).

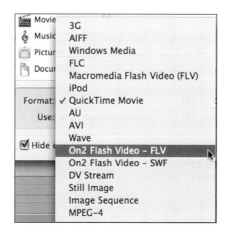

Figure 9-14
Flix Exporter is an option in the QuickTime Conversion settings.

3. Click the Options button. Final Cut Pro opens a Mac-ified version of **Figure 9-4**. Please refer to the instructions in Step 2 of "Outputting an FLV File From After Effects with Flix Exporter," for more details.

4. Once complete, click OK to close the dialog and name and save your file as normal.

Outputting an Intermediate QuickTime File with Final Cut Pro

Final Cut Pro can also output an intermediate QuickTime file for producing your FLV file in Flash encoding programs like On2 Flix Pro or Sorenson Squeeze. The process is similar to After Effects, but there are enough subtle differences that I'll detail it here.

1. Click File > Export > Using QuickTime Conversion. Final Cut Pro opens the QuickTime Save dialog.

2. Click the Format list box, and choose QuickTime Movie.

3. Click the Options tab. Final Cut Pro opens the Movie Settings window.

4. Click Settings to open the Standard Video Compression Settings dialog shown in **Figure 9-15**.

5. In this window:

   • **Compression type** – Choose Animation in the list box.

   • **Frame rate** – Choose Current if the same as your sequence, or choose another target in the list box.

   • **Key frames** – Click the All checkbox.

   • **Compressor depth**

      – When producing alpha channel video, choose Millions of Colors+ (not shown).

      – Otherwise, choose Millions of Colors.

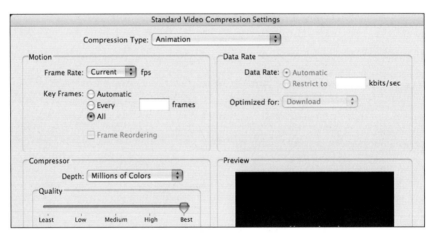

Figure 9-15
Choosing the settings for the QuickTime Animation codec.

   • **Quality** – Drag the slider to Best.

   • Leave all other controls at their defaults.

6. Click OK to close the dialog and return to the Movie Settings window.

7.   Click the Size button to open the Export Size Settings window (**Figure 9-16**). In this window:

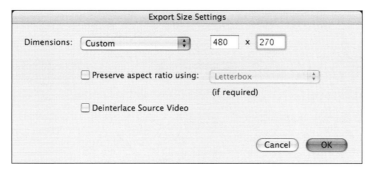

Figure 9-16
Targeting the target output resolution for the intermediate file in Final Cut Pro.

- Assuming that your goal is full-frame (no letterboxing or cropping), aspect-ratio-correct video, do not check the Preserve Aspect Ratio checkbox.

  - If you created a custom preset, or inserted an output resolution that matches the display aspect ratio of the sequence (like 320×240 for SD DV, or 480×270 for HDV), you shouldn't have to click the Preserve Aspect Ratio checkbox.

  - When outputting a resolution that doesn't match the display aspect ratio of the sequence, if you don't check the checkbox, Final Cut Pro will produce the file at that resolution, which will generally distort the aspect ratio of the intermediate file. If you click the Preserve Aspect Ratio checkbox, you can choose to have Final Cut Pro preserve the aspect ratio via letterboxing or cropping, or choose scaling, which will again distort the video.

- **Deinterlace Source Video** – Checking this will not deinterlace your video footage; you must apply Final Cut Pro's deinterlace effect.

8.   Click OK to close this window and return to the Movie Settings window.

9.   Make sure that the Sound checkbox is checked, and click the Sound Settings button to open the Sound Settings window (**Figure 9-17**). Choose Linear PCM as the format, and Channels, Rate and Sample Size as desired. Conform other settings to those shown in the window and click OK to close the window.

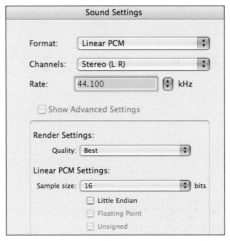

Figure 9-17
Passing through uncompressed sound when creating our intermediate file in After Effects.

10. Accept all other defaults in the Movie Settings window, then click OK and name and store the file in the desired location as normal.

These are the editing programs; now let's move on to the Flash Encoding programs.

Encoding with On2 Flix Pro

On2 Flix Pro is from the developer of the VP6 codec, which probably means that they know their way around the technology. The program is also easy to use, fast and highly functional, with chroma-key capabilities, the ability to create cue points, and lots of other bells and whistles.

Flix Pro is a bit awkward when it comes to encoding files with a pixel aspect ratio that isn't square. Specifically, it looks at the actual pixel resolution, not the pixel aspect ratio, when it "maintains" the aspect ratio. For example, input a 4:3 DV file and choose maintain aspect ratio (which is supposed to be good, right?) and Flix Pro will produce a 720×480 file that's 10% too wide.

In contrast, Squeeze recognizes what you're trying to achieve, and if you enable its equivalent maintain feature, it would force you to 640×480 resolution, which is your true target. The workaround in Flix Pro is to never rely upon the maintain checkbox to constrict you to the right target unless your input file is square pixel and, in most cases, if it is, you'll be encoding to that resolution anyway.

Otherwise, the only interface "gotcha" is that the deinterlacing checkbox is not on the main encoding screen, so you tend to overlook it until you encode DV source video and the artifacts jump out at you. I'll cover where to find it in the workflow discussion, which starts now.

1. Start in File tab. Click the Browse button next to the file Input box, and navigate to and select your target input file (**Figure 9-18**). Flix Pro will automatically store the file in the same folder as the source file and name the FLV file after the

source file. You can change this by clicking the Browse button next to the Output box, changing the location and typing the new name.

Figure 9-18
Inserting our intermediate MOV file into Flix Pro.

2.   On the bottom right of the Flix Pro interface, click the Video Editor button. Flix Pro opens the Editor window (**Figure 9-19**). In this window, you can deinterlace (which I don't need to do since I deinterlaced when creating the intermediate file), apply the Chroma Key effect, adjust color and brightness, crop, fade-in and fade-out and even trim the clip. Click Close in the upper right-hand corner to close the window and return to the main Flix Pro screen.

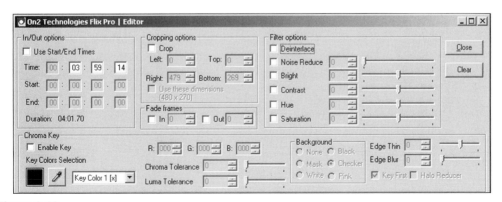

Figure 9-19
Here's where you can deinterlace—if you need to.

3. Click the Vid/Aud tab to open the main encoding settings screen **(Figure 9-20)**. This looks a bit like the Flix Exporter screen and shares much of the same functionality. Here's how to set the controls:

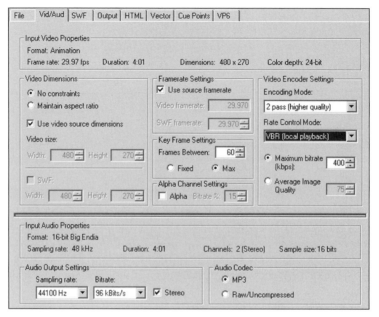

Figure 9-20
The Vid/Aud tab is where you set most encoding parameters for Flix Pro.

- **Video dimensions** – Here's where the square pixel discussion from Chapter 7 will really pay off.

    - Since I'm encoding an intermediate file produced at the same resolution as my target, I clicked the Use video source dimensions checkbox. In this case, either button in the Video Dimensions box would produce the same result.

    - If inputting a file with a pixel display aspect ratio different than 1.0, like DV (4:3 or widescreen) or HDV, click the No constraints checkbox, and uncheck the Use video source dimensions checkbox. Then input your target Video size in the Width and Height boxes, making sure that your output resolution matches the display aspect ratio of the source video. Otherwise, Flix Pro will probably distort the aspect ratio of your file during encoding.

- **Audio output settings** – I'll use these settings; nothing magical here, just select your targets, and make sure to click the MP3 checkbox.

- **Frame rate**
  - If your target frame rate is the same as your source footage, as is the case for my concert footage, click the Use source frame-rate checkbox.
  - If different, uncheck this box and type the desired frame rate in the box.
- **Key frames** – On2 Flix Pro will auto-insert key frames at scene changes. Unless you have some dramatic reason to change this, I would leave the default with Max checked.
- **Alpha channel** – It's not an issue for this concert footage, but when encoding footage with an alpha channel, check the Preserve alpha checkbox. Accept the default Bitrate % or modify as desired (I discuss the Bitrate % allocation in an author's note in Chapter 8).
- **Encoding mode** – Choose 2 pass (higher quality).
- **Rate control mode** – VBR is appropriate for my concert video because it has a mix of high- and low-motion content and will be viewed via progressive download. If you're streaming, be sure to monitor streaming quality to make sure that data-rate spikes don't interrupt the viewing experience.
- Click the Max streaming bitrate (kbps) checkbox, and insert your target.

4. Almost home. Click the VP6 tab to view your advanced encoding options (**Figure 9-21**). Note that the controls in this tab have no effect unless and until you click the enable Advanced Features checkbox. Here are some observations about the controls in this tab:

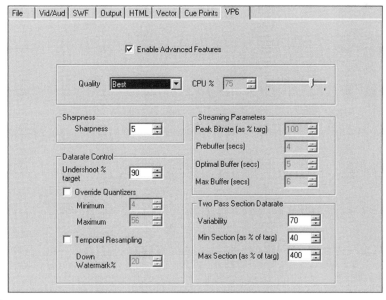

Figure 9-21
Here's where you enable Flix Pro's advanced features.

Author's Tip

Batch Processing in Flix Pro

To batch process multiple files in Flix Pro, choose your settings as described above. Then choose View > Batch Processing to open the Batch Processing window, where you can drag and drop multiple files to encode to these selected parameters. It's a simple but highly effective process, and the help file should answer any questions. Again, it's better for production than experimentation, since, unlike Sorenson Squeeze, it can only encode multiple files to a single set of parameters, rather than one file to multiple parameters.

- **Quality**
    - The default is Good, but so long as the Advanced Features checkbox isn't checked, it has no effect. More specifically, when the checkbox isn't checked, Flix Pro encodes at the Best (slowest and highest quality) setting, even if Good is the grayed-out selection.
    - Choose Good to encode your video faster, but at less quality.
- I discuss the Undershoot % target and Two Pass Section Data rate controls above.
- For the others, read Flix Pro's help file for more details.

5. After selecting all of your options, choose Encoding > Encode to start encoding.

After selecting all of your encoding options, you can save them as a settings file by choosing File > Safe Settings As . . . . You can then reopen and reuse the settings file by choosing File > Open Settings File.

If you're handy with HTML / XML type editing, you can also edit Flix Pro's presets by choosing View > Options, and clicking the Edit in Notepad button. It's a bit scary for beginners, but coders should have no problem with the syntax.

Encoding with Sorenson Squeeze

Sorenson Squeeze is the best all-around encoding utility in the land, and gives Flix Pro a run for its money with Flash encoding. I love its drag-and-drop interface, and the flexible batch-encoding utility. Note that not all versions have On2 VP6 encoding functionality, so if you can't find the presets discussed below, you may not have the right version.

Though Squeeze supports more formats than Flix Pro, it has no chroma-key functionality, so if you want to produce FLV files with an alpha channel, you have to import a QuickTime file as described in Chapter 8.

On the other hand, Sorenson does a better job of recognizing the pixel aspect ratios that it compresses, simplifying the process of producing the right resolution. For example, input a 16:9 DV file and check the "Maintain Aspect Ratio" checkbox, and it will force you to a 16:9 output resolution. Flix Pro doesn't seem aware of display aspect ratio issues, so you have to be much more careful to get it right.

Like Flix Pro, Squeeze has one major interface "gotcha"; you have to manually enable Auto Key frames, which from where I sit makes no sense, and has cost me hours of rework on several projects. I'll describe where to enable this in our walkthrough. Run Squeeze and follow along:

1. Click the Import File button on the top left of the interface, and navigate over and select your file. Squeeze loads it into the Preview and Setting windows.

2. In the Format & Compression Setting window on the left, click the plus sign to the left of the Macromedia Flash Video preset group, and scroll to a VP6 preset that's close to your target. I'll use the VP6_512K preset. To apply it to the file in the Setting window, drag it onto the file (**Figure 9-22**).

Figure 9-22
The main window for Sorenson Squeeze. Note the compression settings on the left, which you drag onto the file in the Setting window.

3. Let's have a quick look at the filters available in Squeeze. In the Filters window on the upper left, double click Custom. Squeeze opens the Filter Settings window (**Figure 9-23**). To apply and customize a filter, drag it onto the target clip.

Figure 9-23
Squeeze's Filter Settings window. Note that Deinterlace is always selected and applied, and note the Noise Reduction capability on the right.

4. Now let's customize our encoding settings. Click the plus sign next to the preset to reveal the audio and video codecs. Double click either the MP3 or VP6 Pro line to open the Audio/Video compression Settings window (**Figure 9-24**).

5. Click the Advanced button on the lower left to expose all encoding options. This is a monster window and I'll describe only the top half, which contains the most relevant controls.

In the top window (**Figure 9-24**):

*   **Audio** – Click the Audio checkbox and choose your target settings. Note that stereo isn't an option.

*   **Video** – Click the Video checkbox and choose On2 VP6Pro in the Codec list box (should already be selected).

*   **Method** – Choose 2-Pass VBR.

*   **Data rate** – Insert your target.

*   **Display Aspect Ratio Policy** – I chose Maintain Aspect Ratio, since that was the default, but since the file input resolution matched the file output, Unconstrained would have also worked.

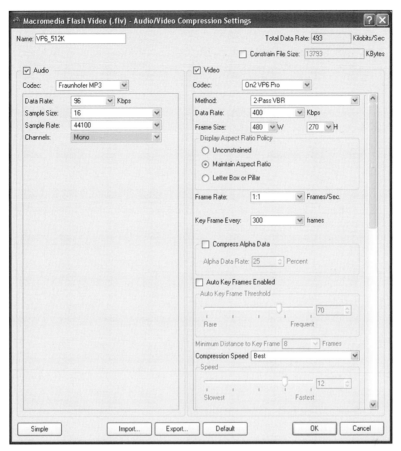

Figure 9-24
Squeeze's Audio/Video Compression Settings window, where you'll find all encoding options. Drag the slider bar on the right to view additional options.

- **Unconstrained** – Squeeze will encode to your target, potentially distorting the aspect ratio.

- **Maintain Aspect Ratio** – Squeeze will force you into an output resolution that matches file display aspect ratio, preventing distortion.

- **Letter Box or Pillar** – Squeeze will output square pixels but insert black bars where necessary to fill out the frame.

- **Frame rate** – 1:1 produces the same rate as the input file. To change, choose a different rate in the Frame Rate list box.

- **Key frame every**: The default is 300 Frames, which is ten seconds in this footage, rather than two seconds like Flix Pro and the Adobe Flash Media Encoder. If I needed the file to be very interactive, I would increase the number of key frames; otherwise this should be fine since I'll be enabling Auto Key Frames in a moment.

- **Compress alpha data** – It's not an issue for this concert footage, but when encoding footage with an alpha channel, check the Preserve Alpha checkbox. I think Sorenson's default Alpha Data Rate Percent of 25% is too high, and would dial it down to 15% and check for edge artifacts. If the video looks clean, you might try even lower (I discuss the Bitrate % allocation in Chapter 8).

- **Auto key frames enabled** – Click this checkbox to enable it, and accept all other default settings.

- **Compression speed** – Choose Best.

6. Drag the slider on the right down to expose all other Advanced Settings, including the VBR controls shown in **Figure 9-1**. I would accept the default on most of these, until a problem surfaces (like low-motion footage that looks too degraded). The only control worth considering is the Drop Frame to Maintain Data Rate checkbox, which may be helpful when streaming video from a Flash Media Server where data-rate adherence is required.

7. Once you've selected all encoding parameters, click OK to close the Compression Settings window.

8. You can add as many source files as you'd like to the Setting window, and as many encoding profiles as you'd like to each source file.

9. When ready to encode, click the Squeeze It! button on the bottom right.

Note that you can save your project by choosing File > Save Project As, which you can recall by choosing File > Open Project. Frustratingly, there is no way to start a new batch; you have to either exit the program, or manually delete all source files in the Setting window.

On the other hand, you can create your own custom presets by right clicking in the Format & Compression Settings window, and choosing New Preset. You can also Import and Export presets by clicking these buttons in the Compression Settings window.

Encoding with the Flash Video Encoder

Let's conclude by working through the encoding process with the Adobe Flash Video Encoder, which we've already seen glimpses of twice before in this chapter with Premiere Pro and After Effects. By way of background, this is the encoder that ships with Flash 8 and Flash CS3.

Though Stefan was able to get his hands on an advance copy of CS3, I was not, but fortunately the changes on the encoding side are very modest. That is, the CS3 version has deinterlacing, which Flash 8 doesn't, which essentially disqualified it for encoding any high-resolution files that weren't first deinterlaced and scaled in a video editor.

Given that the CS3 encoder doesn't have two-pass VBR encoding anyway, I wouldn't use it for my concert. For some talking head videos, however, it produces quite excellent quality, and it can batch process multiple encodes using multiple input files to different output parameters, which is always useful for testing and prototyping. Here's the workflow:

1. Once the Flash 8 Encoder is running, click Add, and navigate to and select your target file. Note that you can select multiple files at one time.

2. Once input into the program, click the Settings button to open the Flash Video Encoding Settings window, and Show Advanced Settings to view all encoding options (**Figure 9-25**).

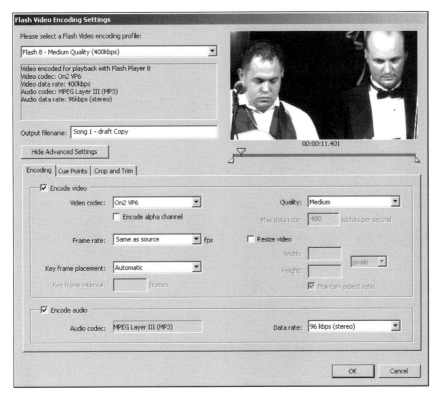

Figure 9-25
The Flash Video Encoding Settings screen from the Flash 8 Video Encoder.

3. In this window, adjust the following settings:

    •   **Output filename** – The encoder will automatically store the file in the same folder as the source file and name the FLV file after the source file. You can change the name by typing the new name in the Output filename text box.

    •   **Video codec** – Select On2 VP6 (should be selected already).

    •   It's not an issue for this footage, but when encoding footage with an alpha channel, check the Encode alpha channel checkbox.

    •   **Frame rate** – My target is 29.97, so I'll leave same as source. Otherwise, click the list box and choose the desired rate.

- **Key frames placement** – If you choose automatic, the encoder will add a key frame every 60 frames; otherwise you can choose Custom and insert a different interval. The encoder does not automatically add key frames upon scene changes. Automatic is fine for my concert footage and should be fine for most other videos.

- **Quality** – My concern is data rate, which is 400 kbps according to the grayed-out box, which is my target for video. To adjust this, click the drop-down list, choose Custom and insert the desired data rate.

- **Resize video**
  - The encoder will encode at the resolution of the source file unless you click the Resize video checkbox. Since I'm encoding an intermediate file produced at my target, I don't need to make a change.
  - To change resolution, click the Resize video checkbox and insert your target resolution.
  - If you click the Maintain Aspect ratio button, the encoder will constrain your typed input to conform to the aspect ratio of the actual pixel resolution, which is desirable when encoding videos with a square pixel aspect ratio (so, with 640×480 video, if you type 320 as the Width, the encoder will constrain Height to 240).
  - When encoding video where the pixel aspect ratio isn't square (like DV or HDV), this produces distorted results. For example, if you input 16:9 DV video and type 640 as Width, the encoder will enter 426 as Height, where for 16:9 display, the correct height is 360.
  - You can achieve the desired results, but only if you deselect the Maintain aspect ratio checkbox and type in a target resolution that matches the display aspect ratio of your source video (like 400×300 for 4:3 DV, or 480×270 for widescreen DV—see discussion in Chapter 7).

4. Once you've finalized all of your settings, click OK to close the Encoding Settings window, and Start Queue in the Video Encoder window to start the batch.

Overall, if you have low-motion, talking-head footage, you should definitely give this encoder a try. It's fast and the quality is quite good. With the Flash 8 (pre-CS3 version), just be sure to deinterlace while creating an intermediate file for your encoding.

Conclusion

Wow, it's been fun; this is my (Jan Ozer) last major section. We've gone from picking a background to keying it out, with a lot of interesting steps in between. In this chapter, you learned how to create intermediate QuickTime files and final FLV files with a bevy of common tools.

Now I hand you off to Stefan Richter, my esteemed coauthor, who will teach you what to do with these files. Enjoy the trip, and I'll see you again at Chapter 19 for the case studies.

CHAPTER 10

Flash Video Concepts

Now that you know how to shoot, process and encode Flash video, it's time to dive a little deeper into the delivery platform that is Flash. In this chapter, you will not only learn Flash's history and its file formats, but also about:

- what "Flash" actually means
- delivery options for Flash video
- Flash video codec evolution
- video capabilities by Player version.

A Brief History of Flash

Flash has come a long way since first released just over ten years ago. Back in the mid-nineties, it started life as an animation package called SmartSketch by a company named FutureWave Software. The driving force behind FutureWave was Jonathan Gay, who is now known as the father of Flash. SmartSketch enjoyed great success as an animation package which brought lightweight, vector-based content to web browsers in a completely new form. Comparable implementations inside a browser environment were based on Java and were quickly replaced by Netscape's plug-in API.

The product was renamed and released as FutureSplash Animator in May of 1996 and you can see a screenshot of the start-up screen in **Figure 10-1**.

FutureSplash Animator was successfully used on projects for MSN, Fox and Disney and it didn't take long for Macromedia to take notice. In December 1996 FutureWave Software was sold to Macromedia, and FutureSplash Animator became Macromedia Flash 1.0. Flash 1.0 was a web animation tool without scripting capabilities or bitmap support, the latter of which was added in 1997 when Flash 2 was released, followed in quick succession by Flash 3 in 1998 and Flash 4 in 1999. This was also the time when the Flash Player reached an installed base of 100 million.

Figure 10-1
FutureSplash Animator later became Flash 1.0.

Other Flash milestones include the following:

- The Flash 5 release in 2000 was the first version of Flash that added improved scripting support, which allowed more experienced users to create intelligent applications that were no longer tied to the timeline.

- Flash MX (Flash 6) was released in 2002. It added support for streaming video via Flash Communication Server, which was released in the same year. Flash MX also allowed for video content to be embedded into the Flash file itself.

- Flash MX 2004 followed—no, not in 2004—in 2003. It added ActionScript 2 support, which pushed Flash development to a new level. Flash Player 7 was the first Player to support progressive video playback.

- Flash 8 in 2005 added the VP6 codec as well as filters, bitmap caching and more.

- Flash CS3 (which is essentially Flash 9) should be released by the time you read this book. This version adds ActionScript 3 support and a new Virtual Machine inside the Flash Player, resulting in an immense performance boost.

What Exactly Is Flash?

What are people referring to when they use the term Flash? Flash can mean a lot of different things to different people and it is important to distinguish the context in which the term is used.

Flash, the File Format

When I speak to a client and refer to building something "in Flash," I am essentially referring to the finished product, the compiled SWF file to be deployed on a web server and served to website users. Every SWF file starts life as an FLA file, the source file which, once compiled, produces a SWF. The SWF file is generally embedded into an HTML page, often displayed alongside traditional image and text content and presented to the user inside a browser.

Figure 10-2 gives a brief overview of the formats and also includes FLV (Flash Video files) for reference.

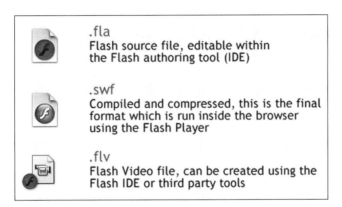

Figure 10-2
Flash file formats and their respective icons (icons may differ depending on installed Flash version).

SWF files can contain a variety of content, ranging from text to sound files, from bitmaps to vector graphics and from XML data to video. SWF has become a universal container for a whole range of media and it offers easy access to external data via SOAP web services, XML or HTTP/S, among others.

The Flash Player

The Flash Player is the most important feature in the Flash platform. The Flash Player is a ubiquitous client that is installed in the form of an ActiveX control to Internet Explorer or as a plug-in to Mozilla-based browsers. One major factor leading to its success is its small file size, currently around 1.4 MB, making it accessible even to dial-up users who can retrieve it in a matter of minutes. According to Adobe, the Flash Player is currently installed on nearly 98% of Internet-enabled desktops; new Flash Player releases achieve over 80% penetration in less than 12 months via an ever more sophisticated distribution and update mechanism.

The Flash IDE

The term IDE stands for Integrated Development Environment and it basically refers to the Flash authoring tool, including Flash CS3 and Flash 8. The IDE is where you create and edit FLA source files and subsequently compile them to SWF format.

Just like the Flash Player, whose releases normally go hand in hand with updates to the IDE, the authoring tool has undergone a huge transformation over the years, moving from an animation tool to a sophisticated development environment that in its latest incarnation supports ActionScript 3.

Looking Ahead

Flash's future continues to look positive. The Flash Player is now the most pervasive piece of software ever, outnumbering even Windows itself, due to its cross-platform support. In one way or another, it could be argued that Flash has won the race inside the browser.

Rather than sitting back and enjoying Flash's success, Adobe is pushing forward with new technologies that leverage Flash as a platform and distribution channel, including Flex 2 and a project code-named Apollo.

Flex 2

Adobe Flex 2 offers developers an alternative way to produce content in SWF format. Flex 2 is a web-application framework that is mainly aimed at producing data-driven applications, delivered via Flash Player 9 and above.

The Flex 2 platform consists of several key elements:

- *Flex Builder 2.* This is an Eclipse-based IDE that allows developers to use a combination of MXML (a form of XML) and ActionScript3 to build sophisticated web applications in a visual programming environment that also offers easy access to the underlying code. **Figure 10-3** shows a screenshot of Flex Builder 2 in design view.

Figure 10-3
The Flex Builder 2 IDE.

- *Flex Framework and SDK.* This is a component-based framework for developing and delivering content in SWF format via the Flash Player. Applications built upon this framework are cross platform, meaning they run on any operating system or device that supports the required Flash Player. In fact, an end user may not see a significant difference from a SWF produced in Flash; the delivered format is still a SWF file but in the case of Flex includes a more sophisticated and powerful web application framework, when compared to a SWF that originated from Flash. Flex is therefore arguably better suited to develop enterprise-level applications than Flash.

- The Flex 2 SDK, class library and compiler are available free of charge. **Figure 10-4** shows one of my own projects, a Flex 2-based video chat application that uses Flash Media Server as its back end.

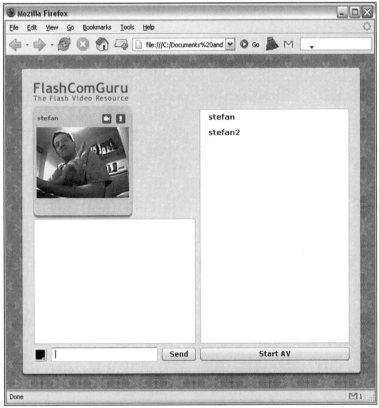

Figure 10-4
FlexVideoChat is a video chat application built using Flex Builder 2.

- *Flex Charting 2*. Flex Charting 2 is an add-on for Flex Builder 2 that provides a library of rich graphs and charts. Drill-downs, rollover effects and data binding are all supported by Flex 2's charting components. **Figure 10-5** shows one of Adobe's Flex sample applications utilizing the charting components.

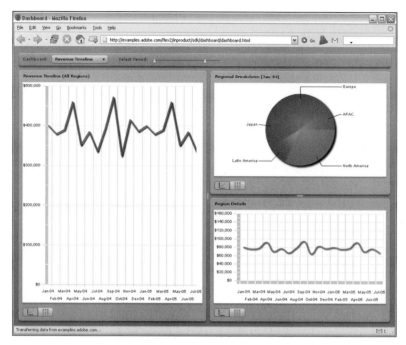

Figure 10-5
A Flex 2 dashboard application.

- *Flex Data Services 2*. Flex Data Services 2 is an enterprise-level server-side data management platform. It extends the client-side Flex framework by providing sophisticated data connectivity and business logic.

More and more Flash developers (as opposed to Flash designers) are adding Flex 2 to their toolkit. I personally use Flex 2 for certain applications that require heavier data interaction, and stick with Flash to build less complex projects or create assets to use within Flex. The line between the two products is still blurred and will likely remain so. What's important to remember is that, whichever product you choose, you are still targeting the Flash Player as your delivery channel. Note that Flex 2 applications require Flash Player 9 or above.

Apollo

Apollo is the code name for a cross-platform desktop runtime that Adobe is currently developing. It will support Windows, Macintosh and Linux operating systems and allows developers to build desktop applications by utilizing traditional web technologies and skills (think Flash/ActionScript, HTML, PDF, JavaScript/Ajax).

Apollo applications behave like "real" desktop programs, run outside the browser and offer many new features when compared to browser-based applications, due to a tighter integration with the user's operating system. Adobe refers to these applications as desktop RIAs (Rich Internet Applications).

It is to be expected that most existing Flash and web applications can be enabled to run inside Apollo with a minimum of effort. Flex 2 applications will be particularly suited for this.

Author's Tip

At the time of writing, Apollo has not yet been released. It is expected to go into public beta in early 2007 with a 1.0 release later in the year. Apollo is a code name that will likely change upon release.

Figure 10-6 shows a screenshot of the San Dimas project, an eBay desktop client developed in Apollo. It can take advantage of the desktop's features and provide things like local storage and desktop notifications very easily, setting it apart from a browser-based equivalent.

You can read more about San Dimas at *http://blogs.zdnet.com/Stewart/?p=197* and find info on Apollo at *http://labs.adobe.com/wiki/index.php/Apollo*.

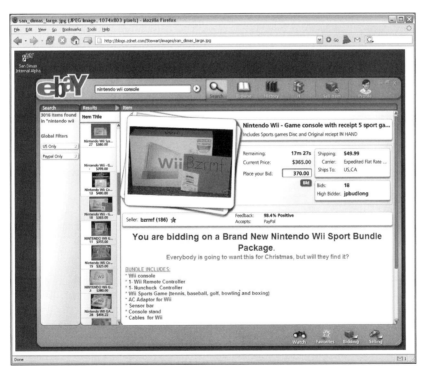

Figure 10-6
San Dimas is an Apollo-based eBay client.

The Evolution of Flash Video Codecs

Initially, Flash video was created by placing sequential video images on the Flash timeline and exporting these as Flash animation. This was primitive and worked poorly with real-world videos.

Then Macromedia released Flash MX with the FLV format and a true video-compression technology called Spark from Sorenson Media that boosted video quality significantly, especially if you used Sorenson's own encoding tool, Squeeze. Still, in use, video quality trailed codecs offered by Real, Microsoft and Apple, and maintaining synchronization between the audio and video components was a significant problem.

Synchronization issues were largely resolved with the introduction of Flash Professional MX 2004, which streamed video from a server rather than including it in the Flash timeline. Then On2 released the VP6 codec for Flash, which achieved comparable video quality to the other codecs available to streaming developers. At this point, Flash's natural advantages, design flexibility and player ubiquity, took hold, and Flash Video began to dominate.

Today, Flash video is the primary codec for many broadcasters, including ESPN and CNN, and is also extraordinarily popular among Fortune 500 and other organizations with a large web presence.

Delivery Options for Flash Video

Support for Flash video content has grown steadily with every recent release of Flash and the Flash Player. Initially the Player's video features were pretty basic, and the main delivery platform for video in Flash was on CD-ROM. Today, you have several deployment methods at your disposal, so let's examine them in more detail.

Embedded Video

Embedding video files into a Flash application has been supported since around 2001/2002 with the release of Flash MX and Flash Player 6. In previous versions, video could only be simulated with a series of bitmap or vector images.

When imported, video is compressed using the Spark codec, then decompressed again when the SWF is played back. Embedded video content and associated SWF files can be placed on and delivered via any standard web server.

Embedding video into your Flash SWF has a number of disadvantages, including:

- **Large file size** – Because the video content is part of the Flash application, the resulting SWF files grow significantly in size.

- **Difficult to update** – Since the video is integrated into the SWF, any updates require editing and re-exporting of the FLA source files, making updates a laborious process.

- **Synchronization issues** – Audio and video tracks tend to get out of sync when video is embedded. This is because the frame rate of the video content may be different from that used in the Flash application.

- **Time restrictions** – The timeline in Flash is limited to 16,000 frames and longer video clips are therefore not supported.

Due to these limitations and the availability of better delivery mechanisms, embedding video is no longer recommended. Some niche cases, such as video used for Button rollover effects, do exist, but in order to deliver any meaningful length of video in Flash, you should now concentrate your efforts on the following methods.

Progressive Download

Added to Flash Player 7, the method of downloading a FLV file progressively into a Flash application was a milestone for Flash video popularity. Most major sites including YouTube and Google Video deploy their Flash video content via progressive download.

With this technique, FLV content is maintained externally from the SWF file and a download into the SWF and subsequently to the user's machine is initiated once the Flash application requests it. This has several advantages over embedded video, including:

- **Easier updates** – Since the FLV is separate from the SWF, you can easily swap content without editing or modifying the Flash application itself.

- **Smaller file size** – No unnecessary video content bloats the SWF.

- **Better playback** – The frame rates of the FLV and SWF operate independently so there are no audio sync issues or premature endings.

- **Fast start-up** – Video playback starts as soon as enough data has been downloaded.

Since progressively downloaded FLV files can be served from any web server, it is the most widely adopted form of Flash video delivery today. Many casual website authors as well as professionals use this method to publish Flash video content quickly and with minimal hassle. This process is being made even simpler by the export features in Flash CS3 and Flash 8 as well as Dreamweaver's video wizard, both of which I cover in more detail in the next chapter.

Streaming Delivery

Streaming delivery is only available when distributing video via a specialized streaming server, such as Flash Media Server. This technique offers many of the benefits of a progressive download, plus a few of its own. It is also well suited to deliver long video files or to distribute video to a large number of simultaneous viewers. Other benefits include:

- **Advanced seeking** – A user can seek to any point within the video without having to wait for this part to be downloaded first, as is the case with progressive delivery. Instead, any part can be accessed after a short buffering time.

- **Efficient use of bandwidth** – Video is delivered as it's being watched, so if the viewer stops watching, little bandwidth is wasted. Progressive delivery delivers the entire file as quickly as possible, which can result in wasted bandwidth if the viewer stops watching.

- **Low system requirements** – Memory and disk space usage is very low when using streaming, as no file is being downloaded.

- **Security** – Files are not cached on the user's hard drive, which complicates copying and repurposing of the streaming content.

- **Live video and recording** – Only streaming Flash video offers the possibility for live video and audio broadcasts as well as recording facilities.

- **Advanced features** – Flash Media Server offers bandwidth detection features and failover capabilities that are hard to replicate on other platforms or delivery mechanisms.

FVSS Delivery

FVSS stands for Flash Video Streaming Service and it is offered by several companies approved by Adobe to deliver globally distributed Flash video streaming services. Currently this service is offered by Akamai, Limelight Networks, VitalStream and Mirror Image Internet. In a nutshell, this service offers a CDN (Content Delivery Network) based delivery for streaming Flash video.

The experience for the user is essentially the same as when video is streamed via a single Flash Media Server, but it offers scalability and availability features that are only possible via a CDN. FVSS is therefore the recommended platform to deliver large volumes of Flash video content to a globally distributed audience. Recent competition and falling bandwidth prices mean that CDN services are now within the financial reach of even small- to medium-sized businesses.

Note, however, that FVSS supports video streaming only. That's because other Flash Media Server features like text chats and custom server side scripts aren't possible on a CDN due to its distributed nature. Live video, however, is being offered by more and more providers and I expect to see a growth in the live Flash video arena over the coming months.

Author's Tip

Note that you can use the same FLV file using either progressive download or streaming (be it via your own server or FVSS), meaning the file itself contains no prerequisites that tie it to one or the other form of delivery.

Flash Player Compatibilities

Each release of the Flash authoring tool saw the introduction of new features that were not previously supported by the Flash Player, meaning that every release of the authoring tool went hand in hand with a new release of the Player. Video features weren't unaffected by this, so you need to be aware which features and video codecs are supported by which version of the Player.

Flash Player 6

Player 6 was the first version to support embedded as well as streaming video. In both cases, the Sorenson Spark codec was utilized to compress the video content.

As embedded video is no longer preferred and progressive download not supported by Flash Player 6, streaming to this player is your only option. Specifically, Flash Player 6 was released at roughly the same time as Flash Communication Server 1.0 (now named Flash Media Server). The server enables live and on-demand streaming Flash video delivery to Flash Player 6 using the Sorenson Spark codec.

Flash Player 7

As the first Player to support progressively downloaded video, again utilizing the Spark codec, Flash Player 7 was a milestone in the evolution of Flash video. Being able to serve video progressively meant that everyone with access to a web server could now deploy Flash video content; no longer was this area reserved to those with a Flash Communication Server license.

Most of the large video portals, including YouTube, were built on top of this technology, serving progressively downloaded FLV files to an audience requiring Flash Player 7 or above.

> **Author's Tip**
>
> Newer Flash Players are always backward compatible with features from the previous Players. This means that you can be certain that Spark-encoded videos that played fine in Player 6 will still work reliably in future versions of the Player in years to come.

Flash Player 8+

Another milestone for Flash video was the release of Player 8 in 2005, as it introduced support for a new, higher-quality codec: On2 VP6. Developers were now able to deliver progressive and streaming Flash video content with much higher video quality at the same bit rate or indeed the same quality at a lower bit rate, saving bandwidth costs. The introduction of VP6 brought Flash into line with other technologies such as QuickTime and Windows Media and meant another push for Flash as a video-delivery platform.

Flash Player 9 did not introduce any significant video features, but it is likely that Adobe will add support for additional video codecs to future versions of the Flash Player.

While VP6 has yet to reach its peak on the Flash video stage, there is no doubt that Adobe is working hard on implementing new codecs and features to the Player.

> **Author's Tip**
>
> It is easy to detect and upgrade a user's Flash Player if needed. You will learn more about this process in the next chapter.

Summary

You should now be aware that not every version of the Flash Player supports all video features and codecs. If you want to have access to both Spark and VP6 in both progressive and streaming form, then Flash Player 8 or above is the version you need to target.

When choosing your codec and distribution technique, you obviously need to be in touch with the Player version installed by the bulk of your target users, especially in situations where they can't auto update to the latest Player.

For example, On2's VP6 codec was widely (but certainly not universally) adopted by general-purpose sites because they knew that their target audience could and would generally update to the latest Player to watch their video. Conversely, in a locked-down corporate, government or institutional environment, where users can't choose to update even if they wanted to, it would be folly to use a codec that the standard machine can't play, which is one of the key reasons many large organizations with large internal video distribution use the Spark codec for their streamed and progressive delivery.

Always ascertain your audience's capabilities first, and then choose the most complementary codec and delivery mechanism. I've summarized these capabilities by Player version in **Figure 10-7**.

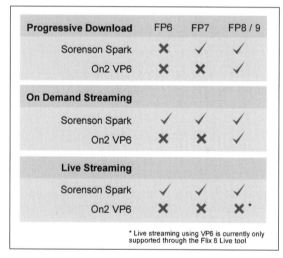

Figure 10-7
Video capabilities and codec summary by Flash Player version.

Conclusion

I hope that this chapter has given you a good overview of some key Flash video concepts as well as the milestones in Flash's 10-year-long history. There is no doubt that this platform, which started life as a simple animation tool, has matured into one of the most popular technologies on the Internet.

It is important to understand that certain Flash video features are only supported by some Flash Player versions, such as the ability to deliver a video progressively or streamed. You will build on this knowledge when moving on to the next chapter, "Deploying Progressive Flash Video."

CHAPTER 11

Deploying Progressive Flash Video

Previous chapters described how to produce high-quality Flash video; now it's time to deploy it. This chapter starts by reviewing three techniques for deploying Flash video files, first by using prebuilt components in Flash, then via Dreamweaver and finally back to Flash to learn how to deploy Flash video via direct coding in ActionScript.

ALERT This chapter uses Adobe Flash CS3 Professional (alternatively you may use Adobe Flash Professional 8). To follow along with the examples, which I recommend, you will need a copy of the program installed on your computer. Should you not own a copy of the program, note that Adobe offers a free 30-day trial version on its website.

Also, note that you can find the files referred to and used in this chapter at *www.flashvideobook.com*. Consider downloading these files now, so they'll be available once I start referring to them.

Next we'll look at the different ways of adding Flash video to a web page, specifically the OBJECT and EMBED tags, the problems created by the Eolas patent and recent related changes to Internet Explorer.

After learning how to work around Eolas-related issues with the SWFObject script library, I'll describe how to add Express Install to your SWFs so all potential viewers can easily update to the latest version of Flash Player and play your gorgeous VP6 encoded video files.

After reading this chapter, you will know how to:

* Deploy Flash video files by using prebuilt components in Flash
* Deploy Flash video files using Dreamweaver

- Deploy Flash video files with Flash using Actionscript
- Work around issues caused by the Eolas patent
- Use Express Install to automatically upgrade your viewer's Player to the version of Flash necessary to play your Flash video files.

Deploying Flash Video—An Overview

If you are new to Adobe Flash and Flash video, you may be unfamiliar with the deployment procedures of the associated formats. Here is an overview of these requirements, which I'll cover in more detail throughout this chapter.

Briefly, to add Flash video to a web page, you'll need to deploy at least two files, an FLV containing the compressed video and a SWF file that serves as the player. Usually, you'll deploy three files, the FLV, SWF and an HTML file that acts as a container for the SWF. As you'll see, this number will grow to include JavaScript and other files in some instances.

Figure 11-1 outlines the three key elements that usually make up a Flash video application. The figure shows a basic web page containing the HTML container (1), the SWF file (2), as well as the FLV video (3), which plays inside the SWF.

Figure 11-1
A typical Flash video application: The *Roanoke Times* Sportscast at *http://blogs.roanoke.com/ sportstimescast.*

The workflow for creating these files varies by application. For example, you can input an AVI or MOV file into Flash, choose player components, and have Flash automatically produce the necessary FLV, SWF and even HTML files. Dreamweaver can't convert MOV/AVI to FLV, but can create simple SWF files and, of course, the necessary HMTL.

In this chapter, I will explain how to deploy files via progressive download, which you can do using any standard web server. In Chapter 17, you'll learn how to serve streaming Flash video, which requires either a Flash Media Server or a Flash Video Streaming Service (FVSS).

Player Components

There are several options for deploying progressive Flash Video content, including developing your own Flash Player. While this may sound challenging to those new to Flash and ActionScript, I'll later describe how to build a simple player using ActionScript (without a component), and you'll see that a hand-coded player does not have to be complex.

To simplify player development, Adobe preinstalls several player components with Flash. Arguably the most popular one is the FLV Playback component, which supports progressive and streaming video, and live and on-demand video. The component also supports cue points, bandwidth-detection features (when used in combination with Flash Media Server 2), understands SMIL (the Synchronized Multimedia Integration Language) and you can customize its look and feel. It also includes all the ActionScript source code, which you can tweak as and when required.

Other commercially available components include:

FLV Player 2.1 by AFComponents *http://www.afcomponents.com/flv/index.htm*. This component is based on Adobe's FLV Playback component and offers similar features.

Flash Video Player 3.1 by Jeroen Wijering *http://www.jeroenwijering.com/?item=Flash_Video_Player*. Jeroen's player supports a variety of playback methods and can also be used without the Adobe Flash authoring tool, which I'll also refer to as Flash IDE, for Integrated Development Environment.

Custom FLV Player 1.0 by Meshybeats *http://meshybeats.com/components/*. This player has been around for quite a while and I like its minimalist look.

Note that, unless a component specifically states otherwise, you'll usually need Adobe Flash to compile a SWF movie containing the player component. When someone mentions a Flash component, they normally refer to a precompiled MovieClip (in this case a video player), that can be installed into the components panel of Adobe Flash and from there be used via drag-and-drop fashion before being compiled to SWF format.

There are some ready-made players in SWF format that you can deploy without any Flash knowledge or even without the need to open Adobe Flash at all. One such example is Jeroen's player, which can be used directly in HTML (as a SWF) without having to compile it first.

Any skilled Flash developer can convert most components into a standalone SWF. This means that you can use a single SWF to play multiple FLV files by passing the FLV reference or FLV URL to the component from the page it is embedded on—a method also referred to as FlashVars. You will learn more on this in Chapter 14, where I also cover other configuration options that make your video player more versatile.

Why Components?

Briefly, components are prebuilt Flash assets that add complex functionality to your application without programming. After installing components into Flash, you deploy them via drag and drop, and configure them via Flash's Property panel, which hides complex ActionScript code and makes the development process more visual and less code-centric.

Components are great for developers because they promote reusable code and often encourage a best-practices approach. A component discretely manages a problem or task without having to be closely linked to other parts of an application. For example, a video player component only deals with playing video and not with data loading or form validation. Usually, you can feed a component the data that it expects (in our case, this may be a URL to an FLV file) and it will work out of the box.

Components also allow novice users to achieve results quickly and usually painlessly. For example, the FLV Playback component lets you publish a Flash Video Player including SWF and FLV without writing a single line of code. The entire procedure is driven by a wizard that kicks into life once you choose Import Video from the File menu in Adobe Flash.

But this functionality comes at a price. Sometimes components introduce unnecessary functionality, adding weight and complexity to an application. They can also be hard to customize in look and feel and functionality. Components are often precompiled so you can't access source code, which complicates matters, especially if you find a critical bug in the component.

The FLV Playback component ships in precompiled format but it also includes full source code. To make sense of the source code and mold it successfully to your needs, you need to be fairly skilled in ActionScript 2. If digging through code is not for you, you can simply skin the component fairly easily, as you will see in Chapter 12.

As with many Internet-related technologies, working with components may be a compromise. Depending upon your project, you may be better served by a component or a custom-written video player, or even a combination of both.

Deploying Progressively Loaded FLV Video Files Using the FLV Playback Component

Let's stop talking about it and produce and deploy a Flash video file with Adobe Flash. This is a great option for novices seeking to quickly encode and upload a video file, or even for experienced Flash programmers who need an efficient, no-frills approach.

Let's use the Import Video dialogue in Flash CS3 or Flash 8, which both present a wizard-style workflow that includes encoding the video file to FLV format and adding and configuring the FLV Playback component. To get started, you'll need Adobe Flash CS3 or Adobe Flash 8 on your system.

I'll be using files you can access from *www.flashvideobook.com*; if you haven't already downloaded these, please do so now. Here are the steps:

1. Create a new Flash document by choosing File > New > Flash Document from the File menu. Select ActionScript 2 as the document type if you see this option.

2. Save the document under the name of "video_import.fla" into the same location as the unzipped source files for Chapter 11 (see **Figure 11-2**).

Figure 11-2
The FLA, Windows Media and QuickTime files.

3. Choose File > Import > Import Video from the File menu. The Import Video wizard opens. You have two options:

   • You choose a local file that exists on your file system, or

   • Point the wizard to a file that is already deployed on the Internet.

If you choose the second option, note the file must be an FLV file or—when distributing files via the Flash Media Server—an XML file containing SMIL content. An SMIL file is nothing more than a pointer to FLV video content, which allows you to keep the video information external to the SWF. You will learn more about Flash Media Server as well as SMIL files in Chapter 17.

I'll assume for this example that you'll convert the supplied WMV file (or MOV file if you are using a Mac, as WMV is not commonly supported there) to FLV format. **Figure 11-3** shows the selected video path as seen on my screen. Note that the path on your computer may vary from mine, depending where you have saved the sample file archive after download.

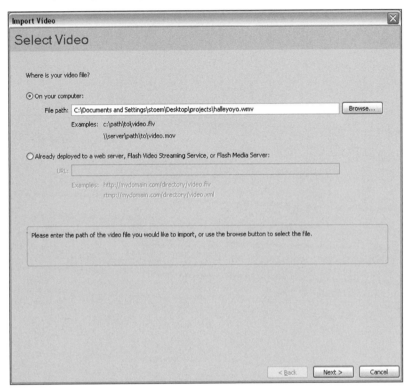

Figure 11-3
The Import Video wizard with the WMV file selected (Mac users should choose the MOV file).

4. Click Next. Flash presents a series of radio buttons for choosing the deployment method. Your choice preconfigures the FLV Playback component with the necessary deployment parameters. The Progressive download option is the default option for this panel, and should already be selected (see **Figure 11-4**). If not, click Progressive download.

5. Click Next. Flash presents the encoding interface from the Adobe Flash Video Encoder (**Figure 11-5**). You should see a preview area with a scrub bar (sometimes referred to as timeline but not to be confused with Flash's own timeline), a time indicator, as well as five different tabs offering options for Encoding Profiles (Video, Audio, Cue Points, as well as Crop and Resize). Note that the interface of the Flash CS3 video encoder differs slightly from that of Flash 8 where most options are accessed via the Advanced Settings button.

    The Encoding Profiles drop-down list offers multiple encoding profiles and defaults to Flash 8, Medium Quality (400 kbps). At a high level, a user can choose between the two Flash video codecs, Spark and VP6, which controls Flash Player compatibility. Specifically, Spark is compatible—when using progressive download—with Flash Player 7 and above, while VP6 only works with Flash Player 8 and above.

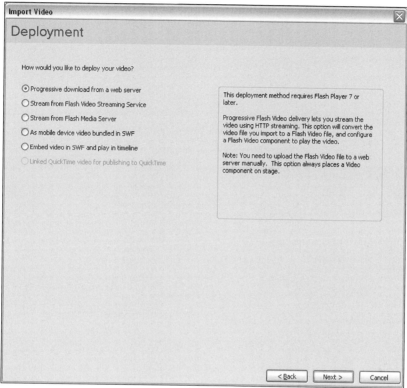

Figure 11-4
The Progressive download method is selected.

Flash Media Server allows you to deploy streaming FLV files, using Spark, since Flash Player 6. You can of course also stream FLV files encoded with VP6 via Flash Media Server, but again your users must have Flash Player 8 (or above) installed to view it. For more details on which codec is compatible with which Player, check Chapter 10.

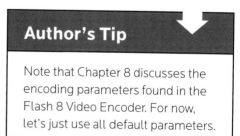

Author's Tip

Note that Chapter 8 discusses the encoding parameters found in the Flash 8 Video Encoder. For now, let's just use all default parameters.

Unless your target viewers can't update to Flash Player 8—say in a highly secure corporate environment—it's probably safe to assume that the penetration level of Flash Player 8 is high enough to deploy VP6 video.

6.   Choose the encoding bit rate (low, medium or high) that matches your target audience's Internet connection. For this example, I'm using the default setting.

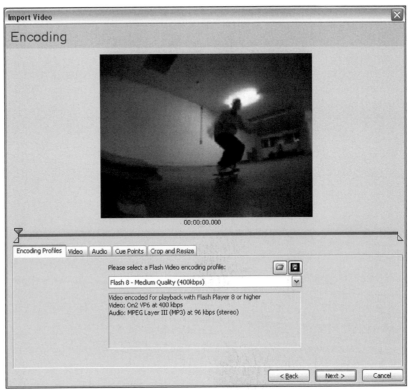

Figure 11-5
The selected Encoding Profiles tab.

7.   Click Next to reach the Skinning panel, which previews the appearance of your finished application. You can preview a variety of player skins and apply your favorite, and even create your own skin and supply its custom URL. For this example, let's choose MojaveExternalAll.swf as shown in **Figure 11-6**.

As you can see, all skins are actually SWF files that you'll need to upload to your web server along with the FLV file and the SWF file you're about to create. If you don't deploy the skin, your remote viewers won't have playback controls, which you clearly want to avoid.

8.   Click Next. Flash displays summary encoding information for your review.

9.   Click Finish to start encoding. The Flash Video Encoding Progress window will open (see **Figure 11-7**) and provide real-time status updates. Depending on the chosen codec, video length, CPU speed and many other factors, this can take a while to complete. Go grab a cup of coffee or indeed consider a nap if you're encoding a feature-length film.

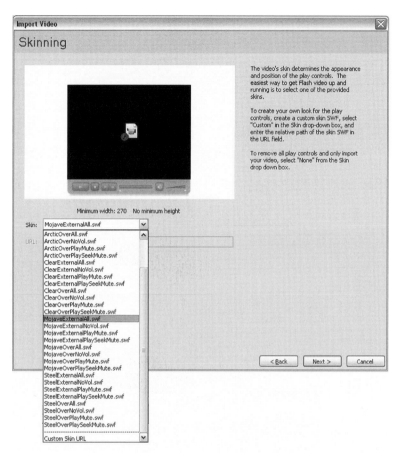

Figure 11-6
Selecting the MojaveExternalAll.swf skin.

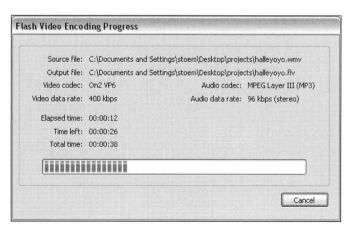

Figure 11-7
The Flash Video Encoding Progress window.

Author's Tip

If you are using Flash CS3 in combination with the latest version of the FLV Playback component, note that the name of the *contentPath* property has changed to *source* in ActionScript 3. In that case, remember to use *source* instead of *contentPath*. The samples in this book use ActionScript 2 syntax.

After encoding, Flash will display a black square representing an instance of the FLV Playback component that is linked to your video. To check its configuration, click the black square, and open the Properties panel by choosing Window > Properties > Properties from the menu bar to reveal the Properties panel, then click the Parameters tab.

If not already selected, click the FLV Playback component to reveal its configuration parameters. You should see the newly encoded file, halleyoyo.flv, in the contentPath parameter, and further down the skin file, ready to go.

10.   Choose Control > Test Movie from the menu bar to preview the player and video inside of Flash. The Flash Player opens and plays the file (**Figure 11-8**).

Figure 11-8
The encoded video plays in Flash.

You are now just one step away from completion. One key element, however, is still missing: the HTML container. Again Flash makes life very easy by offering a painless publishing process.

11.   From the File menu, choose File > Publish. Flash publishes the application and opens your default browser for a preview. If you don't like the look, you can easily change video player skins by clicking that value in the Parameters tab within Flash, which returns you to the same interface shown in **Figure 11-6.**

12.   Once you're happy with the look and feel, upload the contents of your project folder (minus the original halleyoyo.wmv or halleyoyo.mov file) to your web

server and a URL of your choice. Then, of course, link your web to the HTML file you just created to make your new Flash Video file accessible on the Internet.

A last look back at the location to which you have saved the FLA file initially confirms that the necessary files are ready to deploy (see **Figure 11-9**). Use your favorite FTP tool to upload the files, as Flash doesn't provide a facility for this.

Remember to upload the FLV video file, the HTML document, and the skin SWF file, as well as the JavaScript file that Flash CS3 produces (AC_OETags.js), which embeds the SWF into the HTML document. To play the file, you can click on the link on your web page or enter the URL of *video_import.html* in your browser.

Author's Tip

Some users get tripped up when setting up paths to the FLVPlayback skin SWF and to the FLV that's pulled in by the SWF. The path to a skin SWF file is relative to the HTML document (and not to the embedded SWF). The FLV, however, is relative to the embedded SWF. To avoid confusion, we simply place everything in the same folder.

Well done—you've just deployed your first Flash video application.

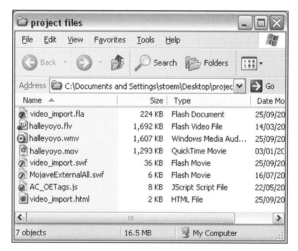

Figure 11-9
Several new files have appeared. Upload all apart from the original WMV or MOV file to your website, and link to the HTML file, not to the SWF or FLA files.

Dreamweaver 8 Insert Flash Video Dialogue

The Dreamweaver Insert Flash Video dialogue enables users with minimal Flash or HTML knowledge to quickly deploy an FLV video file complete with SWF-based player interface. Dreamweaver can't actually produce an FLV file, so you'll have to encode the FLV and perform other encoding-oriented tasks in a separate application.

Still, Dreamweaver's sheer simplicity makes it a great option for deploying Flash video. If you don't have Dreamweaver, consider downloading the free 30-day trial version from Adobe.com.

This lesson uses the halleyoyo.flv file encoded in the previous exercise to illustrate how to deploy Flash video via Dreamweaver. Let's get started.

1. Run Dreamweaver and create a new HTML file by choosing File > New from the File menu. Choose Basic Page > HTML from the New Document dialogue.

2. Choose File > Save As to save the page to the location of your choice. Creating a separate folder for this exercise will facilitate finding all the files created by Dreamweaver.

3. Choose Insert > Media > Flash Video. The Insert Flash Video dialogue opens (**Figure 11-10**).

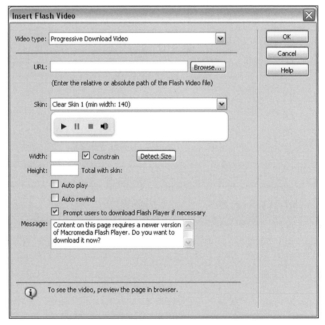

Figure 11-10
Dreamweaver 8's Insert Flash Video dialogue.

4. Click the Video type drop-down menu and select Progressive Download, which is the default option. Your other option is Streaming Video, which you should use when publishing to a Flash Media Server or Flash Video Streaming Service.

5. Click Browse to navigate to the halleyoyo.flv file. If located in the same folder as your HTML file, typing halleyoyo.flv into the URL field should do the trick. Note that the path to the FLV file can also be an HTTP address for previously deployed FLV files.

6. Click the Skin dropdown menu to choose a skin for your player. Like the skins we saw with Flash's FLV Playback component, Dreamweaver's skins are a SWF file containing playback controls that you must deploy with the other HTML, SWF and FLV files. Pick the desired skin, making sure its minimum size fits within the dimensions of your video (min: width 140 pixels in the skin selected in **Figure 11-10**).

7. Click Detect Size to have Dreamweaver detect and enter the resolution of your FLV file in pixels, or type the width and height manually.

8. Next, make some playback-related choices.

    • If desired, click the Auto Play checkbox, which—you guessed it—automatically plays the video once the HTML page and a portion of the video have loaded.

    • If desired, click the Auto rewind checkbox, which automatically rewinds the video after playback. If you leave this option unchecked, the last video frame remains on screen once the video finishes playing, which is useful when that frame includes a message or call to action. Note that viewers can then click to rewind and replay the video.

    • Lastly, you have the option to detect the user's Flash Player version and alert her to upgrade it if necessary. Usually you should leave this option checked as it will ensure that the user is prompted to download the latest Flash Player if the minimum required version was not detected. Note that this detection routine uses JavaScript and does not implement the Express Install feature. It therefore requires a download and install procedure as opposed to the in-page update that Express Install offers, which I describe below.

9. Click OK to close the dialogue. Dreamweaver 8 will create the necessary SWF file and embed it into your HTML document. If desired, choose View > Code from the menu bar to view the code that Dreamweaver generated.

10. Choose File > Save to save the file. To preview the completed page in your default browser, choose File > Preview in Browser. **Figure 11-11** shows the completed page in my browser.

To deploy this player, upload the following files to your web server. They should be located in the same location as the original HTML document. They are:

    • halleyoyo.flv, your FLV file

    • dreamweaver.htm, your HTML document

    • Scripts, a folder containing JavaScript needed for embedding the SWF into the HTML page; this is Dreamweaver's way to circumvent the Eolas issue discussed below

    • Clear_Skin_1.swf, the player skin (which may differ depending on which skin you have chosen)

    • FLVPlayer_Progressive.swf, the player SWF.

Figure 11-11
The completed page showing the SWF and video embedded into the HTML page.

> **Author's Tip**
>
> Note that Dreamweaver 8's skins are somewhat older (going back to Dreamweaver 7) than the FLV Playback skins that ship with Flash 8 and above. As a practical matter, this means that the Dreamweaver 8 skins always float atop the video content, revealing and hiding as the user moves her mouse over and out of the video area, which may not be to your liking, but is your only current option with Dreamweaver. I guess this is another compromise to be considered when simplifying the video-publishing process. Also note that you cannot use Flash's FLV Playback skins within the Dreamweaver wizard.
>
> For more control over skin appearance and operation, you can always fall back to Flash as your development tool. It offers full control on all these aspects, and we will cover design changes in more depth in Chapter 12,"Customizing the FLV Playback Component."

After uploading, navigate to dreamweaver. htm with your browser to see the video playing. To link the player into an existing web page, create a link to the HTML file, not the FLV or SWF.

Playing an FLV File Using ActionScript

There is surprisingly little code necessary to play an FLV video using a bare-bones ActionScript approach, much less than the lesson on the FLV Playback component may suggest. Believe me, that component contains many hundreds of lines of ActionScript code and, while it works well, you should understand that a handcrafted Flash video application can be much less complex. Though you'll probably want to start by using components, hopefully this exercise will both introduce you to ActionScript and make it feel much more accessible.

Don't worry if you are new to ActionScript, as our project is very basic. It does, however, help if you are familiar with basic programming concepts such as variables and functions. In addition, following this tutorial along in Flash will help you understand the workflow better than just reading about it. Upcoming chapters include several examples built in Adobe Flash CS3 that you can work through with me or simply use for reference. But enough talking, let's get started.

1. In Flash, click File > Open and select the file flv_via_actionscript.fla, which I've included in the files you can download from *www.flashvideobook.com*. Once opened, you'll see assets in the file, including the MovieClip video_mc on Stage, which contains a Video object we will use to display our FLV video. Video objects are a special Symbol used to display video in Flash that you create by selecting New Video from the Library pop-up menu, as shown in **Figure 11-12**. A Video object doesn't encapsulate any functionality that a component would offer, but is merely designed to display a live or prerecorded FLV video file. Note that I have already added the Video object for this example and there is no need to create another one.

2. Choose Window > Library to open the Library panel.

Figure 11-12
The Library panel with selected New Video option. This shows how to create a Video object, which I have already done for you in this example.

3. Right click frame 1 of the actions layer and choose Actions, or choose Window > Actions from the menu bar. The Actions panel opens.

4. Type the following code in the Actions panel at around line 11, after the comments (that's the code showing up in a light gray color) that are already present:

```
// specify which file to play
var videofile:String = "halleyoyo.flv";

// create a NetConnection Objecttype
var nc:NetConnection = new NetConnection();
// connect to 'null' for progressive video playback
nc.connect( null );
// create a NetStream object, passing a reference to nc
var ns:NetStream = new NetStream( nc );
// optional: specify a buffer time
ns.setBufferTime(2);
// attach the NetStream to our Video object on stage
video_mc.my_video.attachVideo( ns );

// finally play the video
ns.play(videofile);

// stop the timeline from moving further
stop();
```

This is all you need to play a progressive FLV file in Flash. In fact, you could reduce it even further, but I prefer this approach because it's more readable. Let's walk through the code and see what it accomplishes.

```
var videofile:String = "halleyoyo.flv";
```

The first line identifies the FLV file to play. This example uses a relative path in the same directory as the SWF file we will soon compile, but it can also point to an absolute URL.

```
var nc:NetConnection = new NetConnection();
```

This line sets up an instance of the NetConnection class. NetConnection is always needed to play external FLV files in Flash.

```
nc.connect( null );
```

This line connects the NetConnection instance. The null parameter signifies that we will play a progressive FLV file. To stream an FLV file from a Flash Media Server 2 or compatible media server, we would enter an rtmp address instead of null. Rtmp stands for Real Time Messaging Protocol, a proprietary protocol developed by Adobe, formerly Macromedia, which is covered in more detail in Chapter 17.

```
var ns:NetStream = new NetStream( nc );
ns.setBufferTime(2);
```

Author's Tip

Flash offers extensive and well-structured help files. In order to find out more details on a certain term or object such as NetConnection, simply highlight the item in the ActionScript panel and press F1. The Flash Help panel will open and display information on the selected item. This procedure will work for most terms that are highlighted in blue in Flash's ActionScript editor.

This next piece of code first creates an instance of the NetStream class and then specifies a buffer time of 2 seconds. This directs the Flash Player to buffer enough data to play 2 seconds of video (and audio) before starting playback. Note that this doesn't mean that the actual waiting time experienced by the remote viewer will be 2 seconds; it can take longer or be a lot quicker, depending on the user's connection speed.

When you test the application locally, of course, the video will play straight away. That's because it only takes a split second to fill the buffer from your hard drive, though obviously your mileage may vary over a shaky Internet connection, let alone dial-up.

```
video_mc.my_video.attachVideo( ns );
ns.play(videofile);
```

The next two lines attach the video (our FLV) to be played via NetStream to the Video object my_video, which is placed inside the video_mc MovieClip.

You may wonder why I haven't placed the Video object directly on Stage. The answer is: habit. I guess I could have done that, but it's just more convenient to wrap a MovieClip symbol around it. MovieClips are the nuts and bolts of Flash and are very familiar objects for most Flash developers. I see this technique as a best-practices approach.

5.   Choose Control > Test Movie from the menu bar to preview the application, which first compiles and then plays in the Flash Player, as shown in **Figure 11-13**.

Figure 11-13
The compiled SWF with video playing.

6. Choose File > Publish, and Flash will create and save the SWF and HTML files to the same folder as the project file. Choose File > Publish Settings to explore your publish options in more detail.

To deploy the files you just created, you'll have to upload them to a web server. The required files are the compiled SWF, the FLV video and the HTML document that Flash has produced for you.

Depending on your version of Flash, you may also need to upload a JavaScript file by the name of AC_OETags.js which should be in the same location as the HTML document. This file is used by the HTML document to embed the SWF and to circumvent the Eolas patent issue discussed below.

At the time of this writing, Flash 8 does not produce this JavaScript file and I recommend you refer to the following section for more on the Eolas patent and a best-practices approach to embedding SWF content into HTML documents.

OK, you've created a player and deployed the necessary files, but a video player is not a video player without playback controls. For this purpose, I have prepared another file to demonstrate a simple pause and unpause control.

1. From within Flash, choose File > Open and select and open the file flv_via_actionscript_controls.fla.

2. Choose Control > Test Movie from the menu bar to compile and preview the movie.

   You will notice that I added a button that acts as a play and pause toggle switch once the video starts playing. This button is part of the UI component set that comes preinstalled with Flash. I added it to the Stage by simply dragging it from the components panel. I then selected it on stage and assigned it the instance name of playpause_btn in the Properties panel, which lets me then refer to it from ActionScript. There are also some simple additions to the code that you can see in the Actions panel. Let's have a look.

3. Click on frame 1 to select it and choose Window > Actions from the menu bar to show the Actions panel.

```
playpause_btn.onRelease = function()
    {
            ns.pause();
            if (this.label == "Play")
            {
                    this.label = "Pause";
            }
            else if (this.label == "Pause")
            {
                    this.label = "Play";
            }
    }
```

   `playpause_btn.onRelease` gets invoked when the user clicks on the Pause button.

`ns.pause();` acts as a toggle, pausing playback when playing a video or starting playback if already paused. The rest of the code simply changes the button's label from Pause to Play and vice versa.

I know this is a very basic example, but it hopefully shows how easily you can build your own simple video player in Flash. You can easily customize the controls and produce a totally custom-branded player in no time.

Reviewing all available controls goes well beyond the scope of this book and I would probably still be writing well into the New Year. Fortunately, there are many tutorials on the net covering this and similar subjects, and the Flash community is renowned for its helpful attitude and willingness to share knowledge.

Some destinations you should check out include:

goToAndLearn() *http://www.gotoandlearn.com*

Flash Developer Center *http://www.adobe.com/devnet/flash/video.HTML*

Community MX *http://www.communitymx.com*

Some people may also recommend my own site, *Flashcomguru.com*. The forum and mailing list attracts lots of skilled developers.

Deploying a SWF File

Unless you're new to web development, you've probably seen the traditional technique for embedding a SWF movie into an HTML page. Specifically, this consists of an OBJECT tag with an EMBED tag inside it, which acts as a fallback mechanism. This is the most popular Flash embed method and is the default choice when publishing your SWF from within Flash 8. In Flash CS3, Adobe modified the code for the Eolas workaround included in the Dreamweaver 8.02 update, which I detail later in this chapter.

But before I get too far ahead of myself, let's look at an example of the default Flash embed code:

```
<object classid="clsid:d27cdb6e-ae6d-11cf-96b8-444553540000"
codebase="http://fpdownload.macromedia.com/pub/shockwave/cabs/flash/swflash.
cab#version=7,0,0,0"
    width="550" height="400" id="Untitled-1" align="middle">
<param name="allowScriptAccess" value="sameDomain" />
<param name="movie" value="mymovie.swf" />
<param name="quality" value="high" />
<param name="bgcolor" value="#ffffff" />
<embed src="mymovie.swf" quality="high" bgcolor="#ffffff" width="550"
    height="400" name="mymovie" align="middle" allowScriptAccess="sameDomain"
    type="application/x-shockwave-flash" pluginspage="http://www.macromedia.com/go/
getflashplayer" />

</object>
```

Author's Tip

Why do we need both OBJECT and EMBED tags to embed Flash video into a web page? Briefly, the OBJECT tag targets Internet Explorer, which uses ActiveX controls to play Flash video. In contrast, most other browsers use the Netscape plug-in architecture controlled via an EMBED tag.

However, this is only a rule of thumb, as different browsers on different operating systems may use either tag. For example, Internet Explorer on the Macintosh swaps sides and reads the EMBED, rather than the OBJECT tag. Note that newer versions of Internet Explorer now also work without an OBJECT tag, but I recommend using both tags to ensure maximum compatibility with older browsers and possible future changes.

You don't really have to understand this rather nasty-looking piece of code, but you should be aware of what it achieves, which is embedding a SWF file into an HTML document.

In this example, the embedded SWF movie is called mymovie.swf; if you substituted the name of your SWF file for this, and adjusted other parameters like height and width in both the OBJECT and EMBED sections, you could use this code to embed the SWF file into your HTML document.

Of course, most web-design tools and HTML-authoring programs contain an "insert Flash" option that produces this code for you. As previously mentioned, Flash's publish feature even outputs an HTML document incorporating this code that is ready to upload to your web server. Having said all that, it certainly doesn't hurt to familiarize yourself with the rough syntax in case you need to tweak it here and there.

The Eolas Patent

If you produce or distribute interactive media inside a browser environment, you may be familiar with the Eolas patent and its effects on Internet Explorer. The patent, which was granted to Eolas in November 1998, relates to a "distributed hypermedia method for automatically invoking external application providing interaction and display of embedded objects within a hypermedia document."

Previous versions of Internet Explorer could automatically invoke an external application via ActiveX, which was found to violate the patent. To avoid licensing the patent, Microsoft changed Internet Explorer so that users must "activate" certain interactive content, including SWF files, before playing it. While this may sidestep the patent, it is not a very user-friendly way of presenting content on the web.

For example, suppose you embedded a Flash video into a web page as a design element, choosing autoPlay to play the video when the viewer opens that page. With an Eolas-adjusted version of Internet Explorer, when your viewer opens the page, the video won't play, and Internet Explorer will instead display a dotted outline around content.

If the viewer moves her mouse over the content, Internet Explorer will then display a tool tip advising the viewer to click the content to activate the control and play the video. Obviously, this isn't desirable for many Flash videos.

Fortunately, there is a JavaScript-based workaround that plays interactive content without user activation. Briefly, instead of calling the OBJECT and EMBED tags directly from the HTML page, you add a small JavaScript application that calls the commands instead. This sidesteps the Eolas issues and should also provide a future-proof way to avoid upcoming issues in browsers other than Internet Explorer.

Adobe has released its own Technote on this subject; you can find it at *http://www.adobe.com/devnet/activecontent*. Those new to this concept will also find the Beginner's Guide, located at *http://www.adobe.com/devnet/activecontent/articles/beginners_guide.html* very helpful.

Let's explore how to work around the Eolas issue.

Introducing SWFObject

To simplify this JavaScript workaround, Adobe released an update to web-authoring tool Dreamweaver. Though this works well, it's not the preferred technique to implement the Eolas fix, although it is of course a very usable one.

Instead, the most widely adapted solution appears to be Geoff Stearns's SWFObject, a small JavaScript file that you can freely access from *http://blog.deconcept.com/swfobject*. Let's discuss that approach now.

Using SWFObject

SWFObject (which was formerly known as FlashObject) is a small JavaScript file that simplifies embedding Flash video in a web page and includes Flash Player plug-in detection. It essentially substitutes the entire embed and object code from the page and writes it to the browser via JavaScript, once the HTML document loads. It is also very search-engine friendly, degrades gracefully and can be configured to include Adobe's Express Install feature, which allows you to upgrade the user's Flash Player to the latest version with minimum fuss.

Author's Tip

In terms of embedding a SWF into a web page, SWFObject uses essentially the same JavaScript method that Flash CS3 and Dreamweaver 8 (once updated to 8.0.2) deploy. In this sense, one solution is not preferred over another, nor is one superior from a functionality standpoint. However, SWFObject's code is arguably easier to read and understand and, bundled with the optional Express Install functions, it is also more versatile. On the flipside, SWFObject requires a more manual approach to coding, so if you are unfamiliar with HTML then I suggest you stick with the documents and code that Flash CS3 or Dreamweaver 8.0.2 produce.

The most efficient way to embed a SWF file into an HTML page using SWFObject looks like this (inserted anywhere in between the HTML document's body tags):

```
<script type="text/javascript" src="swfobject.js"></script>
<div id="flashcontent">
    The SWF file will automatically appear here when the HTML page loads. It gets
inserted by SWFObject's JavaScript code.
</div>
<script type="text/javascript">
    var so = new SWFObject("movie.swf", "mymovie", "200", "100", "7", "#FFFFFF");
    so.write("flashcontent");

</script>
```

Let's break this code down into functional sections and examine what they achieve.

The following line of code links the necessary JavaScript files to the HTML document:

```
<script type="text/javascript" src="swfobject.js"></script>
```

The next part creates a <div> that will hold the Flash content:

```
<div id="flashcontent">
    The SWF file will automatically appear here when the HTML page loads. It gets
inserted by SWFObject's JavaScript code.
</div>
```

A new SWFObject is created by this line,

```
var so = new SWFObject("movie.swf", "mymovie", "200", "100", "7", "#FFFFFF");
```

which specifies the SWF to be loaded (movie.swf), assigns it an identifier (mymovie), sets a size (200x100), the Flash Player version needed to view the content (7) and lastly the background color, in this case #FFFFFF, which is white.

Using SWFObject Including Express Install

SWFObject makes it very easy to add Adobe's Express Install functionality to your SWF. Briefly, Express Install is a process that detects a user's Flash Player and, if necessary, initiates an in-page upgrade process that securely installs the latest version of the Player.

After installation, Express Install directs the viewer back to the page that initiated the update, making the upgrade process seamless. It is also possible to send the user to another specified page after the upgrade process is complete.

If you include Express Install in your SWF, viewers with older players will have the chance to automatically upgrade and view your file. If you choose not to include Express Install, the viewer will rely on his browser or operating system to tell her that certain content on the page cannot be viewed, and then will have to manually upgrade to the new player. For this reason, I add Express Install to most SWF files and recommend that you do as well, unless you can be sure that your audience has the required Flash Player version installed.

To implement Express install, you must include the file expressinstall.as in your FLA before you compile it to SWF. Therefore, Express Install can't be added to SWF files if you don't have a copy of the FLA from which it was compiled.

In order to add this code to an existing Flash application, you need to follow these steps:

1. Open an existing FLA in Flash and move all existing content to a frame beyond frame 1.

2. Select frame 1 and bring up the Actions panel by pressing F9.

3. Add the following code to the frame by pasting it into the Actions panel:

```
#include "expressinstall.as"
// initialize the ExpressInstall object
var ExpressInstall = new ExpressInstall();
// if the user needs to upgrade, start the upgrade process
if (ExpressInstall.needsUpdate)
{
  ExpressInstall.init();
  // if expressinstall is invoked, stop the timeline.
  stop();
}
```

4. Place the file expressinstall.as in the same location as your FLA. The expressinstall.as file ships with SWFObject.

The URL for SWFObject again: *http://blog.deconcept.com/swfobject/*

Later in the book you will also learn how to use SWFObject to pass additional parameters to the SWF, for example to specify which FLV video should be played. Externalizing parameters is a powerful feature and I will cover several ways of doing this in Chapter 14.

Author's Tip

It is also possible to export a Flash movie complete with basic Player detection features right from within Flash (if the HTML publish setting is used). You can specify this option via the Publish Settings' HTML tab. Note that this method of Player detection does not utilize the Express Install feature but instead directs users to the traditional download and upgrade process at Adobe.com.

Conclusion

This chapter should leave you with a good understanding of how HTML, SWF and FLV files fit together to make up a Flash video application. You are able to decide which type of player may be better suited for the project at hand and you are also aware of the issues that the Eolas patent introduces, alongside a great way to circumvent them by using SWFObject.

In the next chapter you will learn a lot more about the FLV Playback component and in particular how it can be customized using a variety of methods.

CHAPTER 12

Customizing the FLV Playback Component

Introduction to Skinning and Customization

Adobe's FLV Playback component ships with Adobe Flash 8 Professional and Adobe Flash CS3 Professional, so it's no surprise that it's one of the most widely deployed Flash video components. Many developers and designers use this component daily, due to its versatility and the ability to customize look and feel as well as the code base. The process of changing the look and feel of an existing component is commonly referred to as skinning, and that's what you'll learn in this chapter.

ALERT

This chapter uses Adobe Flash CS3 Professional (alternatively you may use Adobe Flash Professional 8). To follow along with the examples, which I recommend, you will need a copy of the program to be installed on your computer. Should you not own a copy of the program, note that Adobe offers a free 30-day trial version on its website.

Also, note that you can find the files referred to and used in this chapter, including completed skins, at *www.flashvideobook.com*. Consider downloading these files now, so they'll be available once I start referring to them.

This chapter describes three alternatives for changing the look and feel of the FLV Playback component. These are:

1. Modifying existing FLV Playback skins provided as FLA files in Flash 8 and above. Skins are prebuilt controls that manage video playback. Changing the color scheme of these skins is quite simple, but more detailed changes can disrupt normal operation, as the skins are programmatically tied to the component.

2. Importing your own artwork such as play or stop buttons and replacing the controls provided by Adobe. This lets you fully control application look and feel, but requires some ActionScript knowledge to duplicate the capabilities provided by the FLV Playback component. One popular middle ground is to use fewer controls in return for a fully customized look.

3. Using the pre-installed Custom UI components (**Figure 12-1**) and modifying their look and feel, which gives you the best of both worlds in many respects. Briefly, Custom UI components are individual video controls that you can associate with an FLV Playback instance. While you can easily reskin Custom UI components (which you do on Stage like any other MovieClip), they still tap into the underlying code that is tied to them. This eliminates the need to recreate their functionalities (for example, a volume scrub bar) in ActionScript.

Figure 12-1
The FLV Playback component and Custom UI components shown in the components panel.

Author's Tip

Before modifying any existing classes, it's good practice to back them up so you can revert back to the standard configuration if necessary. Though the location of the ActionScript 2 classes for the FLV Playback component will vary by operating system and version, you should be able to find them in the First Run folder in the Classes\MX\video subfolder. If all else fails, search for FLVPlayback.as in Windows Explorer or Finder to locate them.

This chapter describes the process of basic skinning using each of the three methods, concentrating on changes that leave the underlying ActionScript code untouched. This approach is very popular as it yields good results in a short amount of time.

Modifying an Existing FLV Playback Skin

The release of the FLV Playback component has dramatically simplified the process of skinning Flash's video-playback components. The component first shipped with Adobe Flash Professional 8 and included not only the ActionScript 2 source code but also the FLA sources for all the skins available with the component. The ability to edit and recompile the skin source files makes it very simple to completely change the look and feel of the FLV Playback component.

But before you go wild and rip the skin to pieces, remember that each skin is programmatically tied to a component. I recommend only changing what's provided in the skin file rather than adding or deleting items. This minimizes the risk that you'll break any existing functionalities, but also restricts modifications to updating a color scheme and not much more.

In this walkthrough we will use an existing FLV Playback skin as a starting point to create a newly colored skin, using a red theme. To start, you'll need to locate the skins directory containing the FLA source of the skins that ship with Adobe Flash. You will then copy one of the skins and modify it.

Locating an Existing Skin

Locate the Flash installation directory on your hard drive. The skins are contained in a subfolder <language>\Configuration\SkinFLA for Flash 8 or <language>\Configuration\FLVPlayback Skins\FLA\ActionScript 2.0 or \ActionScript 3.0 (depending on which version of the component you are working on). For this example we will use the files from the ActionScript 2.0 folder, which is shown in **Figure 12-2**.

You can open and edit any of these skins directly in Flash, but remember to first save a copy under a new name to avoid overwriting an existing skin. Note that you'll have to export the finished SWF file containing the skin to the <language>\Configuration\Skins folder if you are using Flash 8 or <language>\Configuration\FLVPlayback Skins\ActionScript 2.0 if you are using Flash CS3 before compiling; otherwise, you won't see it in the FLV Playback component's skin drop-down menu.

Some users prefer to copy the FLA file directly into this directory so the SWF automatically exports to the correct location; unfortunately this also means that the FLA file appears in the FLV Playback component's skin drop-down, which is inconvenient and can be downright confusing. For this reason we will keep very organized and will be saving the FLA to the folder containing the FLA source files.

In this example you will modify the skin named SteelExternalPlaySeekMute.fla.

1. In Flash, choose File > Open from the menu bar to open the file SteelExternalPlaySeekMute.fla.

2. Choose File > Save As to save it under the name of RedExternalPlaySeekMute.fla into the same folder alongside the existing skin FLA files.

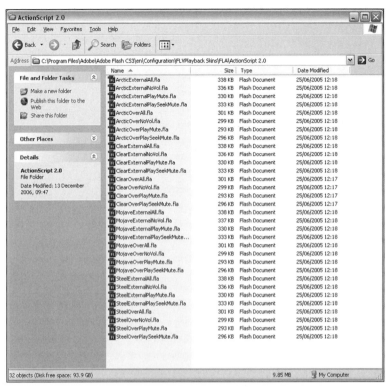

Figure 12-2
The directory containing the skin FLA files.

3. You should see FLA contents shown in **Figure 12-3**, which are the assets that comprise this FLV Playback skin.

You may have expected to find a more complete looking skin—this one looks like it's been hacked to pieces. Unfortunately (or should I say luckily) the skin FLA file is structured differently from a compiled skin, with all assets spread out across the Stage. This reflects the fact that during compilation, the individual assets are automatically aligned, spaced and scaled to size via ActionScript, allowing a skin to accommodate a variety of video sizes. But don't worry, the code that manages this process is already written, freeing you to concentrate on your design changes.

For your reference, note that a basic version of the player, a MovieClip with the instance name of layout_mc, is on the upper left of the Stage, while individual controls and interface elements are on the right and below the player. To check an instance name for a particular Symbol or MovieClip, simply click it to select it. You can then check its instance name in the Property Inspector.

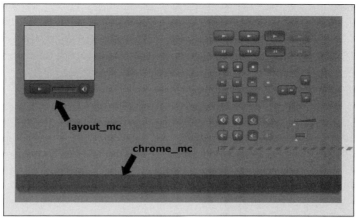

Figure 12-3
The newly saved RedExternalPlaySeekMute.fla skin file with assets on Stage.

Modifying a Skin FLA

The object of this lesson is to customize a player for a website featuring a red color scheme, which involves changing several assets on Stage to reflect this color. At first it may seem like a huge task to change all gray assets to red, but, as you'll see, since many assets are actually transparent, one change affects many assets. Here's how to customize this skin:

1. Double click the large gray panel at the bottom of the Stage. Its instance name is chrome_mc, as you can see if you open the Property Inspector (Window > Properties > Properties).

2. Next, in the Timeline, find the Color Plate layer and unlock it by clicking the little padlock icon (**Figure 12-4**).

Figure 12-4
You can click this arrow (or click Scene 1) to go back to the root of the FLA.

3. Once unlocked, click frame 1 of the Color Plate layer. This selects the gray shape on Stage. You can now change the color using the fill tool.

4. In the Tools panel, click the Fill tool (it looks like a little bucket with a color swatch to the right) and select a dark red color. I chose the HEX value of #990000.

5. That's it! Click Scene 1 or the little arrow shown in **Figure 12-4** to return to the FLA root. I recommend this in order to save the file in the same state as you have found it.

As you can see, most controls in the layout_mc MovieClip on the upper left of the Stage have changed from gray to red. Now, you will update the green highlights inside the button symbols as well as the progress/buffering bar.

Update the Button Controls

Fortunately, most Buttons in the skin are based on a common symbol. Change that symbol and Flash automatically updates the appearance of all Buttons, simplifying the skinning process. Here's how you go about this task:

1. If the Library panel is not open, Choose Window > Library from the menu bar to open it.

2. In the Library panel, double click the Skins folder to expand the contents.

3. Double click the _SquareButton folder to open it.

   The three MovieClips you should see are SquareBgDown (the Button's down state), SquareBgNormal (the Button's normal state) and SquareBgOver (the Button's over state), as shown in **Figure 12-5**. You will have to modify all three separately; let's start with the SquareBgDown symbol.

4. Double click the SquareBgDown icon inside the Library to open it in edit mode on Stage.

5. Select the Zoom tool (the magnifying lens-looking icon) from the Tools palette and zoom in on the symbol until you can see all the details. If you cannot see the Tools palette, choose Window > Tools from the menu bar to open it.

6. Using the Selection tool (which you can access from the Tools palette—it's the black arrow), click through the figure and note the three rings that comprise the signal. Then click and highlight the inner ring.

7. Choose Window > Color Mixer from the menu bar to open the Color Mixer panel. Alternatively, you can use the fill tool from the Tools panel.

8. With the inner ring selected, click the Fill tool in the Color Mixer (the paint bucket with a color swatch next to it). Type #990000 (or any desired color) as the hexadecimal value, and then press Enter to set the color. Then open the Color Mixer again and set the transparency value by typing in 35% or adjusting the slider.

Figure 12-5
The Library panel showing the contents of the _SquareButton folder.

9. Repeat step 8 for each of the other rings (the middle and outer ring) but use the following color values:

    • For the middle ring, choose a more vivid red such as #D50000 and choose a 100% alpha transparency (solid fill).

    • For the outer ring, choose the same color as in step 8 (I used #990000) and 35% for alpha transparency. The result should look similar to **Figure 12-6**.

10. Click Scene 1 or the little blue back arrow in the Timeline header to exit Editing mode. Back on Stage, you will notice that four buttons in the skin have changed their appearance, even though you edited only one symbol.

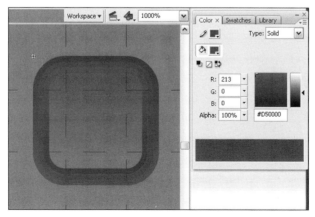

Figure 12-6
The fully edited SquareBgDown symbol.

Repeat steps 4 to 8 for the remaining Button symbols, SquareBGNormal and SquareBGOver, unlocking any layers if necessary (locked layers are recognizable by a small lock).

It's impossible to cover all the customization options available to you, and for brevity's sake I won't go over them in detail here. A few points to note, however, are:

- Some Button symbols remain unaffected from the changes you just made. This is due to the fact that they have a slightly different shape and are therefore not based on the common symbol that you just edited. If desired, you can edit the remaining buttons in the folder "Forward and Back Buttons" in the Library.

- You haven't made any changes to the Buffer or Progress bar, yet these controls should appear red due to the color changes you made to the underlying chrome_mc MovieClip.

11. After completing your modifications, export your finished skin to the <language>\Configuration\ FLVPlayback Skins\ActionScript 2.0 directory (if you are using Flash CS3) or the <language>\Configuration\Skins folder (if you are using Flash 8) inside the installation directory so it will show up in the FLV Playback component's properties panel as an available skin. To export the SWF:

- Choose File > Export > Export Movie, navigate to the target folder, and click Save.

- Accept all defaults in the Export Flash Player dialog, and click OK.

- Choose File > Save to save the edited FLA file in case you need to make any further changes at another time.

You can see the completed red skin in **Figure 12-7**, shown alongside the standard gray design. You can access newly created skins by dragging an instance of the FLV Playback component onto the Stage and selecting a skin from the Parameters tab. Skins are also available during the Import Video wizard, which will be covered later in the book.

Figure 12-7
The original gray skin and completed red colored skin. Small difference in this grayscale image, huge difference in your web page.

Where to Go from Here

Among the files you downloaded for this chapter is NewSteelExternalPlaySeekMute.swf, which incorporates the changes discussed above. Take a look to preview the appearance of a finished file, but note that certain controls are missing from this skin as it is based on a different FLA.

Don't hesitate to experiment; after all, you're working on a copy of a skin so if things don't go according to plan, simply save another copy and start again—there's no right or wrong way when it comes to being creative.

Adding Custom Designs to the FLV Playback Component

Sometimes you have to create a completely custom user interface for the FLV Playback component, especially when the job requirements go beyond simple video playback and call for an elaborate and branded experience. In these cases, you can use your own controls with the FLV Playback component. This approach offers complete creative freedom; you can literally implement whichever look you or your design department sees fit. The downside is that, for some more complex controls, you would have to recreate most provided function-alities—which is nothing short of reinventing the wheel.

Still, you should be aware of this option, so I'll demonstrate with a very simple example in which you will add a custom-designed play and pause button to your video player applica-tion. Note, however, that there is a third option available to you described in the next section. I recommend you read the entire chapter before deciding which approach is best suited for your particular project.

Should you have any problems following along with the steps outlined below, note that the completed application is also available with the sample files for Chapter 12. The file name for the completed application is flvplayback_customcontrols_complete.fla.

1. To get started, choose File > Open from the menu bar and open the file flvplay-back_customcontrols.fla, which is included in downloadable files available for this chapter, in Flash.

   You will see an FLV Playback component on Stage that is set up to play a video. If you check the component's skin property in the Parameters tab (Window > Properties > Parameters, or click the Parameters tab in the Properties window) you'll see that it is set to None. It is therefore configured not to use a skin. Note that the component's instance name is myplayer.

2. You will now add a play button to the component. To do this, create a new symbol by choosing Insert > New Symbol from the menu bar. The Create New Symbol dialogue opens.

3. Give the new symbol a name of play_pb, select Button as the Type by clicking the associated radio button, and then click the OK button to close the dialogue.

Author's Tip

Developing more complex controls such as a scrub bar or a load progress indicator is not a trivial task. In fact, it isn't something you can undertake if you are completely new to ActionScript. It's therefore important to have a clear idea of the methods of customization that are available to you and choose one that offers the best compromise between your own abilities and the functionalities requested by your client.

In my experience, most clients simply care about a working application—how you get there is up to you. A client will usually not pay any bonuses if the code you have written has been tailor-made for her project.

The FLV Playback component is the typical example of a real time saver when it comes to rolling out Flash video applications. Rather than developing each control from scratch, you can either reskin it to tweak the color scheme a little bit or even modify the look and feel in more detail using Custom UI components. Only if this option still doesn't offer the desired level of control would I recommend you try adding your own controls to the component. And in that case, I would also argue that you can safely do away with the FLV Playback component altogether, as writing a custom video player is probably much easier at this stage than fitting everything around the FLV Playback component.

As usual, choosing a course is up to the programmer. Your design department will love you if the player looks exactly as they intended and the client will be happy with a fully functioning (and good-looking) application. So simplify your life by leveraging any components that meet your requirements. This will allow you to deliver on schedule and move on to the next exciting project.

4.   You now find yourself in symbol Editing mode. Click the Rectangle Tool from the Tools palette, draw a rectangle on Stage and give it an outline and fill color of your choice.

5.   Click the text tool and add a Play label to the rectangle you created in step 4. Your button should now look similar to **Figure 12-8**.

Figure 12-8
The Play_pb symbol; pretty sexy, eh?

6.   Repeat steps 2 to 5 to create another symbol pause_pb with the text label Pause.

7.   Click Scene 1 or the little blue back arrow in the Timeline header to exit Editing mode.

8. Drag an instance of the play_pb and pause_pb symbols out of the Library and onto the Stage. Using the Properties panel, give each button an instance name of play_pb and pause_pb, respectively.

9. You're almost done. You now need to assign the two button symbols as controls to the FLV Playback component. You do this by highlighting frame 1 of the actions layer and pressing F9 on your keyboard to bring up the Actions panel.

10. Enter the following code into the Actions panel:

```
myplayer.playButton = play_pb;
myplayer.pauseButton = pause_pb;
```

This piece of code assigns the play_pb as the control to use for playing the video and pause_pb as the control for pausing the video. The syntax for this command is simple; myplayer identifies the FLV Playback Component instance, playButton and pauseButton the property to be set, and play_pb and pause_pb as the controls assigned for each property. You'll notice that playButton and pauseButton turn blue in the Actions panel; this means that Flash recognizes the term as one of the FLV Playback component's properties and therefore applies syntax highlighting to it.

11. To test the application, choose Control > Test Movie from the menu bar. The application compiles and starts playing.

Since the component is set to autoplay, it starts playing upon opening. You can use the pause button to pause playback and the play button to restart it. **Figure 12-9** shows the completed player with custom controls.

Figure 12-9
The completed application with custom play and pause controls.

While these are very basic controls, you can see how easy it was to make them work in conjunction with FLV Playback. Most importantly, the only code you wrote were the two lines that assign the newly created symbols to the actual player. It could hardly be easier.

The component supports many more assignments that you can use in this way, including backButton, forwardButton, stopButton and others. Why not try adding some rollover effects or a rewind button next?

Author's Tip

What Are Custom UI Components?

The FLV Playback Custom UI buttons are designed to be used in conjunction with the actual FLV Playback component, but without using one of its provided skins. The Custom UI components are easily modified in Flash, right inside the FLA file (this is not possible with the main FLV Playback component as it is a compiled clip). Once dragged on Stage, you can edit them via the Library (all assets are automatically added there once you drag one of the symbols out of the Components panel) or by double clicking the component (just like any other MovieClip).

When changing the symbols within a Custom UI component, note that you must design the new controls at the correct size from the start, since resizing Custom UI components may compromise their functionality. It is therefore best to make any design changes "in situ," ideally next to the FLV Playback component that has been scaled to the size of the video that is to be played back.

Using the FLV Playback Custom UI Controls

In my final example, I will describe the Custom UI controls included with the FLV Playback component in Adobe Flash 8 and Adobe Flash CS3. These controls are in a way very similar to the last approach in which you created your own buttons to use as controls for video playback. The major difference is that Custom UI controls provide more complex functionality under the hood that you don't need to recreate when you update the look and feel of these components.

Adding a SeekBar Component

Now let's add a SeekBar to the application you just completed. This will illustrate how quickly and easily Custom components let you add uniquely designed controls to your Flash video application.

1. Choose File > Open from the menu bar to reopen the file flvplayback_customcontrols.fla. Remember that this is one of the files you can download from *www.flashvideobook.com*.

2. Choose File > Save As to save it under the new name of flvplayback_customUI.fla. Alternatively, you can open the file flvplayback_customcontrols_complete.fla included with the downloadable files and save this under the name of flvplayback_customUI.fla.

You will now add a SeekBar to this application. This SeekBar will behave exactly like the one built into one of the original FLV Playback skins, except you can directly edit and modify this Custom UI scrub bar on Stage. There is no need to edit an external skin file as was the case in the previous section; instead Custom UI components can be modified directly on Stage within the application you are building.

3.   Choose Window > Components from the menu bar to open the Components panel.

4.   If you are using Flash 8, click the FLV Playback Custom UI node to expand it. In Flash CS3 the Custom UI components can be found alongside the FLV Playback component under the Video category.

5.   Drag an instance of the SeekBar component on Stage and place it underneath the FLV Playback component that is already there. Your application should now look somewhat similar to **Figure 12-10**.

   Notice that a new folder by the name of FLV Playback Skins has been added to the Library (choose Window > Library if necessary to open this panel). This indicates that there are editable assets inside.

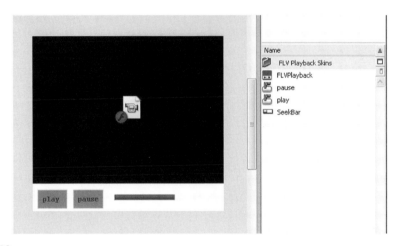

Figure 12-10
A SeekBar component has been added.

6.   Click the new SeekBar component, and in the Properties panel, type seek_bar into the instance name box. You can now access the component via ActionScript.

7.   Click Frame 1 of the actions layer and choose Window > Actions to open the Actions panel.

8.   Add the following code underneath the existing lines of code:

```
myplayer.seekBar = seek_bar;
```

   This assigns the Custom UI component seek_bar as a control for the player component on Stage.

9.   Choose Control > Test Movie from the menu bar to test the application.

The application compiles and starts playing and you will notice that the SeekBar updates as the video plays, and that you can scrub forward and back by using the little triangular handle.

So far, so good, but the look and feel of the new SeekBar is still that of the standard Custom UI component, which doesn't match our other custom button controls. Let's change that . . .

Updating the Look and Feel of the SeekBar

As mentioned earlier, the Custom UI components can be edited directly on Stage (or in fact via the Library) once they have been added to the application. You will now do just that:

1. First, let's resize the SeekBar so that it fills the available space nicely. Click the SeekBar and choose Modify > Transform > Scale from the menu bar. You can then use the resize handles to update the component's dimensions. **Figure 12-11** shows my updated interface.

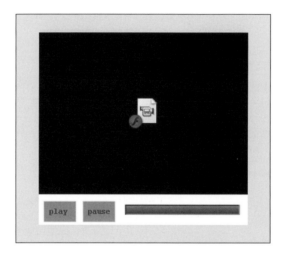

Figure 12-11
The resized SeekBar.

2. Double click the SeekBar to enter Symbol Editing mode. Double click again on the MovieClip called progress_mc on the progress layer to access its assets. You can now update the look and feel of this asset.

3. Choose Window > Color Mixer from the menu bar to open that panel. The Seek-Bar has a gradient color that you can adjust by clicking the tiny swatches below the gradient bar and choosing a color in the Mixer. I chose a yellow as the first color of the gradient and an almost white color for the second. You can see the result in **Figure 12-12**.

4. Double click any empty area on Stage to return to the SeekBar editing screen.

5. Click frame 2 of the assets layer to access the little scrubber triangle. Double click the little triangle to enter its Editing mode.

6. Layer 1 contains the actual triangle while the layer underneath acts as the hit area for the control that responds to mouse clicks. Let's assume that the triangle is too small to be usable on its own, and replace it with a larger symbol.

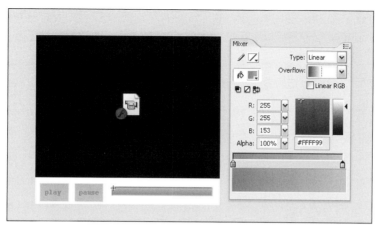

Figure 12-12
You've changed the SeekBar color.

7.   Delete the little black triangle and use one of the drawing tools to draw another shape in its place. I chose a circle. Change the colors as desired.

You can see the results of my efforts in **Figure 12-13**. When compiled, the application will use this circle symbol as the scrub control.

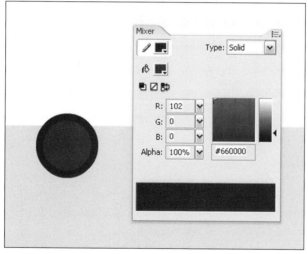

Figure 12-13
I'm using a circular control as the SeekBar handle, replacing the little triangle.

8.   After completing your new scrubber, double click anywhere on the Stage a few times to return to the main Timeline. Alternatively, click Scene 1 or the little blue back arrow in the Timeline header to exit Editing mode.

9. To test the application choose Control > Test Movie from the menu bar. The application compiles and starts playing. You can see the completed application in **Figure 12-14**.

Figure 12-14
The completed SeekBar component.

You will see a visually updated SeekBar with a yellow background color. The scrub control itself now looks like a little circle and the whole design ties in better with the look and feel of the play and pause buttons.

You could easily take this example further by changing the SeekBar's outline (or even remove the outline altogether), or by adding other Custom UI Controls such as a VolumeBar and modifying its look and feel to suit.

Conclusion

You've come a long way in this chapter and have now learned the basics of modifying and reskinning the FLV Playback component. Hopefully this knowledge will come in handy when you are next tasked with designing and building a branded Flash video application.

In the next chapter you will learn all about cue points, including how they can aid navigation inside a video and ways of synchronizing external assets during video playback.

CHAPTER 13

Using Cue Points

Cue points are events that fire during the playback of Flash video, which act as programmatic triggers to which you can tie other events and actions. Cue points therefore make it very easy to add richer functionality to your Flash video applications that goes far beyond standard audio and video playback.

Common uses for cue points include, but are not limited to:

- Display of chapter titles
- Navigation within a video
- Synchronization of external assets such as graphics or slides
- The display of closed captions (also referred to as subtitles)
- Invocation of external URLs
- Loading of other video, audio, image or text content.

This chapter will describe how to use cue points and the various cue point types. You will use that knowledge to construct a simple application that processes cue points that you have added to an FLV file.

In this chapter you will learn about:

- Cue points and how to deploy them
- The difference between the three types of cue points, and knowing when to use them
- How to insert and invoke cue points in your Flash video application
- How to use the FLV Playback component to process cue points in your FLV Video files.

ALERT

!

This chapter uses Adobe Flash CS3 Professional (alternatively you may use Adobe Flash Professional 8). To follow along with the examples, which I recommend, you will need a copy of the program installed on your computer. Should you not own a copy of the program, note that Adobe offers a free 30-day trial version on its website.

Also, you can find the files referred to and used in this chapter at *www.flashvideobook.com*. Consider downloading these files now, so they'll be available once I start referring to them.

Introduction to Cue Points

You can use cue points to trigger pretty much any event or action that you could otherwise invoke manually or through ActionScript code. This functionality makes it possible to let the video tie in closely with other elements within your Flash application, or even on the web page.

Figure 13-1 shows a very simple example in which I have added several navigation cue points to the FLV video. When this screenshot was taken, a cue point that had been triggered contained a name property of Title that I displayed above the video component. As the video plays, more cue points are encountered and the chapter title changes again and again, and is always relevant to the video then being viewed. You will learn how to add and invoke cue points later in this chapter.

Figure 13-1
The cue point with the name property "Nollie Railslide" is triggered and displayed above the video.

There are three types of cue points, each suited for a particular use. Once you know how cue points differ from one another, you will be able to pick the right type for your requirements. The three types of cue points are:

- Navigation cue points
- Event cue points
- ActionScript cue points.

Most Flash video encoding tools can now add cue points during encoding. For example, the latest versions of both Sorenson Squeeze (4.5) and Flix Pro (8.5) let you add at least navigation cue points to your files.

Inside the Industry

 Cue-point naming conventions are not consistent between different encoding tools and you will see cue points referred to as chapters, markers or chapter markers. It's also not always clear which type of cue point you are adding when using a third-party encoder; in my opinion, the Adobe Flash Video Encoder is the best tool in this respect, as it sticks well to the naming conventions.

My feeling is that Sorenson Squeeze only supports navigation cue points, whereas Flix Pro supports both navigation and event cue points, though this isn't clearly spelled out. This isn't a huge issue as the differences between these types of cue points are not always significant.

Technically, the biggest difference between navigation and event cue points is that a navigation cue point gets added to the FLV as a key frame so viewers can directly seek to it. In contrast, an event cue point is simply a bunch of data positioned at a certain time in the video and does not get added as a key frame.

ActionScript cue points cannot be added during the encoding process but can only be added once the video has been imported in Flash. You can attribute this to the fact that the Flash application has to manage and track ActionScript cue points, so it's a feature that is closely tied to the Flash authoring tool.

Some FLV Playback component skins can automatically sense the presence of navigation cue points and allow the user to skip forward and back through a video from cue point to cue point. The skin titled SteelAllExternalAll.swf is such a skin (**Figure 13-2**), and it includes forward and back buttons that navigate from chapter to chapter. Look for skins with the word "All" in the name, as these skins contain the necessary buttons for navigation cue point support, amongst other controls.

Besttrick Rail

ALEX GORGES

Figure 13-2
SteelExternalAll.swf is one of the skins that includes controls to skip between navigation cue points.

Cue Point Types

You already know that the FLV format supports three types of cue points. Let's have a look at each type in more detail and find out about the differences and similarities.

Navigation Cue Points

Navigation cue points are (unsurprisingly) designed to be used to navigate within a single video file. Each navigation cue point specifies a point in time to which viewers can directly navigate, which makes navigation cue points ideal for breaking a long video into several chapters.

Navigation cue points are also commonly used in talking-head video presentations that are accompanied by a slide show. In such a case, navigation cue points allow users to skip forward and backwards to the slides that most interest them, which is much more convenient than seeking randomly within the video. ActionScript code that triggers a certain slide at a certain time (usually when the navigation cue point is encountered) needs to be added to the application to facilitate this. Or, you could add navigation cue points to the start of each song in a concert video, allowing viewers to seek to their favorite songs.

Note that both navigation cue points and event cue points (which are covered next) are added to the video during encoding and cannot be edited or removed after encoding.

Event Cue Points

Event cue points are similar to navigation cue points except that you cannot easily seek to them. For this reason, as a rule of thumb, if your goal is to create a cue point viewers can seek to, use a navigation cue point. Otherwise, use an event cue point. For example, event cue points are popular for triggering specific actions at certain times within the video, such as to show closed captions, load external assets, show or hide images, and so on.

As mentioned previously, event cue points are part of the FLV file and cannot be removed or edited after encoding. If you need to add additional cue points or remove any, you'll need to re-encode the source footage (or use ActionScript cue points, which are covered next).

ActionScript Cue Points

ActionScript cue points are unique in that they do not form part of the FLV video file. Instead, ActionScript cue points are part of the SWF application and are tracked separately by the Flash Player as the video plays.

ActionScript cue points offer similar functionalities as the other cue points but are more flexible because they can be added, edited and deleted after encoding. This is why ActionScript is the default cue-point type when adding cue points to an already encoded FLV file. Moreover, ActionScript cue points can only be added *after* encoding, which is why no encoding tools can insert ActionScript cue points.

ActionScript cue points offer less temporal precision during playback than navigation or event cue points and may be up to a tenth of a second out of sync to the specified time. This doesn't matter in most scenarios, but you should nevertheless be aware of it.

Author's Tip

As you may know, you can't seek to a segment of a progressively downloaded FLV video that has not yet been downloaded. This directly affects the usability of navigation cue points, as your viewers may not be able to access all parts of the video right away. Instead, they have to wait for the entire video to download before they can access all navigation cue points.

To circumvent this, you could deliver your FLV video in streaming format via the Flash Media Server, since you can seek to any point in a streaming video file even if it hasn't been viewed previously.

Or, you could use navigation cue points in a progressively downloading FLV video by including some ActionScript code in your application to enable the cue points sequentially as the video downloads. To illustrate this, imagine a video player that includes five thumbnail images off to the side of the interface. Clicking on one of the thumbnails would normally take the viewer to a navigation cue point. However, unless that part of the video has already been downloaded, the button action would simply fail.

Some simple ActionScript logic could use the FLV's metadata to enable each thumbnail as the video downloads. As you probably know, metadata contains, amongst other data, all cue-point information and is available as soon as an FLV file starts downloading. Your code could compare the cue-point time codes with the status of the downloading FLV video and enable each thumbnail as the video is cached, resulting in a very robust and usable user interface. You could even gray out disabled buttons to signal the viewer that they are not yet clickable. Adding this logic is, of course, not a requirement but it is recommended if you want to build a fail-proof application. Note once again that you only need to worry about this issue when you are deploying your FLV files via progressive download.

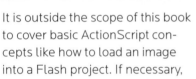

Author's Tip

Remember: only the Flash IDE itself allows you to work with ActionScript cue points. Video-encoding tools only support navigation and event cue points.

Author's Tip

It is outside the scope of this book to cover basic ActionScript concepts like how to load an image into a Flash project. If necessary, please refer to the Flash Help files for more details on topics such as loading external assets at runtime.

Adding and Processing Cue Points

The best way to learn about cue points is to use them, so let's do it. For this exercise, you'll need Flash Professional 8 or Flash CS3 and the downloaded files for Chapter 13 from www.flashvideobook.com.

To start, run Flash and open the file flvplayback_adding_cuepoints.fla. The file contains a text field on Stage with the instance name of caption—this is where the chapter titles as specified by the navigation cue points will appear during playback.

Encoding with Cue Points

In this example, you will add cue points to and encode the file wkhall.wmv (if you are a Windows user) or wkhall.mov (if you are using a Mac, as WMV files are not usually supported on a Mac) to FLV format. You can find both files amongst the downloaded files for Chapter 13. More specifically, you will add navigation cue points to jump forward and back within the video and use event cue points as well as ActionScript cue points to load external assets during playback.

I've already added the code to handle this logic to frame 1 of the actions layer. Feel free to check it out by selecting frame 1 and choosing Window > Actions from the menu bar.

All that's missing now is an FLV video file with added cue points. Let's supply that now:

1. From within Flash, choose File > Import > Import Video from the File menu. The Import Video Wizard opens.

2. Click the On your computer radio button, which is the topmost radio button.

3. Click Browse, and navigate to the file wkhall.wmv if you are on Windows or choose wkhall.mov if you are using a Mac. Both files should be located in the same folder as the FLA file you just opened. Click Open to load the file, and then Next to continue with the wizard.

4. Click the Progressive download from a web server radio button, then Next. The Encoding dialogue opens.

5. Leave the default Encoding Profile selected and click the Cue Points tab (see **Figure 13-3**). If you're running Flash 8, click the Show Advanced Settings, then the Cue Points tab. The interface is slightly different from that shown from Flash CS3, but it works identically.

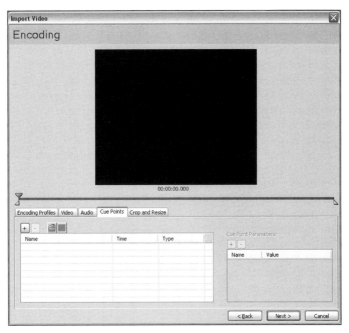

Figure 13-3
The video encoding wizard with selected Cue Points tab.

6. Let's insert an event cue point to load and display an image named 7k_logo. jpg when the video starts to play. Click and drag the seek bar beneath the video preview (the blue line) to about 1 second into the video. Don't worry if the time is not totally exact.

7. In the Cue Points tab, click the + sign to add a new cue point. Flash adds a new cue point to the list.

8. Change the name of this cue point to "imageloader" and leave the Type set to the default value of Event.

9. In the Cue Point Parameters list on the right, click the + sign to add a parameter (the URL of the image to be loaded) to the cue point. Be sure that you select the imageloader cue point when you add the parameter.

10. Type "myurl" in the Name field and "7k_logo.jpg" in the Value field, as shown in **Figure 13-4**.

11. Click and drag the video scrub bar to roughly 9 seconds into the video.

12. Click the + sign to add a new cue point, but this time choose Navigation as a type and type "Session start" as the name.

13. Scrub to different points in the video and repeat step 12, adding two or three additional navigation cue points. Refer to **Figure 13-5** to see my results. Click Next to continue.

Figure 13-4
The imageloader cue point has been added and additional parameters have been assigned to it.

Figure 13-5
Several cue points have been added ready for encoding.

14. Choose the skin titled SteelExternalAll.swf from the Skin drop-down menu. As you recall, the inclusion of "all" in the title means that this skin automatically handles navigation cue points. Click Next to continue.

15. Review the advice on the next screen and then click Finish to start the encoding process.

    After encoding, you will see that an instance of the FLV Playback component has automatically been added to the Stage. Please click this component and type "player" for the Component name in the Parameters tab of the Properties panel (**Figure 13-6**).

    A closer look at the Cue Points line in the Parameters tab also reveals that all the cue points you just added are listed there (also shown in **Figure 13-6**).

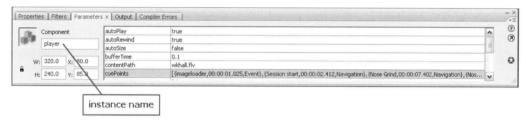

Figure 13-6
Cue points are displayed in the Properties panel of the FLV Playback component.

    Let's test the application to check what happens up to this point.

16. Choose Control > Test Movie from the file menu to compile and run the SWF file.

    You should notice some trace statements in the Output panel describing the name, time and type of cue point that the FLV Playback component encounters. The code that generates these traces has already been added to frame 1 of the actions layer.

    As the video plays, the ActionScript code loads the jpg that you specified in the first event cue point and places it on Stage. Subsequent navigation cue points are used to display chapter titles. You can also use these cue points to skip forward and back through the video. Give it a try by clicking the respective buttons on the component. **Figure 13-7** shows the player in action.

> **Author's Tip**
>
> To build more advanced cue point functionalities, check out the Flash Help files. There are several methods which you can leverage in your applications, including the find-NearestCuePoint() method, which allows you to detect the cue point nearest to the current playback time, for example after a user has seeked to a new point within the video.

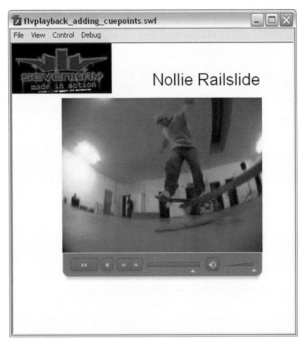

Figure 13-7
The player showing the image loaded into the top left corner and the cue-point name displayed on the right.

Should you have problems recreating this example, note that I have provided a completed file amongst the sample files. The name of the file is flvplayback_adding_cuepoints_complete.fla.

As a last step, you will add one final cue point, this time an ActionScript cue point.

Adding an ActionScript Cue Point

The final cue point will remove the logo that the first cue point added to the application.

Why are we using an ActionScript cue point here? It's mainly for demonstration purposes—we could have used an event cue point but in that case we wouldn't be able to add it after encoding, or edit or remove it later.

1. Click the FLV Playback component on Stage to select it.

2. Click the Parameters tab on the Properties panel.

3. Double click the line titled cuePoints. The Flash Video Cue Points dialogue opens.

4. Click the + sign to add a new cue point and change the name of this cue point to "unload."

    Note that "unload" is just a meaningful term that I chose here for the name property of this particular cue point. The actual unloading of the image is triggered by a piece of code that simply reacts to a cue point type of ActionScript—once this is encountered, the image is unloaded and removed from the application.

You can find this code in lines 39 to 42 on frame 1 of the actions layer. Here's what it looks like:

```
else if (evt.info.type == "actionscript")
{
    // unloads the jpg
    unloadMovieNum(5);
}
```

5. Update the Time property of this cue point to be just a fraction later than the last cue point currently in your list. In my case I added a time of 00:00:14.000.

6. Make sure the cue-point type is set to Action-Script. Click OK when you are finished.

You have successfully added an ActionScript cue point.

You can see my finished example in **Figure 13-8**. The player now contains a series of cue points of different types.

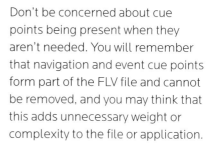

Author's Tip

Don't be concerned about cue points being present when they aren't needed. You will remember that navigation and event cue points form part of the FLV file and cannot be removed, and you may think that this adds unnecessary weight or complexity to the file or application.

You can easily ignore unused cue points by not deploying any code to react to them, or even by disabling them within Flash via the Parameters tab of the Properties panel.

In addition, unused cue points in your FLV file do not affect the performance of your application or video. Even a few additional key frames from navigation cue points won't significantly add to file size or detract from video quality.

Let's test the application again to see what happens when the new ActionScript cue point is encountered.

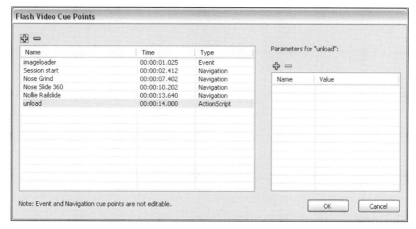

Figure 13-8
Three types of cue points have now been added.

7. Choose Control > Test Movie from the menu bar to compile and view the application. You should notice that the logo is being removed programmatically towards the end of the video when the ActionScript cue point is encountered.

Feel free to modify the time property for this event to see how it affects the application.

Processing Cue Points

Cue points have no value without mechanisms to react to them during playback. Fortunately, Flash makes it very easy to process cue points, especially if you use the FLV Playback component in your application. This component will automatically display the added cue points in its Property panel, making it easy to see the names and times of cue points present in the FLV.

In addition, the component offers several mechanisms for processing and reacting to cuePoint events. Whenever a cue point is encountered, the FLV Playback component will dispatch a cuePoint event that you can listen to from within your code. Here's a piece of code that you can use to capture cuePoint events dispatched from the FLV Playback component:

```
var listener:Object = new Object();

listener.cuePoint = function( evt:Object ):Void
{
        trace(evt.info.name);

        trace(evt.info.time);

        trace(evt.info.type);
}

player.addEventListener("cuePoint", listener);
```

Let's walk through this code step by step:

1. The first line creates a simple object that acts as our Listener. The FLV Playback component dispatches a cuePoint event that the application can react to.

2. The listener.cuePoint function on line 2 captures the event and processes it. In this example I simply trace the properties of the event object. The Flash ActionScript documentation tells me that the event object (here referred to as evt) contains an info property that in turn contains properties describing the cue point itself. These properties are name, time and type but can also contain additional parameters.

3. The last line simply adds the listener object as a Listener to the player on Stage and specifies the cuePoint event to be the event to listen to. Now whenever a cue point is encountered, the listener.cuePoint function will automatically be invoked.

In this fashion, the FLV Playback component informs its environment that a cue point has occurred, and sends along relevant parameters, so your application can react accordingly. It's what programmers call an event-driven architecture—a flexible and powerful way of creating object-oriented applications.

I have included an FLA sample file that already contains the code described above. You can find this file amongst the sample files for Chapter 13 under the name of flvplayback_navigation_complete.fla.

If you are not familiar with basic programming concepts, then the sample code provided in this chapter may be a bit hard to grasp. What you should take away from this example is the knowledge that there are mechanisms you can use to react to certain events during video playback.

Conclusion

Cue points are an immensely useful mechanism that allow you to tie video and external content together in ways that would otherwise be nearly impossible to achieve. In this chapter you have learned the different types of cue points supported by Flash video, along with their individual use cases as well as implementation.

For more details I recommend you have a browse through the Flash Help files, and in particular the Flash Video topics. In the next chapter you will learn how FLV and SWF files tie in with their surrounding web environment and how you can use this to your advantage.

CHAPTER 14

Controlling Your Content

Introduction

To the casual observer of web-based Flash video, it may appear that SWF files live their own little lives within an HTML document, and seldom seem to tie in closely with the surrounding elements on the page. Yet if these same observers dug a bit deeper, by viewing the HTML source in their browser for example, they would notice that Flash needs to interact and play well with either the application server that generated the page, or the HTML code itself.

Take YouTube as a prime example. Could you imagine how much manpower it would take to build their Flash video player like the ones we created in Chapter 11, where we manually imported each video into Flash, encoded and then exported the player as a SWF file along-side the FLV video? Given YouTube's volume, this just wouldn't be workable; instead they needed to create some sort of automated system.

While I have no idea what YouTube's encoding solution looks like (trust me when I say that they do not encode videos by hand) I can tell you that the Flash video player they are using is configurable on the fly, based on parameters passed to it by the enclosing page. Think about this for a minute and it will make perfect sense—a single SWF file that can accept an external parameter (such as the name of the FLV file it should play) enables a much more versatile and dynamic set-up.

Rather than hard coding the FLV filename into the FLA and exporting a player (SWF file) that can play only one video, it is much more efficient to store playback information like the filename and other playback options externally. This could mean a database, an XML file or simply a hand-coded HTML page.

In any case, the SWF will become much more versatile once it can accept such parameters. As you'll read in this chapter, the best thing is that such functionality is easily added to any Flash application. In fact, there are several mechanisms to choose from, and in this chapter you will learn about:

- How to pass parameters to a Flash application using the FlashVars method

- Utilizing the LoadVars Object for configuration

- How XML can be used to feed data to Flash

- Detecting the end of a video, as well as subsequent looping

- How to play videos back to back.

Let's get started.

ALERT This chapter uses Adobe Flash CS3 Professional (alternatively you may use Adobe Flash Professional 8). To follow along with the examples, which I recommend, you will need a copy of the program installed on your computer. Should you not own a copy, note that Adobe offers a free 30-day trial version on its website.

Also, note that you can find the files referred to and used in this chapter at *www.flashvideobook.com*. Consider downloading these files now, so they'll be available once I start referring to them.

Using FlashVars for Configuration

The FlashVars method allows you to pass variables to a SWF file using the Object and Embed tags in the HTML document. Any variables that you pass to the SWF are available on _level0 of your Flash application before the first frame gets executed. As you may be aware, the first document that opens in Flash Player is called _level0. Levels are a way of specifying absolute paths to assets within the Flash application and they start at an index of 0.

FlashVars is arguably the most commonly used method for passing external parameters to a SWF file. FlashVars is compatible with Flash Player 6 and above, which basically makes them universally usable.

The syntax for passing a variable filename with a value of myvideo.flv looks like this:

Object tag:

```
<PARAM NAME=FlashVars value="filename=myvideo.flv">
```

Embed tag:

```
<EMBED SRC="myswf.swf" FlashVars="filename=myvideo.flv">
```

Any additional variables must be separated by the "&" sign. For example, to pass another variable called headline with a value of "My Video" into the SWF and make this available on _level0 of your application for further processing in ActionScript, the syntax would look like this:

Object tag:

```
<PARAM NAME=FlashVars value="filename=myvideo.flv&headline=My Video">
```

Embed tag:

```
<EMBED SRC="myswf.swf" FlashVars="filename=myvideo.flv&headline=My Video">
```

In addition, note that certain characters must be URL encoded before being passed to Flash, which replaces the alphanumeric character with the hexadecimal combination for that character. Such characters include #^%&@)!@)$(% and many others. Adobe has provided a technote on this subject that can be found at *http://www.adobe.com/go/tn_14143*.

FlashVars Example

Let's examine how to use the FlashVars method to configure an application that utilizes the FLV Playback component. As you may know, the FLV Playback component contains a contentPath that is automatically filled with the correct FLV filename if you import a video via the import video dialogue. Alternatively, you can set this value manually via the Properties panel (see **Figure 14-1**).

Please remind yourself of this fact by opening the file flvplayback_flashvars.fla in Flash 8 or Flash CS3. You can find the file amongst the sample files for Chapter 14, which you can download from *www.flashvideobook.com*.

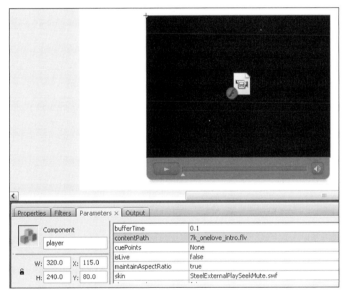

Figure 14-1
The FLV Playback component with its contentPath property set to 7k_onelove_intro.flv. You should delete this value now.

1. Double click the contentPath property and press Delete to delete the value for `contentPath`, thereby removing the value for the FLV file. Later you will set this property through ActionScript.

   At this stage, the application would not play a video since no file is identified to be played. In the next steps, you will configure the application to accept an external parameter and then pass this parameter to the FLV Playback component.

Author's Tip

If you are using Flash CS3 in combination with the latest version of the FLV Playback component, note that the name of the `contentPath` property has changed to `source` in ActionScript 3. In that case, remember to use `source` instead of `contentPath`. If you are using the book's sample file, then no changes need to be made; the component used here is the ActionScript 2 version and uses the `contentPath` property.

As I mentioned earlier, all variables passed into the Flash application via the FlashVars method are present on _level0 of our application. In our example, _level0 refers to the main timeline and that's where we will add the necessary logic.

2. Click frame 1 of the actions layer to select it and choose Window > Actions from the menu bar to open the Actions panel.

3. Add the following code to the Actions panel:

```
player.contentPath = filename;
```

This line of code assumes the presence of a variable called `filename` (this is the variable that we will pass via FlashVars) and assigns the value of this variable to the `contentPath` property of the FLV Playback component on Stage (the component's instance name is `player`). Assuming that the filename variable contains a valid filepath, then the application will play this file as soon as it loads.

Complete the following steps to wrap up this example.

4. Compile the FLA to a SWF by choosing File > Export > Export Movie from the File menu, choosing a name of flvplayback_flashvars.swf.

5. In the HTML editor of your choice, create a new HTML document, save it to the same location as the FLA and SWF files that you have just been working on, and add the following code to it:

```
<html xmlns="http://www.w3.org/1999/xhtml" xml:lang="en" lang="en">
<head>
<meta http-equiv=»Content-Type» content=»text/html; charset=iso-8859-1» />
<title>flvplayback_flashvars</title>
</head>
<body bgcolor=»#ffffff»>
    <object classid=»clsid:d27cdb6e-ae6d-11cf-96b8-444553540000»
codebase=»http://download.macromedia.com/pub/shockwave/cabs/flash/
swflash.cab#version=8,0,0,0» width=»550» height=»400» align=»middle»>
        <param name=»allowScriptAccess» value=»sameDomain» />
        <param name=»movie» value=»flvplayback_flashvars.swf» />
        <param name=»quality» value=»high» />
        <param name=»bgcolor» value=»#ffffff» />
        <PARAM NAME=FlashVars VALUE="filename=7k_onelove_intro.flv">
        <embed src="flvplayback_flashvars.swf"
FlashVars="filename=7k_onelove_intro.flv" width="550" height="400"
```

```
align="middle" quality="high" bgcolor="#ffffff" allowScriptAccess="sam
eDomain" type="application/x-shockwave-flash" pluginspage="http://www.
macromedia.com/go/getflashplayer" />
        </object>
</body>
</html>
```

This code embeds the SWF file called flvplayback_flashvars.swf into the HTML document and adds a variable by the name of filename to the SWF via FlashVars (highlighted in bold).

This code may look complex, but you should be familiar with it by now (and you can copy it from the flvplayback_flashvars.html file included with the download-able files). In addition, you may remember from Chapter 11 that this method of SWF embedding can have some minor problems, like the Eolas "Click to activate this control" issue. In a moment, we'll examine the equivalent SWFObject syntax, which avoids Eolas and is a bit cleaner.

6.   Open the newly created HTML document in a browser to preview it.

Figure 14-2 shows the application playing the video in Internet Explorer.

Figure 14-2
The path to this video is passed to the SWF via the HTML document using the FlashVars method.

In Chapter 11, you learned about SWF Object, the preferred way of adding a SWF file to an HTML document. The equivalent SWFObject code to the previous example looks like this:

```
<script type="text/javascript">
        // <![CDATA[
        var so = new SWFObject("flvplayback_flashvars.swf", "flashvarsmovie",
"550", "400", "7", "#FFFFFF");
        so.addVariable("filename", "7k_onelove_intro.flv");
        so.write("flashcontent");
        // ]]>

</script>
```

You can see that SWFObject offers the addVariable method, which allows you to pass name and value pairs to the SWF. The line that takes care of this task in this example is `so.addVariable("filename", "7k_onelove_intro.flv");`

You can find the completed HTML file using this technique in the downloadable files for this chapter, in the same folder as the FLA file you loaded at the start of this example (flvplayback_flashvars_swfobject.html). It achieves the same results as the previous and more elaborate object/embed syntax. For more information on SWFObject, please consult Chapter 11, "Deploying Progressive Flash Video."

Summary

You just created a Flash video player that does not rely on hard-coded values inside the SWF itself in order to play an FLV video. Instead, this player can receive its configuration from the HTML document that it is embedded in. This set-up makes the SWF much more versatile, as you no longer have to open Flash and export a new SWF file every time you want to update the video content. Instead, you can simply edit the HTML document and pass a new FLV reference to the player.

It's not hard to see how you can take this example a step further by generating the entire HTML document on the fly using an application server of your choice. This will open the door to integrating this player with a database backend, amongst other things. Such a set-up would not be far away from implementations that many of the major video portals use today.

In the next section we will look at one way of letting the Flash application itself request the configuration data by connecting directly to an application server before playback begins.

Using the LoadVars Object for Configuration

This headline must sound a bit confusing to those new to Adobe Flash. LoadVars Object? What on earth is that?

In a nutshell, LoadVars is a technique for loading data from an external server into a Flash movie (SWF). Flash offers many different ways to access remote data and the LoadVars Object is popular and fairly easy to implement.

So, how does it differ from the FlashVars method? Firstly, LoadVars does not require the HTML document to pass any data to the SWF. Instead, by using the LoadVars Object, the SWF can, once loaded, request any necessary data such as filename, buffer time and other video information directly from an application server. In real-life terms, this means that the SWF will connect to a script (for example, a CGI, JSP, PHP, ASP, ColdFusion or any other application server) and directly load data from there. Moreover, the LoadVars Object can also request data from static files such as a plain-text file, which can be useful if the configuration data rarely changes.

LoadVars really starts to shine when used in conjunction with an application server and FlashVars. Imagine a web page that passes a userid to the SWF. The SWF can then process this userid and pass it (via LoadVars) to an application server, which in turn queries a database and returns all available videos for that particular user to the SWF. You can see the flow of this process in **Figure 14-3**.

Figure 14-3
The Flash application makes a request to the database via a script, which in turn returns data back to Flash.

The SWF would then present this information to the user and allow her to choose a video to play, for example by presenting a list. You can probably imagine that this is pretty powerful stuff.

So that was the theory; let's take a look at a more practical example in which you will learn how to load two pieces of information from an external text file. I won't be using an application server in this example, as this would go beyond the scope of this book. If you are already familiar with a particular application-server technology, then it will be very easy for you to port this example from a static text file to a dynamic set-up.

The Configuration File

This example is based on the FLA file from the previous section on FlashVars. I have already prepared all source files for you and you can find them in the LoadVars directory of the downloadable files for Chapter 14. If you're jumping in mid-chapter, note that you can download all source files for this book from *www.flashvideobook.com*.

Let's start by looking at the file containing the data that we want to return to the SWF once requested. Open the text file config.txt in your favorite text editor, and you'll see the following contents:

```
filename=halleyoyo.flv&headline=Skateboard Action
```

This file contains two variables, separated by an "&", that will be passed to Flash:

- `filename` with a value of halleyoyo.flv
- `headline` with a value of Skateboard Action

You will use the first variable to play the specified video and the second to display a headline above it. Note that both variables are separated by an "&". Again, this format is called URL-encoded output and it's the format that Flash expects when using LoadVars.

To find out more about URL encoding you may check the technote at *http://www.adobe.com/go/tn_14143*.

The ActionScript Code

Close the text file and open loadvars.fla in Adobe Flash 8 or Adobe Flash CS3. The contents of this file are almost identical to the one from the FlashVars section. Note the following changes:

- A textfield with the instance name of header has been added to the Stage
- There are some code changes on frame 1 of the actions layer.

The code changes are significant and require a closer look. Here's the new code:

```
var lv:LoadVars = new LoadVars();
lv.onLoad = function (success:Boolean)
{
        if (success)
        {
                trace("Data loaded, starting playback");
                header.text = lv.headline;
                player.contentPath = lv.filename;
        }
        else
        {
                trace("Error loading data.");
        }
};
lv.load("config.txt");
```

The first line creates a new LoadVars Object that will receive the data loaded from the text file.

The onLoad handler on the following line is automatically invoked when data (from the text file in this case) has finished loading and it will return a Boolean value that is either true or false. If the value is `true` then the data loading process was successful and the code in the `if (success)` part of the if/else statement executes. Otherwise a trace message will indicate that data loading has failed.

Any variables loaded from the text file are automatically assigned to the lv object as properties, which means that our headline from the text file is now saved into the variable `lv.headline`. Likewise the filename variable is now saved as `lv.filename`.

Both variables are now available to the application and can populate the `header` textfield on Stage as well as set the `contentPath` property on the player.

The last line `lv.load("config.txt");` initiates data loading by calling the LoadVars Object's load method and passing it the path to the text file that holds the data. This can be a relative path as in this example, or a fully qualified URL.

Testing the Application

You can now test this application by choosing Control > Test Movie from the menu bar. The application will compile the SWF and start playing. You should see some trace statements in the Output window indicating that data has loaded, and the headline textfield should be populated and the video should start playing.

This method of configuring a Flash video application can be very convenient as it allows non-technical users to update filenames and other parameters without having to know either Flash or ActionScript.

Author's Tip

Crossdomain Security
Several data-loading methods, including the LoadsVars Object, are subject to certain security restrictions within the Flash Player environment. Specifically, for security reasons, a SWF file playing in a web browser is not allowed to access data that resides outside the exact web domain from which the SWF originated. This may prevent you from accessing data on a domain (for example siteB.com) that is different from the SWF's originating domain (for example siteA.com). Cross-domain data loading can be configured via a cross-domain policy file called crossdomain.xml. For more info on this, check the Adobe technote at *http://www.adobe.com/go/tn_14213*.

Note that your SWF will not be restricted by this policy if both the SWF file and the data to be loaded (in this case, the text file) reside under the exact same domain, such as siteA.com.

You can try this yourself by copying another flv file into the directory you've been working in and change the text file to reflect the name of the new video. When you then restart the SWF file (for example, by simply dragging it into a browser window) you will notice that the added FLV is now playing—without having to make any changes inside Flash.

Of course, the configuration text file could also be dynamically generated by an application server or you could even point the LoadVars Object's load method directly to a script. This would then look something like this:

```
lv.load("http://www.myserver.com/config.php");
```

As long as the output of the config.php PHP script is formatted in a URL-encoded syntax, then Flash will process and work with it. This is very powerful and can form the basis of an entirely database-driven Flash application.

Author's Tip

Flash to Browser Communication

Flash is also able to communicate with the browser, and JavaScript in particular, directly in a bidirectional way using a feature called *ExternalInterface* that works in Flash Player 8 and above. Prior to Flash Player 8 there were other ways to communicate with the browser but ExternalInterface is now the recommended method for JavaScript-ActionScript communication.

ExternalInterface enables you to call JavaScript functions from ActionScript and vice versa. It is supported by all major browsers on Windows and Macintosh.

The specific usage of ExternalInterface is outside of the scope of this book. However, a great example on controlling a Flash video player can be found in the Flash Help files (choose Help > Flash Help from the menu bar to show it) under the topic of Learning ActionScript 2.0 in Flash > Working with External Data > About the External API > Controlling Flash Video with the External API.

In the next section you will learn how to leverage XML files to achieve a similar configuration set-up.

Using an XML File for Configuration

Using XML to load data into a Flash movie at runtime is becoming increasingly popular as XML is now the de-facto standard for sharing data between systems, especially over the Internet. The main difference between XML and plain text is that XML structures the data in more consistent and understandable ways, usually in a tree-like format.

Here is an example of a simple XML document:

```xml
<?xml version="1.0" encoding="UTF-8"?>
<videos>
  <item>
    <url>video1.flv</url>
    <title>My first video</title>
  </item>
  <item>
    <url>video2.flv</url>
    <title>My second video</title>
  </item>
  <item>
    <url>video3.flv</url>
    <title>My third video</title>
  </item>
</videos>
```

As you can see, this XML tree contains a root tag of videos, which in turn contains a series of item nodes. Each item node describes a video with URL and title. In this chapter you will learn how to load and parse an XML document in Flash and then configure a video player with that data, which is similar to how you used the LoadVars Object in the previous example to load data from a text file.

Examining the Files

The previous XML sample code contains the main data as well as some nodes (such as the item nodes) that are used to keep the actual data (url nodes, title nodes) organized. Distinguishing data from the organizational structure is often referred to as XML parsing, or walking the XML tree.

You can find the XML document used in this in the xml_config folder under the ingenious name config.xml. This file contains information on two videos:

```xml
<?xml version="1.0" encoding="UTF-8"?>
<videos>
  <item>
    <url>halleyoyo.flv</url>
    <title>Skateboard Action</title>
</item>
<item>
    <url>yannic.flv</url>
    <title>Yannic rips it up</title>
  </item>
</videos>
```

As you can see, it is the <url> and <title> nodes that we're interested in. Once loaded, we will configure the Flash application to play one of the two videos at random.

Let's examine the ActionScript code that's responsible for loading and parsing this file.

1. Open xml_config.fla in Flash 8 or Flash CS3. You can find the file in the xml_config folder of the downloaded files for Chapter 14 alongside the other assets needed for this walkthrough.

2. Click frame 1 of the actions layer and choose Window > Actions to open the Actions panel.

    Notice that the code here is almost identical to that in our previous LoadVars example. The process of loading XML is indeed very similar to loading data from a text file (after all, XML is just another text format) with one main difference: an XML file must be parsed once received in Flash. Let's learn how to do that.

Here's the complete code listing:

```
var myxml:XML = new XML();
myxml.ignoreWhite = true;
myxml.onLoad = function(success:Boolean)
{
    if (success)
    {
        trace("Data loaded, parsing XML");
        var myData:Array = new Array();

        var videosNode:XMLNode = myxml.firstChild;
        var totalItems:Number = videosNode.childNodes.length;

        for (var i = 0; i < totalItems; i++)
        {
            var urlNode:XMLNode = videosNode.childNodes[i].firstChild;
            var urlValue = urlNode.firstChild;

            var titleNode = urlNode.nextSibling;
            var titleValue = titleNode.firstChild;
            myData[i] = ( {url:urlValue, title:titleValue} );
            trace(myData[i].url + " - " + myData[i].title);
        }
    }
    else
    {
        trace("Error loading data.");
    }
};
myxml.load("config.xml");
```

This code not only loads the XML document (the load process is kicked off by the last line) but also parses the XML document by first grabbing the root node

```
var videosNode:XMLNode = myxml.firstChild;
```

then determining the number of items (or item nodes)

```
var totalItems:Number = videosNode.childNodes.length;
```

and finally it loops over all the item nodes and breaks them down into nodes and node values. I'm also creating an array by the name of myData, which holds the XML data in the form of an object for each url and title pair:

```
myData[i] = ( {url:urlValue, title:titleValue} );
```

Having access to the XML contents in an array format makes it very easy to handle in ActionScript. In essence, this ActionScript code translates the XML document to an array of Objects for easier handling in Flash.

3.   Test this application by choosing Control > Test Movie from the menu bar.

While the video will not yet play, you should see some trace statements in the Output panel as **Figure 14-4** shows.

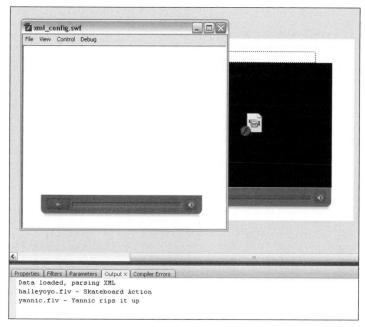

Figure 14-4
A first test shows that the XML file is being loaded and successfully parsed.

Adding Some Randomization Logic

The trace statements indicate that the XML document has been loaded and parsed success-fully and that you can now use this data to configure the player on Stage.

Find the trace statement that reads:

```
trace(myData[i].url + " - " + myData[i].title);
```

and insert the following code right after the closing curly bracket on the next line, so that it reads:

```
    trace(myData[i].url + " - " + myData[i].title);
}

var seed = Math.round(Math.random()*(myData.length-1));
header.text = String(myData[seed].title);
player.contentPath = String(myData[seed].url);
```

I've included a copy of the completed exercise with the source files. The name of the final FLA is xml_config_completed.fla.

This newly added code creates a variable called "seed" which is assigned a random number between 0 and 1 in this case. Note how the random number is generated based on the length of our array minus one. This makes the code universally usable even with a large number of items in your XML file (and subsequently in the array).

The next two lines:

```
header.text = String(myData[seed].title);
player.contentPath = String(myData[seed].url);
```

simply assign the title variable to the header textfield on Stage and set the contentPath property of the FLV Playback component, playing the video.

This little script is perfect for playing a random video from a large selection provided in the XML configuration file. You could imagine putting this player on your homepage to create the effect of constantly updated video content. As long as you have a few dozen videos available, then most return visitors are likely to see a new video each time they come to your site.

Testing the Player

Choose File > Publish Preview > HTML from the menu bar to preview the application in your default browser. Once the first video plays, refresh the page in your browser a few times and you will notice that either one or the other video plays at random. If you refresh the pages often enough, you will get a better feel for the randomness that the script has added.

Try building on this example by encoding a few more FLV videos and adding their details to the XML document. Or why not add another node to the XML to dynamically set the buffer time of the video? The possibilities really are endless and anything you can configure manually in Flash by changing the parameters of the FLV Playback component can just as easily be externalized and provided via XML.

An external configuration file provides a scalable and maintainable video player that separates the presentation layer (your player) from the business logic (as provided by the XML file), rather than mixing both parts in ActionScript, which would make the application much harder to update.

Reliably Detecting the End of an FLV Video

As your Flash video applications become more complex, you'll find that the ready-made functions within Flash become less useful without some modification. Conversely, no matter how diverse your requirements, you'll likely find some Flash mechanisms that you can build upon to shape and create something completely original, which is a common thread throughout Flash development.

Love it or hate it, this is how Flash development has always presented itself: as a bit of a challenge at times, but one that can be mastered.

I like to compare Flash to a big box of Lego bricks, the mixed variety that lets you build a million and one things depending upon what comes to mind, rather than the boxed set that lets you build just one shape, say a race car, and only if you follow the instructions to the letter. That's not my idea of fun. Flash is a lot like the big box of Legos, offering and encouraging creative ideas to (sometimes) solve complex problems without prescribing a particular way to solve them. For this reason, there is often more than one way to complete a particular task, including detecting the end of a playing FLV video file, which you should bear in mind throughout the remainder of this book.

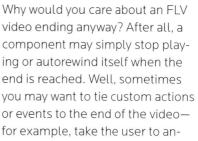

Author's Tip

Why would you care about an FLV video ending anyway? After all, a component may simply stop playing or autorewind itself when the end is reached. Well, sometimes you may want to tie custom actions or events to the end of the video—for example, take the user to another page, open a pop-up window or simply play another video. Being able to programmatically catch the end of playback is crucial in order to make these features happen.

If you search the Internet for the solution to a Flash or ActionScript query, you may encounter several different solutions and more often than not there will be no right or wrong alternative. It will be up to your experience and judgement to determine which solution may be the one best suited for your particular challenge.

For example, if you're using the FLV Playback component, you'll find it offers its very own and easy-to-use method of detecting the end of playback and allows you to capture this event in your ActionScript code. Otherwise, a custom written player must utilize the NetStream Object directly in ActionScript. This approach involves a little extra code but is easy to master. Let's examine both options.

Detecting the End of a Video Using FLV Playback

The main difference between the FLV Playback component and the custom written ActionScript approach is that the component adds a layer of abstraction to the underlying and often complex code, which is hidden from view in the component.

The abstraction layer contains a number of methods and events that can make our lives a little easier—and this is something that most components have in common. In the case of detecting the end of a video that is played using FLV Playback, we need to hook into a specific event called `complete`. This event is dispatched when playback is completed.

I've prepared an example file that you can find amongst the sample files for Chapter 14, in a subfolder called detect_end. The name of the FLA is flvplayback_end.fla, and you should open this in Adobe Flash 8 or Adobe Flash CS3 if you want to test the application.

This application holds an instance of FLV Playback on Stage with an instance name of player. I've added all the necessary code to frame 1 of the actions layer, which looks like this:

```
var completeListener:Object = new Object();
completeListener.complete = function(eventObject:Object):Void
{
    trace("video ended");
};
player.addEventListener("complete", completeListener);
```

This creates a plain object named `completeListener` to which I've attached a `complete` function, which dispatches a `complete` event when playback finishes. All I've done in this example is added a trace statement that will indicate that the video has ended.

Press Control > Test Movie to see it in action. Allow the video to play to the end and watch the Output window for trace statements. You will see that the line

```
trace("video ended");
```

gets invoked once the `complete` event is received, displaying "video ended" in the Output window.

To turn this into a more useful example, you could add a getURL statement (to open a website URL) instead of the trace in order to send the user to another page or website after the video finishes, and have the video content act as some sort of interstitial.

To accomplish this, simply replace this line:

```
trace("video ended");
```

with this:

```
getURL("http://www.flashvideobook.com ");
```

Of course, you can substitute the URL of your choice here.

To test the application in Flash, choose Control > Test Movie from the menu bar. You will see that once the video finishes playing the user is directed to another URL.

In the next section, I'll show you how to achieve the same result using an entirely Action-Script-based approach.

Detecting the End of a Video Using ActionScript

For this example, I have modified a previous example from Chapter 11, which covered basic playback of an FLV video in Adobe Flash using an entirely ActionScript-based approach (the file used in Chapter 11 is called flv_via_actionscript_completed.fla). The example file here uses the existing file, plus a few new additions.

1. Open the file actionscript_end.fla in Adobe Flash 8 or Adobe Flash CS3. You can find this file amongst the sample files for Chapter 14 in a subfolder called

detect_end. I won't review the existing code from the first example, which you can read about in Chapter 11, but will focus on the changes instead. Let's examine them in more detail.

2. Click frame 1 of the actions layer to select it and open the Actions panel by choosing Window > Actions from the menu bar.

The code section that deserves your attention is this:

```
ns.onStatus = function (info:Object)
{
    trace(info.code);
    if (info.code == "NetStream.Play.Start")
    {
        stopping = false;
    }
    else if (info.code == "NetStream.Play.Stop")
    {
        trace("playback is about to end");
        stopping = true;
    }
    else if (info.code == "NetStream.Buffer.Empty")
    {
        if (stopping)
        {
            trace("video ended");
        }
        else
        {
            trace("buffering...");
        }
    }
    else if ("NetStream.Buffer.Full")
    {
        stopping = false;
    }
}
```

As you may remember, ns is an instance of the NetStream class used to play video content in Flash. The onStatus handler is automatically invoked when certain events happen during playback. In total there are eight different onStatus events that you can listen for in your code and they also contain certain error messages.

Each event dispatches an info object containing a code property that we'll use here. I've added a trace statement to display the value of this code property in Flash's Output panel when you test the application.

3. Choose Control > Test Movie from the menu bar and allow the video to play to the end (it's a very short clip).

The Output panel will show the following text:

```
NetStream.Play.Start
NetStream.Buffer.Full
NetStream.Buffer.Flush
NetStream.Play.Stop
playback is about to end
NetStream.Buffer.Empty
video ended
```

The lines starting with "NetStream" are being output by the trace statement that reads:

```
trace(info.code);
```

The other two lines are other traces that are added to highlight important logical steps. To understand what these statements are, and why they are triggered in this particular order, I must explain a few details about how Flash handles video playback and buffering. I'll cover that in the following section.

Understanding Video Buffering in Flash

All videos in Flash use a buffer, even if it's a very small one. As you probably know, a buffer allows for some data to be received by the user's machine before playback begins. The larger the buffer, the more data needs to be received initially, and the longer it takes for playback to begin.

Flash uses the buffer during playback to counteract any changes in connection speed or bandwidth spikes in the video, thereby assuring smoother playback. A 5-second buffer stores 5 seconds of video, which will play even if the user's Internet connection drops completely. Once the buffer is empty (all 5 seconds worth of data have been viewed), the application must rebuffer and playback will stop, as many dial-up users can confirm.

The only way to ensure a completely smooth playback is to load the entire length of the video into the buffer, which isn't practical as it can delay playback for long periods of time. Moreover, such tactics can easily cause memory issues on the user's machine and should be avoided.

But connection troubles aside, a buffer is always present and will always be empty at the end of playback. This fact is leveraged by the ActionScript code we just reviewed. But how can the code distinguish an empty buffer at the end of the video from an empty buffer that may occur during playback due to the aforementioned connection-speed issues?

Conveniently, the NetStream Object's onStatus event will let us know when playback has stopped, meaning that no more data is being sent by the server. The info.code property for this is a string of:

```
NetStream.Play.Sto
```

But you can't assume when you encounter this string that playback has actually stopped, since the buffer on the user's machine still needs to empty for playback to be truly complete. To account for this, you must set a variable indicating that the video is about to stop, which you can accomplish like this:

```
else if (info.code == "NetStream.Play.Stop")

{

        trace("playback is about to end");

        stopping = true;

}
```

I gave my variable the name stopping but you may choose any name that you see fit. What's important here is that I set this variable to true, indicating that the video is about to end and we're just waiting for the buffer to empty. In contrast, if we encounter a NetStream.Buffer.Full string, stopping is reset to false, indicating that playback is not complete and that the previous empty buffer was caused by midstream rebuffering.

The second step involves checking the info.code property for the empty buffer:

```
else if (info.code == "NetStream.Buffer.Empty")
{
        if (stopping)
        {
                trace("video ended");
        }
        else
{
                trace("buffering...");
}
}
```

Once I encounter the string NetStream.Buffer.Empty I simply check if the stopping variable has been set to true previously

```
if (stopping)
```

and if it has, then I indicate to the user (in this case by means of a simple trace statement) that the video is complete. At this point you could hook other logic into the application's flow, like opening a browser window as outlined in the previous example that used the FLV Playback component.

Looping Playback

Another useful bit of functionality you can add once playback has finished is to rewind and restart the video to create looping-video playback.

With the logic provided by the last two sections, we can now add this feature very easily. Once again, I will demonstrate how to achieve this using the FLV Playback component as well as the ActionScript approach. The implementations are almost identical, as they both require you to add the same two lines of code which involve seeking back to the beginning of the video and issuing a play command. Here's how you loop video playback:

1. Open the file flvplayback_loop.fla in Adobe Flash 8 or Adobe Flash CS3. You can find the file in a folder called detect_end, which is a subfolder of the files you can download for Chapter 14.

2. Click frame 1 of the actions layer and choose Window > Actions from the menu bar to open the Actions panel. You will see the following lines of code:

   ```
   var completeListener:Object = new Object();
   completeListener.complete = function(eventObject:Object):Void
   {
       player.seek(0);
       player.play();
   };
   player.addEventListener("complete", completeListener);
   ```

   As you can see, the changes from the previous example are minimal. I simply added two new lines of code:

   ```
   player.seek(0);
   player.play();
   ```

   This instructs the FLV Playback instance (with the name of player) to seek to time 0 (which is the beginning of the video) and then play.

3. Choose File > Publish Preview > Default from the menu bar to preview the application in your default browser.

You will notice that the video automatically loops back to the beginning once the end has been reached. The ActionScript-based approach is almost identical with only one small difference: you need to call the seek and play methods on the NetStream instance and not on a player component (after all, no component is being used).

I have added the completed file to this chapter's sample files. You can find it under the name of actionscript_loop.fla.

1. Open the file actionscript_loop.fla in Adobe Flash 8 or Adobe Flash CS3.

2. Click frame 1 of the actions layer and choose Window > Actions from the menu bar to open the Actions panel. The relevant code looks as follows:

```
else if (info.code == "NetStream.Buffer.Empty")
{
   if (stopping)
   {
      trace("video ended");
      ns.seek(0);
      ns.play();
   }
```

Instead of calling player.seek(0) you need to specify the NetStream Object's instance of ns instead. The same applies to the play command.

3. Test this application by choosing Control > Test Movie and see the video play and loop in your default browser.

In the next section you will learn how to load and play another FLV file after playback has finished in order to facilitate back-to-back playback of multiple files.

Playing Videos Back to Back

I am sure that you can see where this next example is going. Again, there are very few changes that have to be made to the existing code.

Implementation Using FLV Playback

As you recall, the FLV Playback component receives information about which video to play via its contentPath property (or the source property if you are using the ActionScript3-based FLV Playback component in Flash CS3). You therefore need to update this property every time you wish to play another video. Let's examine the details.

You can find a sample file for using FLV Playback amongst this chapter's sample files in a subdirectory called detect_end. The file you are looking for is named flvplayback_backtoback.fla.

1. Open flvplayback_backtoback.fla in Adobe Flash 8 or Adobe Flash CS3.

2. Click frame 1 of the actions layer and choose Window > Actions from the menu bar to open the Actions panel. You will see the following lines of code:

```
var completeListener:Object = new Object();
completeListener.complete = function(eventObject:Object):Void
{
    player.contentPath = "clip2.flv";
};
player.addEventListener("complete", completeListener);
```

This really couldn't be much simpler. Remember that we set the initial contentPath property via the Property Inspector's Parameter tab to clip1.flv and that the autoPlay and autoRewind options have been enabled (set to "true") by specifying a value of true, as shown in **Figure 14-5**.

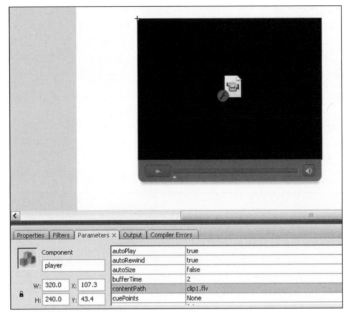

Figure 14-5
contentPath, autoPlay and autoRewind are already configured.

Author's Tip

Playing just two videos may seem rather limiting—there could be cases where you would prefer a whole list of videos to play one after the other.

In these cases, you should consider setting up an array of videos in Flash. If you are familiar with arrays then you will know that they allow you to store multiple values (in this case the URLs of several videos) inside a single variable. This makes it easy to keep track of the currently playing video using yet another variable; you may call it currentVid.

The currentVid variable would specify the current index of the array, keeping track of which video is playing and incrementing this index every time a video finishes.

This set-up allows for playlists of virtually unlimited length. I have included an example named playback_array.fla for your reference amongst the source files for this chapter. You may want to check out the completed example before trying to implement this yourself.

For this reason, there is only one line of code necessary to play another video after the initial video has finished. The following line of code simply sets the contentPath property to the new video's URL:

```
player.contentPath = "clip2.flv";
```

3. Choose File > Publish Preview > HTML from the File menu to preview the application in your default browser. You will see that the second video will start playing as soon as the previous video has finished.

Implementation Using ActionScript

Adding back-to-back playback to the ActionScript-based player involves a few more changes, although even those are fairly simple. You can find the sample file, actionscript_backtoback.fla, amongst this chapter's files in a subdirectory called detect_end.

1. Open actionscript_backtoback.fla in Adobe Flash 8 or Adobe Flash CS3.

2. Click frame 1 of the actions layer and choose Window > Actions from the menu bar to open the Actions panel.

    The first change that I have made when compared to the initial example (flv_via_actionscript_completed.fla) of Chapter 11 is right at the top of the code listing where I added:

    ```
    var videofile1:String = "clip1.flv";
    var videofile2:String = "clip2.flv";
    ```

    Instead of just one videofile variable, you are now dealing with two. This also means that the play statement further down now needs to read

    ```
    ns.play(videofile1);
    ```

    The last change involves the code section that detects the end of playback, which happens just underneath the line that listens for the NetStream.Buffer.Empty string.

    ```
    [...] else if (info.code == "NetStream.Buffer.Empty")
    {
        if (stopping)
        {
            trace("video ended");
            ns.play(videofile2);
        }
    [...]
    ```

    Instead of seeking back to the beginning as you have done in the section covering looping playback, you now play another file. You can easily do this via the line that reads

    ```
    ns.play(videofile2);
    ```

This line is self-explanatory; it simply plays the video URL that is stored in the videofile2 variable that was set up at the top of the code listing.

3. Choose File > Publish Preview > HTML to preview the application in your default browser. You will see the first video playing, followed by a second one.

Conclusion

You covered a lot of code-heavy ground in this chapter and, if you are new to Flash and ActionScript in particular, then this may not have been the easiest of subjects to digest. If nothing else, you are now armed with a small library of examples that you can either build upon yourself or task a developer to take to the next level.

You have learned some Flash video's advanced capabilities and I've hopefully made it clear that in Flash development, you can solve almost any problem in a variety of creative ways. The tools are at your disposal; it's now simply a matter of putting them to good use.

The next chapter will build upon the knowledge gained up to now and explore more advanced video effects and playback configurations.

CHAPTER 15

Advanced Effects and Playback Options

The introduction of Flash 8 saw the addition of the BitmapData class, a highly versatile object that allows for the varied manipulation of bitmaps inside a Flash movie at runtime. With its help, you can create very complex images and effects, some of which are ideally suited for video content.

Through the BitmapData class, you can now apply filters like drop shadow, blur, glow, bevel, gradient glow, and gradient bevel to MovieClips, buttons and text. All that's required to add these effects to on-demand or even live video is to first convert your video object on Stage into a MovieClip.

You can also use color filters to edit a MovieClip's brightness, contrast, saturation, and hue. You can apply filters using the Flash user interface or via ActionScript.

In this chapter, you will learn how to create a glow effect in Flash and ActionScript and also familiarize yourself with the creative opportunities that alpha channel video has to offer, as well as other creative effects. In particular, I will cover:

- How to create a glow effect in Flash via the Filters menu
- Creating the same glow effect with ActionScript
- How alpha channel video can be leveraged
- A technique for generating video snapshots
- The pluses and minuses of full-screen Flash video
- Processing metadata
- Statistics and reporting.

ALERT

This chapter uses Adobe Flash CS3 Professional (alternatively you may use Adobe Flash Professional 8). To follow along with the examples, which I recommend, you will need a copy of the program to be installed on your computer. Should you not own a copy of the program, note that Adobe offers a free 30-day trial version on its website.

Also, note that you can find the files referred to and used in this chapter, including completed skins, at *www.flashvideobook.com*. Consider downloading these files now, so they'll be available once I start referring to them.

Creating a Glow Effect in Flash

Let's first review how to apply a filter effect to a MovieClip using Flash's Filters panel, then explore how to add a filter effect using ActionScript. To follow this example along, which I recommend, run Flash and open the file filters_via_ide.fla. This file is virtually identical to the example from Chapter 11, "Playing an FLV File using Actionscript." You will use this file as a basis to apply the filter effects.

1. Click the video_mc MovieClip on Stage.

2. Choose Window > Properties > Properties from the menu bar.

3. In the Properties panel on the lower left, click the Filters tab to open the Filters panel.

4. From the Filters panel choose the + sign. The Filters menu will open.

5. Choose Glow from the menu (**Figure 15-1**).

Flash will apply the default red glow to the video_mc MovieClip, which will appear around the outside of the movie. Once you apply the Glow filter, you'll see controls for modifying properties like color, blur and strength to the right of the Filter panel.

You can use these to modify the default setting, perhaps changing the color to a dark gray, blur to around 15, strength to about 75% and the quality to high to achieve a subtle, shadowy glow. To test output, compile your movie by choosing Control > Test Movie from the menu bar.

You can find the completed file amongst the source files under the name of filters_via_ide_completed.fla.

Figure 15-2 shows the completed effect. Depending on the settings that you have used, your output may look slightly different.

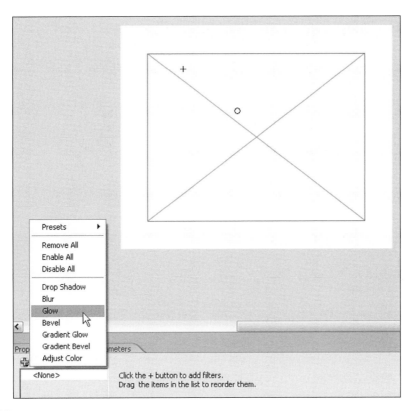

Figure 15-1
The Filters menu with selected Glow option.

Figure 15-2
The completed Glow effect applied to a Movieclip containing a video.

Creating a Glow Effect Using ActionScript

The Filters menu is a convenient way to add effects to a MovieClip (or video contained within it) and it yields quick results. However, in more elaborate applications, it may be preferred or even required to add these effects at runtime—perhaps to create an effect that's tied to a certain user interaction.

Applying effects using ActionScript is often preferred, as it is more flexible than selecting objects on Stage, assigning properties to them and so forth. A little bit of code really goes a long way, as you'll see in this next example.

1. Open the filters_via_as.fla file and click frame 1 of the actions layer.

2. Choose Window > Actions to open the Actions panel if it is not already showing.

    Firstly, note the import on line 12:

    ```
    import flash.filters.GlowFilter;
    ```

    This imports the GlowFilter class, which is required to add a glow effect programmatically. I have also added the following new function on lines 33 to 39:

    ```
    function addGlowFilter()
    {
        var filter:GlowFilter = new GlowFilter(0x666666, 1, 15, 15, 0.75,
        5, false, false);
        var filterArray:Array = new Array();
        filterArray.push(filter);
        video_mc.filters = filterArray;
    }
    ```

    When invoked, this function will create an instance of the GlowFilter class (line 35) with the following parameters:

    *   0x666666 specifies the color for the glow effect in hexadecimal format

    *   1 specifies the alpha transparency for the glow effect, with 1 being no transparency

    *   15 specifies the amount of horizontal blur

    *   15 specifies the amount of vertical blur

    *   0.75 specifies the strength of the glow

    *   5 specifies the quality (5 being high quality)

    *   false specifies that the glow is not an inner glow

    *   false specifies that it is not using a knockout effect.

    Finally the addGlowFilter function is invoked on line 41:

    ```
    addGlowFilter();
    ```

You have now recreated the glow effect in ActionScript. Using ActionScript allows you (for example) to add additional flexibility to your applications, like tying the effect to a user action, something you couldn't accomplish when using the Filters panel.

3.   Compile the file by choosing Control > Test Movie from the menu bar. You will see the same glow effect around the video object as in the previous example.

There are many other filter effects to explore, many of which can be invoked via the Filters panel or manipulated in more detail using ActionScript. Most filters and effects can be mixed and matched, applied sequentially or in parallel. Some filters offer tremendous potential for very sophisticated effects such as sharpen, saturation and threshold manipulation. Others like bevel, gradient bevel and drop shadow offer unique creative opportunities to blend Flash video into other elements of the overall HTML interface.

We're obviously just touching the surface here, but sometimes it's stimulating and illuminating to explore how these effects are being used around us. I strongly recommend checking out Mario Klingemann's website (*http://www.quasimondo.com*), which features a variety of downloadable source files, most of which are directly related to Flash's BitmapData and Filters features. Grant Skinner's Gallery Incomplet (*http://incomplet.gskinner.com*) also showcases several examples utilizing both live webcam video in combination with Filters and BitmapData manipulation (see **Figure 15-3**).

Figure 15-3
Grant Skinner's Gallery Incomplet.

Finally, if these examples have whetted your appetite for more filters, then I highly recommend you check out The Fuse Kit (*http://www.mosessupposes.com/Fuse/index.html*) by Moses Gunesch. His AS2 engine classes make working with BitmapFilters a piece of cake and also add powerful tweening capabilities.

Now let's explore another creative feature introduced by Flash 8: deploying video with an alpha channel.

Using Alpha Channel Video

In this chapter you will learn how you can integrate alpha channel video into a simple Flash movie and how it differs from a regular video file.

Use Cases for Alpha Channel Video

As you may recall from Chapter 9, On2 VP6 video now supports an 8-bit alpha channel. This means that specially processed video can be displayed above other Flash content with a transparent background.

Author's Tip

Alpha channel video can have a significant hit on CPU usage during playback. While you cannot see the transparent areas in the video, they are nevertheless present and need to be decoded and displayed. The more you can crop your content around the subject the better, as this reduces the computational load during playback. Use transparency sparingly, particularly if you are targeting older machines.

Usually, to accomplish this effect, you shoot your video in front of a green or blue screen. As detailed in Chapter 9, you then remove that background during postproduction using a process called chroma keying, and ultimately create an FLV file with an 8-bit alpha channel.

Alpha channel footage can be useful in several scenarios. Firstly, it is often used in presentation-type materials where a speaker, often in a full body shot, talks to the user about a certain subject matter. The speaker can be displayed above any other Flash content, be it static or dynamic. We're suddenly breaking outside of the box that is a square-viewing window. Other creative possibilities enabled by this feature will become clear once you add this piece of video to a Flash application.

Example: Interacting with an Alpha Channel Video

I've prepared an example to showcase some of the unique features of alpha channel video. The footage is of my coauthor, Jan Ozer, discussing how to light a green-screen shoot. If you have access to Flash 8 or Flash CS3 then open the file alphachannel.fla now. You can also run the completed application by opening the file alphachannel.html directly in a browser. You can find both files amongst the book's sample files for Chapter 15.

I am again using the existing player from Chapter 11 as the basis for this example. I have added a MovieClip video_mc on Stage and also created another MovieClip that holds three JPG images as well as some microphones that will be draggable (see **Figure 15-4**) once the application is compiled.

Figure 15-4
The alpha channel application as seen in Flash.

I won't review the ActionScript code here, as it's pretty self-explanatory and really doesn't relate to the fact that the video has an alpha channel. FLV video with an alpha channel becomes transparent automatically, no switches to set, no knobs to turn. Objects on layers beneath the video show through automatically, and objects above can obscure it, just like any other Flash object.

The result is that when a user moves her mouse over one of the three thumbnail images, it triggers a change in the main background image, sending that MovieClip to either frame 1, 2 or 3. This lets the user change the background appearance at runtime. To add some depth to the layout, the user can also drag the microphones into position as shown in **Figure 15-5**.

Note that the code controlling video playback is set up to provide looped playback and you may remember this snippet from Chapter 14. To test the output, choose Control > Test Movie from the menu bar.

Figure 15-5
Jan quickly fills us in on green-screen lighting before the arctic winter sets in.

You can now change the image in the background by hovering over one of the three thumbnails and drag the microphones on top of the video. As you can see, the areas around Jan are totally transparent.

Showcase Links

Adobe's Studio Experience piece was a groundbreaking implementation of alpha channel technology (*http://www.adobe.com/products/studio/experience/*). Not only does it use alpha channel video extensively but it also allows the user to interact with the video content itself. It's one of the earliest pieces to make use of Flash 8's new alpha channel feature.

If you are feeling adventurous, point your browser to Hethuisvanmorgen (*http://www.hethuisvanmorgen.nl/*), a site by the Dutch network provider KPN. The title loosely translates to "The house of tomorrow" and the site uses alpha channel video extensively. It achieves some nice effects by placing objects both in front and behind the video content, adding a layer of depth to the experience.

This wraps up the section on alpha channel video. Next I will show you how to produce image snapshots of video content at runtime.

Figure 15-6
Adobe's efforts with alpha channel video saw a few jaws dropping at the time.

Video Snapshots Using BitmapData

As mentioned previously, the BitmapData object is very versatile when it comes to creating and manipulating bitmaps in Flash. For example, you can take a snapshot of any object in Flash and save it into a BitmapData object, ready for further manipulation. Think of a BitmapData object as a container for image data, or even as an actual image that you can't see but which can be made visible by applying its data to a MovieClip inside the Flash application.

In this example, I will demonstrate how to create snapshots (you may call them screen grabs) from the currently playing video. This might come in handy if you are ever tasked with building a widget that allows a user to mix video elements with photographic material or that maybe serves as some kind of indexing engine.

Author's Tip

Note that it is very CPU intensive to actually save images to an external server or database when using ActionScript 2. This is because ActionScript 2 would require you to process the image data pixel by pixel, converting it to String format and then sending it off for further processing. An application server such as PHP, ASP or ColdFusion would then be required to reassemble the image.

On the other hand, ActionScript 3 working in combination with Flash Player 9 makes it possible to apply a JPG or PNG compression algorithm to the bitmap data inside Flash Player 9 before transmission—a much more efficient way to achieve the same goal.

It does not take much imagination to come up with a few use cases of such an application. With Action-Script 3 being a fairly young language, it's a given that we have only seen the tip of the iceberg of what is possible when it comes to Rich Internet Applications of this kind.

I have tried to keep the following example basic and it will hopefully provide some inspiration and ideas. When completed, you will be able to grab snapshots from a running video and display them inside another MovieClip symbol.

As a basis, we will again use a similar video player as the one from Chapter 11 "Playing a FLV file using Actionscript." To complete the walkthrough, follow these steps:

1. Open the FLA file titled snapshots.fla in Flash 8 or Flash CS3.

    As you can see from **Figure 15-7,** the interface now differs slightly from the original player of Chapter 11. Specifically, I added an empty MovieClip with the instance name holder to the Stage and also positioned a Button component underneath the video window.

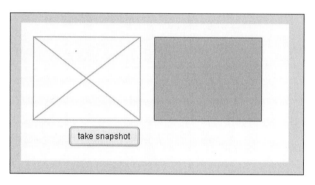

Figure 15-7
The initial layout of the snapshots application.

    You will augment the existing code to add the snapshot functionality. When the user clicks the "take snapshot" button, it will call a function that takes a BitmapData copy of the currently playing video and displays it in the empty holder MovieClip.

2. Click frame 1 of the actions layer.

3. Choose Window > Actions from the menu bar to open the Actions panel.

4. At the top of the code at line 13 insert the following code:

```
import flash.display.BitmapData;
```

    This statement imports the BitmapData class, which enables the snapshot functionality that you are about to add. Next, you will assign a function to the Button that will execute the actual snapshot.

5.   Scroll down to around line 33 and before the `stop()`; statement add this onRelease handler:

```
btn_snapshot.onRelease = function()
{
    var bmdata = new BitmapData(160, 120);
    holder.attachBitmap(bmdata, 5);
    bmdata.draw(video_mc);
}
```

Let's analyze what this code accomplishes.

Firstly, it creates a local instance of the BitmapData class named bmdata to which you're passing a width of 160 and a height of 120, matching the video object's dimensions.

The next line attaches the newly created bmdata instance to the holder MovieClip at a depth level of 5 (I chose 5 just at random; you may pick any other unoccupied level).

Note that, up until now, the snapshot copy would not have been displayed; in fact, you haven't even taken the copy yet. This happens on the last line where the BitmapData class's draw method is called and passed a reference to the source of the data that is to be copied, in this case video_mc.

6.   Test the application by choosing Control > Test Movie from the menu bar. You can click the Button to take snapshots during playback, as shown in **Figure 15-8**.

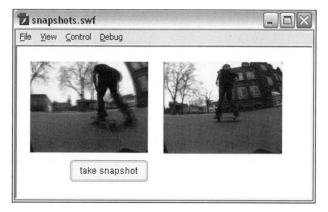

Figure 15-8
The completed snapshots application.

And there you have it—video snapshots in just a few lines of code. It would be no major task to expand on this example, maybe creating some sort of gallery layout with multiple snapshots.

Playing Full-Screen Flash Video

Full-screen video may sound exciting, and certainly millions of YouTube watchers seem to love it, but understand that playing full-screen Flash video has some disadvantages compared to other technologies. That's because, unlike players like the Windows Media Player, the Flash Player can't access acceleration features on your graphics card that not only scale video to arbitrary resolutions with minimal involvement of the host CPU, but also deploy filters that improve video appearance.

In contrast, the Flash Player simply blows the video to a larger size in the Windows GUI, which can make the video appear pixelated and accentuate artifacts. It's basically nothing more than watching a video through a magnifying glass.

This doesn't mean that Flash is behind the times. Rather, because Flash *doesn't* use the graphics hardware, and works *within* the operating system's GUI, it's much easier to integrate into web pages, and much more interactive—witness the alpha channel video discussed previously. It just doesn't scale as efficiently or attractively as other technologies.

That's the bad news out of the way. The good news is that in this chapter you will learn to scale the SWF and Flash Player playback window to any arbitrary size. The code provided will also allow you to resize the playback window on the fly, should you wish to do so.

Inside the Industry

New Flash Player 9 Features

Adobe recently released an update to Flash Player 9 that adds full-screen capabilities to any Flash application coded for this feature, provided it is viewed through this updated version of the Flash Player (version 9.0.18.60 or greater, to be exact). This Flash Player is a beta version that also targets some Linux operating systems.

The new full-screen feature allows Flash content to take over a user's entire screen, filling more than just the browser window, even if the browser window wasn't set to full screen by the user. This makes for a very immersive, TV-like experience, especially when used to display video content. The latest ActionScript 3.0 based version of the FLV Playback component (as shipped with flash CS3) also supports this feature.

Despite this built-in full-screen support, my previous warnings in regards to CPU usage still apply. I've noticed an increase of CPU usage of up to 100% on my desktop PC (up from 20% CPU usage to 40%) when I use the full-screen feature. While 40% CPU usage is acceptable in some circumstances it could have a detrimental effect on older machines. I suspect that this will become less of an issue as CPU power increases among end users and Adobe's technologies are further enhanced. I also haven't tested the feature in ActionScript 3, which may also have a positive effect on CPU usage.

You may have come across a similar feature on Google Video or Youtube where a user can choose a full-screen option. We won't go as far as full screen, but the underlying logic can easily be repurposed in this way if needed.

The usual approach to scale a Flash video (or more precisely, scale the video object inside the SWF movie) is to deploy a piece of code called a Stage Listener. This code reacts (or "listens") to any changes in the SWF size and then recalculates sizes and, if necessary, positions of objects like the video display object, play button, pause button and other controls within the SWF.

So, for example, suppose your SWF was embedded into your HTML page at a size of 100% by 100% (and therefore takes up as much space as it can). When a user resizes the browser window, the Stage Listener can detect these changes and react to them. How it reacts depends on your application, which will become clearer as you work through this next example.

Adding the Stage Listener

To add the Stage Listener, follow these steps:

1. Open the file flv_listener.fla in Flash. It can be found among the sample files for Chapter 15.

   Note that the video_mc MovieClip is positioned at point 0,0 and resized to precisely match Stage size. This will simplify this example by keeping the resizing logic as simple as possible. Adding other elements to this movie should become a lot easier once you've mastered the basics. My goal for this chapter is to explain the relationship between the SWF movie's size, the space it is allocated on the HTML page and the logic that resizes the video_mc MovieClip and the video that it contains.

2. Highlight frame 1 of the actions layer and choose Window > Actions from the menu bar. The Actions panel appears.

3. At around line 11 add the following code:

   ```
   // Stage aligned top left
   Stage.align = "TL";
   // Prevent stage from scaling with the browser window.
   Stage.scaleMode = "noScale";
   ```

   These two lines (plus comments) will align the SWF inside the Flash Player or browser. TL indicates that we want to orient towards the top left corner. This is important when it comes to resizing and repositioning objects as they are scaled from their top left corner.

   A scaleMode of noScale means that the size of the content is fixed and that it remains unchanged even as the size of the Flash Player window (or browser window) changes. Using this feature allows us to manage the sizing inside the Stage

Listener code that is about to be added. Without it, the Flash Player would auto-matically scale the content according to the Publish Settings applied to the FLA.

4. Scroll down to around line 29 and under `ns.play(videofile);` add the following code:

```
var sizeListener:Object = new Object();
sizeListener.onResize = function()
{
    video_mc._width = Stage.width;
    video_mc._height = Stage.height;
}
Stage.addListener(sizeListener);
sizeListener.onResize();
```

This code creates an object named `sizeListener` to which we add a callback function `onResize`. This object is added as a listener to the Stage, a top-level class that we can access anywhere in our code.

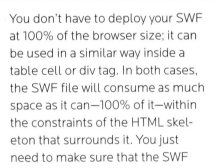

Author's Tip

You don't have to deploy your SWF at 100% of the browser size; it can be used in a similar way inside a table cell or div tag. In both cases, the SWF file will consume as much space as it can—100% of it—within the constraints of the HTML skel-eton that surrounds it. You just need to make sure that the SWF is embedded at 100% and not at a fixed size.

It doesn't take much imagination to see the potential for more features here; for example, the resizing of a div could affect the Flash con-tent size, effectively opening the door to manipulating the video player size on the fly. This is easily achieved through the help of some JavaScript.

What occurs inside the `onResize` function is the inter-esting part and is the nuts and bolts of this applica-tion. Here, the video_mc's size is set to the Stage's current size (note that there is no underscore when we access `Stage.width` or `Stage.height`), effectively resizing it to the same size as the Stage.

The last line invokes the `onResize` function once, in-dependent of an actual resize action by the user. We do this in order to force a resize to the initial browser or Flash Player size upon start-up—otherwise our video_mc movie may remain in its initial 320×240 size until the user decides to resize the browser, which may never happen.

To see this resize functionality in action, we need to make one more change to our document's Publish Settings.

5. Choose File > Publish Settings from the menu bar to open the Publish Settings dialogue.

6. Click the Formats tab. Make sure that only Flash and HTML are checked, as seen in **Figure 15-9**.

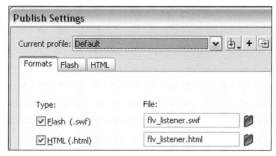

Figure 15-9
The selected Formats tab.

7. Choose the HTML tab and from the Dimensions drop-down menu choose Percent. For Width and Height enter 100, as shown in **Figure 15-10**.

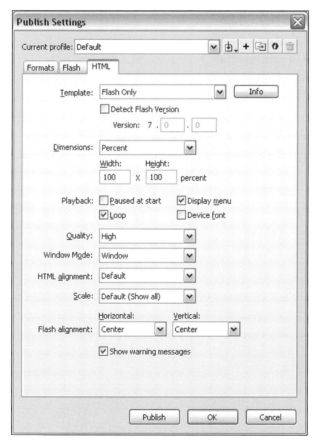

Figure 15-10
The selected HTML tab with dimensions set at 100%.

8. Click OK. You are now ready to publish the movie and test it inside an HTML wrapper.

9. Choose File > Publish Preview > Default (HTML) from the menu bar.

Your default browser will open and the newly generated flv_listener.html will appear. It includes the published SWF file flv_listener.swf, which will more or less fill the browser window.

Try resizing the browser window to see how the Flash content reacts. As expected, the Flash movie will retain the size of the browser window, following its exact dimensions. Note how the video's aspect ratio gets distorted, as there isn't any logic present to take care of that.

Why not try adding this functionality as an exercise? Here are some tips outlining the necessary steps:

- capture the video's initial display size before running the Stage Listener for the first time

- use the captured values to determine the video's aspect ratio

- apply the aspect ratio to your calculations inside the Stage Listener's onResize function.

The FLV file's metadata may also help you when it comes to gathering information about an FLV video file and the next chapter will cover just that.

Author's Tip

You can also implement a similar approach to on-the-fly resizing if your application uses the FLV Playback component (as opposed to a pure ActionScript-based implementation). The main difference is that you may not set the component's width and height directly when using the component; instead you need to use the `setSize` method. For an FLV Playback component with an instance name of myplayer this would look as follows:

```
myplayer.setSize(Stage.width,
Stage.height-45);
```

You would add this code to the onResize handler and 45 pixels are subtracted from the Stage's height to allow space for the component skin.

Processing FLV Metadata

You couldn't be blamed if the term FLV metadata sounded a bit dry to you, but it is in fact a fairly easy yet important topic. Metadata, in general, is described as data about data, and in this case it is data about video data: the FLV video itself. Metadata is usually added to the video file during encoding, but can be added later, and can contain information identifying:

- video duration

- width and height

- video data rate

- audio data rate

- frame rate

- and other properties.

You can normally count on width, height and duration being included in the metadata, though some older versions of Flash encoding tools add the wrong values. This fact doesn't make life easier, so if in doubt you should re-inject the metadata using one of the tools mentioned below.

The Importance of Metadata

Many Flash video players and components rely on the correct metadata to lay themselves out on screen. To accomplish this task successfully, they must process the width and height properties supplied in the metadata.

Similarly, a scrub bar can only function correctly if the duration value is correct. In many cases, the duration value embedded in FLV metadata approximates the actual duration but is not exact. In other words, it will not always match the value of the NetStream.time property when the playhead is at the end of the video stream.

You can add metadata to the FLV file during encoding or at a later stage. In most cases, metadata won't be a concern, since it's added automatically by tools like On2's Flix Pro, Sorenson Squeeze or the Adobe Flash Video Encoder. However, in some cases, the FLV's metadata

Author's Tip

When you deploy videos via Flash Media Server, you have another option for obtaining duration data. Specifically, you can request duration from the server before playback starts.

However, when deploying progressive Flash video, the correct duration metadata must be present. Otherwise, the scrub controls may not function correctly or other timing-related issues may pop up.

may be missing or incomplete. It is then advisable to inject the necessary metadata using freely available tools that are built for this particular job.

FLVMDI

My personal favorite is called FLVMDI, which stands for FLV MetaData Injector and you can find at *http://www.buraks.com/flvmdi*. I find it easy to use and particularly like the variety of command-line options. A GUI version is also available. FLVMDI is a product of the Manitu Group, the same people who brought us Captionate (*http://www.buraks.com/captionate/*).

FLVMDI lets you add your own custom metadata information, such as author information, to FLV files, and offers batch processing functions that can update a folder full of FLV videos in a matter of seconds. In addition to this, it analyzes the FLV file, determines its video properties and adds all the standard metadata properties to your video. FLVMDI is a Windows executable.

FLVTool2

Another popular metadata injector is FLVTool2 (*http://inlet-media.de/flvtool2*), which is open source and available for Windows, Linux and Mac OSX, and supports a similar feature set as FLVMDI.

Both tools will process an existing FLV file, examine its structure and inner working and write this information back into the file. You can also use these tools to generate XML files containing the metadata information, which can be handy when you need access to this data outside of Flash.

Reading and Processing FLV Metadata in Flash

If you are using a component like the FLV Playback component, then you usually don't have to worry about metadata processing yourself—the component will handle all this for you. It can, however, be handy to know how to catch and process the onMetaData event in Action-Script, especially if you are building your own custom player or component.

The onMetaData event fires automatically when the Flash Player receives descriptive information embedded in the FLV file. All you need to do is to define the onMetaData() handler for the NetStream object. This handler will be triggered after a call to the NetStream.play() method, but before playback has actually started.

Example

I know this must be getting really boring by now, but we will once again use our (by now well-known) player from Chapter 11 as a starting point to add the onMetaData handler.

1. Open the file metadata.fla in Flash Professional 8 or Flash CS3. One significant difference between this player and the one from Chapter 11 is the fact that the video_mc movie on Stage is sized to 160 by 120 pixels. This is much smaller than the actual size of the video we are about to play. In this example you will use the onMetaData event to resize the video_mc before playback begins.

2. Highlight frame 1 of the actions layer and choose Window > Actions from the menu bar to open the Actions panel if it is not already showing.

3. At around line 20 and just after this line

    ```
    var ns:NetStream = new NetStream( nc );
    ```

    insert the following code:

    ```
    ns.onMetaData = function(info:Object)
    {
        for (var i:String in info)
        {
            trace(i + " = " + info[i]);
        }
        video_mc._width = info.width;
        video_mc._height = info.height;
    };
    ```

    This code adds the onMetaData handler to the NetStream instance and firstly traces out all the metadata information available in the file. The functionality providing the resize action is added by the last two lines:

    ```
    video_mc._width = info.width;
    video_mc._height = info.height;
    ```

    Here, the video_mc's width and height is set to the values supplied by the metadata. Let's test the movie to see the effect this has on the video display.

4. Choose Control > Test Movie from the menu bar. You will notice that, once the movie starts playing, the video_mc MovieClip on Stage is immediately resized to the values supplied by the FLV's metadata. You will also see traces in the Output window that show the following:

```
canSeekToEnd = true

audiocodecid = 2

audiodelay = 0.038

audiodatarate = 128

videocodecid = 4

framerate = 14.9699859619141

videodatarate = 700

height = 230

width = 320

duration = 29.72
```

This is all the metadata information contained in this FLV. The `videocodecid` value specifies the video codec used. Currently I am aware of the following values and their associated codecs:

```
2: Sorenson H.263
3: Screen Video
4: On2 VP6
5: On2 VP6 with Transparency.
```

Other codecs may be added in future versions of Flash and the Flash Player.

Statistics and Reporting on Progressive FLV Delivery

If you stream your FLV videos via the Flash Media Server, you can access live playback statistics via the server's management console. You will learn more about this in Chapters 16 to 18. However, Progressively downloaded—as opposed to streamed—Flash video files (FLV) are handled by web servers like any other media file; they are served up upon request by a client, in this case the browser with embedded SWF. Because FLV is a fairly young format, you may have to add the necessary MIME type to your web server's configuration, which tells it how to handle the file and serve it appropriately. The required MIME type that you need to add is video/x-flv with a file extension of .flv.

Depending upon the configuration of your web server, you may be able to gather various kinds of statistics about the popularity of your FLV videos. A web server logs requests and file accesses alongside certain anonymous user information. These details may contain:

- the IP address of the computer that is requesting the FLV
- the duration of the page view that contains the FLV
- the type of web browser that received the FLV, among others.

There are a multitude of programs on the market that can process web-server log files. Some are free and a few that come to mind include:

- Analog (*http://www.analog.cx*)

- Webalizer (*http://www.mrunix.net/webalizer/*)

- Google Analytics, formerly Urchin (*http://www.google.com/analytics*)

- Weblog Expert (*http://www.weblogexpert.com*).

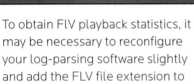

Author's Tip

To obtain FLV playback statistics, it may be necessary to reconfigure your log-parsing software slightly and add the FLV file extension to the recognized list of download-able files. Otherwise, it may be possible that, while present in the actual text logs, the information about FLV files gets lost in the generated reports—the log parser will ignore it unless told otherwise.

But there are dozens of others out there and chances are that you have already used one. The one thing to remember is that it is easy to track performance of your FLV videos once they are deployed.

Should you wish to more precisely track the playback of your videos, then this, of course, is also possible. There are many different ways to achieve this, such as timed requests to a so-called clear GIF tracking image to which you pass additional parameters. Requests for this image will once again show up in your web-server log files and can be processed from there. For more information on this kind of tracking method check *http://en.wikipedia.org/wiki/Web_bug*.

Other, more Flash-specific, tracking methods may include remoting calls that write tracking data directly to a database or calls to any application server, which again can log this information either to a text file or to a database. The possibilities in this area are truly endless and it is entirely possible to develop a video player in Flash that tracks all user interactions such as play, pause, volume changes, restarts and time watched. In fact, Flash is the ideal platform for such applications and similar tracking functionality has been used in banner ads for a long time.

Conclusion

After you've read this chapter, I hope you appreciate the creative possibilities offered by Flash video. Like no other video technology, it allows you to break out of the rectangle and add author-time as well as run-time effects to your applications, as the sections on filter effects and BitmapData have demonstrated. Rest assured that I was barely able to scratch the surface here. If you need some more inspiration, then have a search around the Internet, maybe starting at Adobe's Flash Video Gallery, which can be found at *www.adobe.com/products/flash/flashpro/video/gallery/*.

You have also enhanced your knowledge of alpha channel video by adding interactivity to an FLV file with alpha channel and explored FLV metadata and reporting techniques.

The knowledge you have gained in this and previous chapters should give a good foundation for the next section of the book, which is devoted to Flash Media Server, its installation, capabilities and features.

CHAPTER 16

Introduction to Flash Media Server

When people talk about Flash video, they quite often mention Flash Media Server in the same breath, and for a reason. At the time of this writing, Flash Media Server is the only production-ready platform that can stream FLV video files (as opposed to serve them progressively).

In this chapter, I will introduce you to Flash Media Server, its history, licensing options and capabilities. I will walk you through a typical installation routine and give you an overview of the server's folder structure, pointing out common pitfalls. In the last section you will learn how to connect to the server using Adobe's efficient RTMP protocol.

In order, the main topics covered are:

- An overview of Flash Media Server
- Installing Flash Media Server in Windows
- Examining the Server's folder structure and creating an application
- Server connection tips and examples.

ALERT

This chapter uses Adobe Flash CS3 Professional (or Adobe Flash Professional 8) as well as Flash Media Server. To follow along with the examples, which I recommend, you will need a copy of both programs installed on your computer. Should you not own a copy, note that Adobe offers a free 30-day trial version of both Flash and Flash Media Server on its website. I will detail the installation of Flash Media Server in this chapter.

Also, note that you can find the files referred to and used in this chapter, including completed skins, at *www.flashvideobook.com*. Consider downloading these files now, so they'll be available once I start referring to them.

Overview of Flash Media Server

Flash Media Server started life in 2002 as the Macromedia Flash Communication Server MX 1.0. Version 1.5 soon followed in early 2003 and 1.5.2 was released in May, 2004. The next major release was in November, 2005, where Macromedia changed the name to Macromedia Flash Media Server 2.

Soon thereafter, Adobe completed its takeover of Macromedia, though the server is still called the Macromedia Flash Media Server 2, which often is abbreviated to FMS2 or simply FMS. Note that, at the time of this writing, FMS still installs under Macromedia's brand, accounting for the multiple mentions of Macromedia in this chapter.

The version number is often omitted and I will follow this tradition for the remainder of the book. So when I talk about Flash Media Server or FMS I am actually referring to Flash Media Server 2.

So, why the name change? That's a tricky question, as the main features haven't really changed from Flash Communication Server to Flash Media Server. I put the name change down to a refocusing as well as a marketing exercise; Flash video was heating up as a technology and Macromedia may have found the term "communication server" misleading for potential customers.

Macromedia also had its own communication platform in the form of Breeze (recently rebranded to Adobe Connect), which incidentally is built on top of Flash Media Server, and clearly tried to focus the Flash platform more towards media delivery than communications. But make no mistake—Flash Media Server still contains all the features of Flash Communication Server, and more.

In a nutshell, FMS enables a Flash application in the form of a SWF file to send or receive live or on-demand video and audio content as well as other data, such as text.

The SWF is uploaded and served via a web server (FMS does not serve SWF or HTML files) and sometimes, especially in a development environment, the web server may reside on the same machine as FMS. In most cases, however, the FMS machine is a separate, physical machine to the web server.

I like to compare this set-up to a database server such as MS SQL or MySQL, which does not need to be present on the same physical machine as the web server. The database server can be located halfway around the world, yet your database connection will still work reliably.

This is very similar to how FMS operates—a SWF will make a connection to FMS after it is executed inside the user's browser. The SWF doesn't care where it was being served from, as long as the RTMP connection string inside the SWF points to the right place, it will attempt to connect to FMS. If this connection succeeds, then the application can use FMS's features.

Capabilities

Outside the obvious capabilities such as on-demand streaming delivery of FLV video files, the server offers an array of other features, including:

- Live video, audio and data communications, including video conferencing
- Enhanced seeking support
- Clustering and failover support
- Audio and video recording
- MP3 streaming
- Total scriptability through ActionScript
- SSL support
- Origin/Edge deployment.

I will cover many of these features in more detail later in the book.

Examples

One of FMS's unique capabilities is the ability to allow web users to broadcast audio and video via their webcam and microphone, right from within their browser. Several sites and services that leverage these features have recently appeared, with one of the more high-profile examples being Userplane, now part of AOL.

Countless dating sites now also leverage Flash Media Server to enable their communities to create video profiles, text chats or even live AV chatrooms. It doesn't take much imagination to see why the adult market has also shown an interest in this technology.

Odeo is another example of a service that allows its users to create instant podcasts by recording audio through their Odeo Studio application, shown in **Figure 16-1**.

Figure 16-1
Odeo Studio is Odeo's online audio recorder.

Adobe Connect (formerly Breeze) is arguably the most high-profile application running on Flash Media Server architecture. It's a feature-rich service delivered right inside the browser via a special version of the Flash Player. **Figure 16-2** shows a screenshot of the product, still sporting its Macromedia branding.

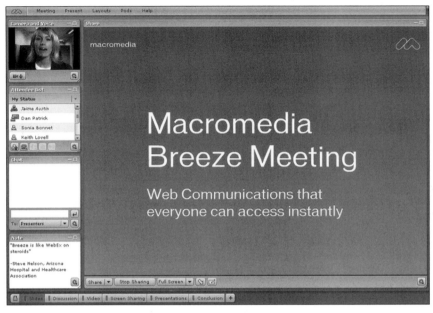

Figure 16-2
A Breeze Meeting room.

Editions and Pricing

Flash Media Server is configured by a license file. Depending on the license type, the server will run with more or less capacity, whereby capacity is measured (and limited) in terms of concurrent connections and bandwidth throughput. Connections effectively mean number of concurrent users, as in most set-ups each user will use one connection, for example to play a video file. The different capacity limits are offered in four editions of Flash Media Server:

- **Developer Edition** – The free Developer Edition allows 10 connections with un-limited bandwidth throughput. From Flash Media 2.0.3 onwards, you can use the Developer Edition for commercial projects and it is no longer a mere trial edition.

- **Professional Edition** – The Professional Edition targets small- to medium-sized deployments and offers a configurable capacity limit, which can be applied via one of three interchangeable license profiles, which I describe below. The Professional Edition retails for USD $4,500.

- **Origin Edition** – The Origin Edition is aimed at large deployments and enter-prise-level applications and forms part of an Origin/Edge architecture, requiring one or more Edge Editions. A single Origin license supports 5,000 concurrent connections. Pricing is available on request and will approximate several tens of thousands of dollars for a complete Origin/Edge network.

- **Edge Edition** – The Edge Edition cannot be used on its own but must be tied to an Origin server. An Edge Edition does not have any connection limits as the Origin Edition, to which a user ultimately connects, is already limited in capacity. Every Edge server requires its own license and it resides on a separate physical machine to the Origin.

Inside the industry

When Macromedia released the initial version of FMS, there was an outcry in the developer community because new low limits on concurrent connections dramatically boosted pricing for high-connection/low-bandwidth type applications. In an unprecedented move and in reaction to community feedback, Macromedia changed the licensing terms for the Professional Edition not long after the release of Flash Media Server 2. It was decided that a more varied usage pattern needed to be supported through additional license profiles.

Professional Edition Profiles

Adobe now offers three license profiles for the Professional Edition. When you purchase a Professional Edition you are able to switch from one profile to another at any time, at no extra cost. The profiles are:

- **Profile 1** – Allows a maximum of 150 concurrent connections at unlimited bandwidth throughput. This profile facilitates a high-bandwidth, low-connection set up, which is most common when streaming large video files.

- **Profile 2** – Allows for up to 1,000 concurrent connections up to a maximum bandwidth throughput of 40 Mbps. This profile balances connections and bandwidth more evenly and allows for a higher number of potentially lower-bandwidth streams to be served.

- **Profile 3** – Allows for up to 2,500 concurrent connections at a maximum bandwidth throughout of 25 Mbps. This profile is aimed largely at applications with a high connection count and low bandwidth throughput, such as multiplayer games.

Confused? Sorry, but I'm not done yet . . .

The Professional and the Origin Editions can also be stacked, meaning that you can increase the connections and bandwidth limits by purchasing additional licenses. Note, however, that only one license profile can be stacked at any one time, meaning that you cannot mix and match Profile 1 with Profile 3 to achieve over 2,500 connections at unlimited throughput. If you want to stack licenses, then each license must be configured to use the same profile.

Phew, that's it in a nutshell—a big nutshell.

It's no secret that Adobe was heavily criticized for its FMS licensing terms (though since Macromedia reportedly cost 3.4 billion, perhaps the pricing is understandable). At $4,500 for a Professional License, it is out of reach for many smaller companies and Flash Media Server licensing has had a negative effect on Flash video adoption (especially streaming Flash video), which is still perceived as being more expensive when compared to other technologies.

Of course, server licensing costs are only one part of the equation, as Flash Media Server offers more than just streaming video. On the flipside, though not everyone leverages these additional features, everyone must pay for them as there is no streaming-only Edition.

One way to outsource any licensing costs to a third party is the delivery of streaming Flash video via a CDN.

Limitations of CDN Delivery

Many Content Delivery Networks (CDN) offer Flash video streaming services, but do not allow users to upload server-side code, thereby limiting the server's capabilities to some extent. However, this limitation is understandable, as the type of nonstreaming applications that developers can implement using Flash Media Server (such as text chats, video recordings, etc.) are not well suited for a distributed environment. If you need such applications, you should either host FMS yourself or choose from one of the many Flash Media Server hosting providers. A list of providers can be found on my website at *http://www.flashcomguru.com/ articles/hosts.cfm*.

It remains to be seen what Flash Media Server 3 (which is currently under development) will bring to the table in terms of pricing, licensing and editions. A drop in the overall cost for streaming Flash video would be a positive development.

Installing Flash Media Server

Flash Media Server is available for both Windows and Linux operating systems, while applications that leverage FMS can be developed on any platform that produces SWF files, the major ones being Windows and Macintosh.

Operating Systems

According to the system requirements, FMS will run on Windows 2000 Server and Windows 2003 Server (Standard Edition), while on Linux you must run either Red Hat Enterprise 3 or 4. I can confirm, however, that the server will very happily run on Windows XP (Home and Pro) and can also be installed on other Linux flavors. However, in both cases Adobe will not provide installation support.

On the Linux front, I've heard of successful deployments on SuSE, Debian, Gentoo, Fedora and others. The key here is to use the −platformWarnOnly flag during install, circumventing the OS check. Note that there are two libraries needed by FMS that are not always included in certain Linux distributions (libssl.so.4 and libcrypto.so.4), and others may be missing as well, depending upon your flavor of Linux. As long as you know that a missing library may prevent the server from running you should be able to recognize and fix the problem fairly easily. If you get stuck, try a Google search for "platformwarnonly" and the Linux flavor you're installing on, and you should find some helpful results.

If in doubt, I recommend you stick to Red Hat Enterprise 3 or 4 as those are the Linux distributions that are officially supported.

Hardware
In terms of hardware, it's a simple case of the bigger the better. Adobe lists a 3.2-GHz Pentium 4 with 1 GB as a requirement but you can get away with a lower specification if you expect fairly low traffic. When serving videos, the CPU of the server can often be a limiting factor, so you may want to consider a beefy set-up to avoid being limited by your hardware. After all, it would be regrettable if CPU limitations prevented you from distributing all the streams you're paid for.

Installation on Windows
I will describe installing FMS on Windows because most readers will have access to a Windows machine to follow along with the lesson. For Linux users, note that all server configuration options are identical on Windows and Linux once the server is up and running.

Let's review the installation process and initial configuration options. Installing FMS is straightforward and requires the following steps:

1. Download the installer from Adobe.com. The Free Developer Edition is as functional as the Professional Edition but has a concurrent connection limit of 10. At the time of writing, the latest available version of Flash Media Server is 2.0.3.

2. Double click the Installer to run it. The Welcome screen appears. Click Next, and read and accept the license agreement.

3. The admin set-up dialogue appears, as shown in **Figure 16-3**. Type a username and password, which you'll also use later to administer, monitor and debug the server. Click Next when complete.

   A bit of background information: the values here will be written to the fms.ini file that resides in the /conf subdirectory within the installation directory. Many other values in fms.ini are also used across a variety of XML configuration files and the server username and password are destined for a file named Users.xml. Fms.ini offers one centralized place to make most important configuration changes, if required.

4. The port configuration dialogue appears. You should leave the default ports of 1935 for the main server port and 1111 for the admin port untouched. However, you should add additional ports to the server.

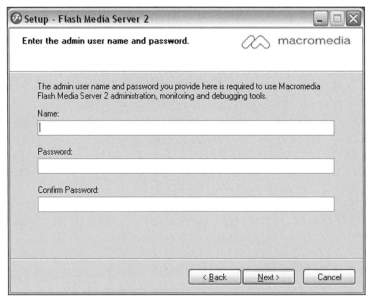

Figure 16-3
Admin username and password dialogue.

For example, add port 80 and 443 to achieve maximum reach to users behind firewalls, as some firewalls may block traffic on port 1935. You can see my final port settings in **Figure 16-4**.

Remember that port 80 is usually used for http web traffic while port 443 is the SSL port. Both ports are often open on most firewalls to pass web traffic through, and are therefore ideally suited for use with FMS.

However, if you already have other services running on either port 80 or 443 then stick to port 1935 for now. Click Next to continue.

5. You can now select an installation location. I usually accept the default location, which on my system is C:\Program Files\Macromedia\Flash Media Server 2 as seen in **Figure 16-5**. After entering the location, click Next to continue.

6. Select a Start Menu Folder and click Next.

7. You can now review your configuration options, as shown in **Figure 16-6**. If acceptable, click Install to install the server or click Back to make any required changes. This is also the last opportunity to abort the install process.

Figure 16-4
Server and admin ports are configured.

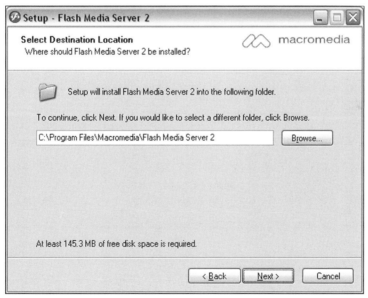

Figure 16-5
The Select Destination Location dialogue.

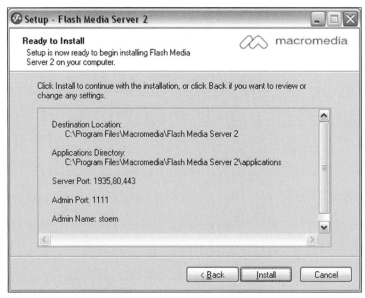

Figure 16-6
Review your installation settings on this dialogue.

8. Installation can take a few minutes. Once complete, you'll see the dialogue shown in **Figure 16-7**.

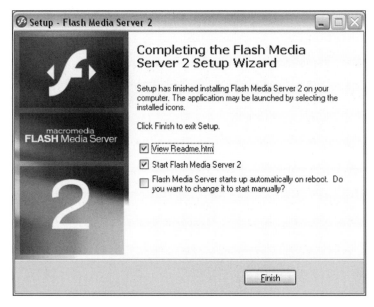

Figure 16-7
This dialogue indicates that the installation is complete.

You can now choose to start the server right away, view the Readme file and disable automatic start-up. This can be useful if you are running Flash Media Server in a development environment where it is used intermittently. In a production environment, you should make sure that the option for manual start-up remains unchecked. Click Finish when you are done.

Congratulations! You have successfully installed Flash Media Server. Now let's verify the installation.

Verifying the Installation

To verify that the server is up and running, you can check Windows' Services panel, which is available at Start > Control Panel > Administrative Tools > Services. The two required services are Flash Media Administration Server and Flash Media Server (FMS). If the Status of both of these services is not Started, then select each service in turn and then press the Start button. Alternatively, right click on each service name and choose Start. Windows will attempt to start the service, and should succeed.

 ALERT There are many software programs that can interfere with Flash Media Server functionality, resulting in errors messages and failed connection attempts, rendering the server unusable. One such piece of software is NetLimiter but I've also encountered problems with Cingular's wireless networking software, certain Antivirus software packages (though McAfee VirusScan works fine with FMS) and other products that intercept system calls and interfere with Flash Media Server's socket actions.

The only way to fix this problem is to uninstall the software in question, as simply disabling it will usually not help. Note that this only applies if FMS is installed on the same machine as the software in question. You may run any such software on your machine if you use FMS on a remote server. However, if you install FMS locally and are also running NetLimiter, for example, then FMS will not work properly.

Flash Media Server also ships with a Management Console that you can use to monitor, administer and configure certain aspects of the server. To access Management Console, choose Start > All Programs > Macromedia > Flash Media Server 2 > Management Console. The Management Console (as shown in **Figure 16-8**) will open in your default browser.

The Management Console is a Flash application that uses Flash Media Server's Admin API to connect to and administer the server. Let's have a quick look at its capabilities.

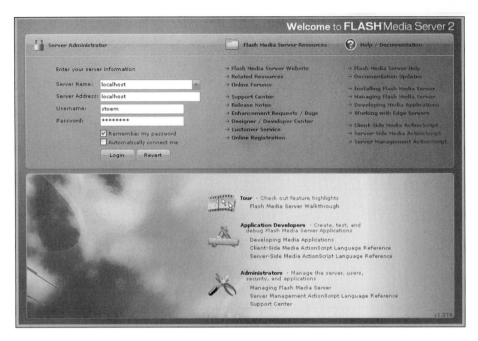

Figure 16-8
Flash Media Server Management Console's login screen.

Using the Management Console
Before you can administer the server, you must log on using your server admin username and password.

1. At the login prompt, enter a server name (this can be any descriptive name), server address (this can be localhost if FMS is installed locally, otherwise specify an IP or domain name) and your username and password.

2. Click Login. The interface has three main areas to administer applications, users and the server itself (or, indeed, multiple servers).

3. Have a look around the different sections to familiarize yourself with the interface. The console also features links to Help content.

Though we look at some Management Console functions below, covering all options goes beyond our scope. I recommend you consult the Flash Media Server documentation for help on its features and capabilities.

Examining the Server's Folder Structure
The following section is critical, as there is a direct relationship between Flash Media Server's folder structure and application logic, including locations in which your FLV videos will be stored. Placing your FLV files in the right location to make them available for streaming is one of the most common stumbling blocks for new users and even experienced users often struggle with this.

RTMP Connections

Connections to Flash Media Server are made using a protocol called RTMP, which stands for Real Time Messaging Protocol. It is a proprietary protocol developed by Macromedia (now Adobe). To send or receive any data to and from Flash Media Server, you must first connect to it using an RTMP connection string, similar to the way you use http to connect to a web server and request a web page.

RTMP connections are persistent for the duration of a session, so once you connect you can send and receive data without having to reconnect. Likewise, the server can send data to you without you (the client) having to request it. This allows for powerful two-way communications.

A connection string for Flash Media Server always starts with rtmp, which specifies the protocol, followed by the server address and optional port, an application name and an optional application instance name, as shown here:

RTMP connection string syntax:
rtmp://server[:port]/application/[instance]

RTMP connection string example:
rtmp://flashcom.mysite.com/videoplayer/myinstance

With this as background, let's learn more about the relationship between connection strings and application directories.

The Applications Directory

The applications directory can be described as the root of the server. It's where applications are created and the associated assets, including FLV videos, are commonly placed. The name of each application will directly affect the connection string you will use to connect to the server, and it is therefore important to understand this relationship.

On a Windows server, the default location for your applications directory is usually C:\Program Files\Macromedia\Flash Media Server 2\applications, or, more generally speaking, a folder by the name of applications within your chosen installation directory. Under Linux, you can typically find the installation directory at /opt/macromedia/fms/. You can see a screenshot of my applications directory in **Figure 16-9**.

Creating an Application

To accomplish anything with FMS, you need to create an application, which you do by creating a new folder inside your server's applications directory. Each new folder may optionally contain a server side ActionScript file, the code that is executed depending on certain conditions such as application start-up, client connections or logoff.

The server side files (file extension .asc) expose functionalities like bandwidth detection and stream length requests to your Flash video player, some of which we will cover in a later chapter. The FLV Playback component requires its own special server side ActionScript file, which you must deploy before you can use the component in conjunction with FMS. Again, I will cover this later in the book.

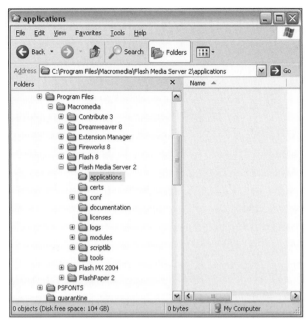

Figure 16-9
Flash Media Server's applications directory is where applications are created (but no web facing files such as SWF or HTML are deployed here).

I have created a new application called streamvideo by creating a folder of the same name inside the applications directory, as you can see in **Figure 16-10**. You will now do the same.

1. Navigate into the applications directory and choose File > New > Folder to create a new directory and name it streamvideo. This creates a new application.

2. Open up the Management Console again and log on to the server using your server details.

3. Choose View Applications.

4. Click the New Instance . . . drop-down menu to expand it. You should now see the streamvideo application.

5. Press Enter to start the application. **Figure 16-11** shows the application running on my server.

Well done—you just created and started your first application using the Management Console. Obviously, this was merely a simple exercise to show how you can start applications from the console. Usually an application starts automatically when a user connects, so there is no need to start applications from here. Instead, the Management Console is usually used to debug an application when there are problems.

I hope you can see how the creation of a folder inside the applications directory effectively creates an application on the server. You will learn how to connect to an application from within a Flash application later in the chapter.

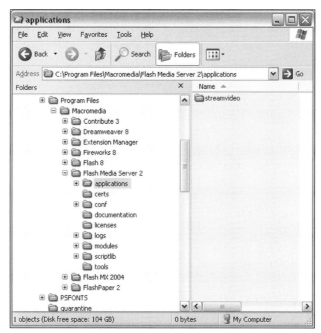

Figure 16-10
I've created an application called streamvideo.

Figure 16-11
The Management Console with the loaded streamvideo application.

Application Instances

Notice that the application you loaded into the Management Console is actually loading up with an instance name of _definst_.

ALERT FMS will automatically create application instances for you if you do not specify them in the connection string. If you omit an application instance name from the RTMP string, then you are always connecting to _definst_, the default instance of your application.

Author's Tip

While application instances are separated by default and cannot access each other's data, there are ways to connect them. For example, in a chat application, you could allow users to move from one "room" (an application instance) to another, or make it possible for the rooms to share data. For pure on-demand streaming, however, such logic is seldom necessary.

However, one requirement that you may encounter is to share video files between application instances or actual applications. There are several ways to achieve this via the server's XML configuration (one option is to use FMS's virtual directories feature), which I will outline later in this chapter.

For example, both of these connection strings will connect to the default instance _definst_:

String 1: *rtmp://flashcom.mysite.com/streamvideo/_definst_*

String 2: *rtmp://flashcom.mysite.com/streamvideo*

String 1 explicitly connects to _definst_, the default instance. String 2 omits the instance name from the connection string, which means that it too connects to _definst_, but only implicitly.

It is critical to know which instance you are connecting to, as this will affect the necessary location for your FLV videos.

By default, videos in one application instance are not available to another. This means that users who connect to *rtmp://flashcom.mysite.com/streamvideo/room1* cannot access or view videos that users connecting to *rtmp://flashcom.mysite.com/streamvideo* can. Note that *flashcom.mysite.com* is just an example domain; you should substitute it with your server's actual domain name or IP address.

To see the relationship between applications, connection strings and folder structure, have a look at **Figure 16-12**. It shows how the connection string ties in with the applications, and their respective folders, on the server. Note that I am using the server name localhost here, as my server is running on my local development machine.

In this example I have created a total of three different applications, each one of which would encapsulate a specific purpose—for example, related to a particular website. Since I didn't specify any application instances, all three RTMP strings will connect to *_definst_*.

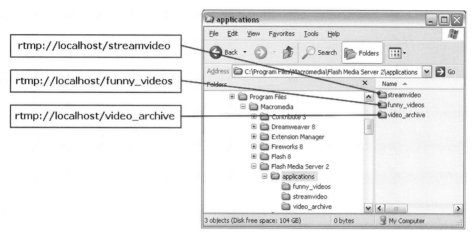

Figure 16-12
RTMP connection strings and their relationship to the application folder structure. All three RTMP strings are in fact connecting to _definst_.

Where to Place Your FLV Files

You have now learned how to reflect application names (and folder locations) in RTMP strings. Now, I will explain how application instances determine where you must store associated FLV files.

By default, you must store FLV files in a folder named streams inside the application's folder, so for the streamvideo application, the folder structure would be /streamvideo/streams.

But, you don't place your files directly into this folder. Instead, you must create a subfolder named after the instance that you are connecting to. For the default instance, name this folder _definst_.

Continuing with our streamvideo application example, to make videos available to users who connect using the default instance (for example, using the connection string *rtmp://localhost/streamvideo*) you must place the FLV files into the /streamvideo/streams/ _definst_ folder.

Similarly, to make videos available to users connecting to an instance of room1 (using the connection string rtmp://localhost/streamvideo/room1) place the FLVs into a subfolder named room1, again within the streams folder. **Figure 16-13** shows three video files that will be available to any clients connecting to *rtmp://localhost/streamvideo* (or *rtmp://localhost/ streamvideo/_definst_*).

You will learn to stream Flash video files via Flash Media Server in the next chapter, and the relationship between instances and FLV file locations should become even clearer then. But enough with the theory—let's take a closer look at how to establish a connection to the server.

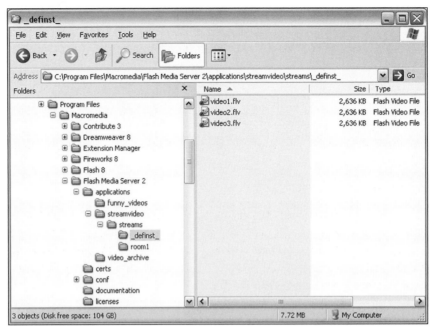

Figure 16-13
The video files shown here are placed to be accessed by streamvideo's _definst_ application instance.

RTMP Connection Routines

As I mentioned already, RTMP stands for Real Time Messaging Protocol and it is the standard way for Flash Media Server to communicate with its connected clients. To better understand the intricacies of the server and how you connect to it, it's worthwhile examining the protocol in more detail.

This will help you ensure that viewers who wish to connect to the server to view a video will be able to do so without effort. As you know, firewalls and system security settings are getting increasingly more stringent and unless you know how to circumvent the majority of these issues you may be denying some of your users access to the video content that they wish to see.

Protocols and Ports

You may remember that Flash Media Server prompted you during install to enter the ports on which to run the server. You may have left the port settings at the standard port of 1935 or you may have added additional ports, such as 80 and 443, as I suggested.

To ensure maximum availability, I recommend that you always add these ports if your server is a production server. I will presume for the rest of this chapter that the server you are configuring is indeed a production server, as only production servers have a need for high availability and accessibility.

The main reason to add ports 80 and 443 to the server's configuration is that the Flash Player (from version 6.0.65.0 or later) will attempt to connect to these ports should the default port of 1935 not be reachable, as when a firewall blocks web traffic on ports other than port 80 or 443, the standard http and https ports. Nonstandard ports such as 1935 are often blocked on corporate firewalls and having alternative back-up ports helps ensure a high availability of your server.

Standard RTMP Connections

To allow the Flash Player to make several connection attempts, you must use the following syntax when attempting a connection:

rtmp://server/application/[instance]

This tells the Flash Player to use standard RTMP on up to three ports; 1935, 80 and 443. A connection on port 443 is only attempted if port 1935 fails and port 80 is only attempted if ports 1935 and 443 fails. Finally (if all RTMP attempts fail), the Player will also attempt a tunneled connection on port 80 (more on tunneling in the next section). Specifying an application instance name is, as always, optional.

So the automatic connection sequence carried out behind the scenes by the Flash Player when trying to connect to

rtmp://server/application/[instance]

is as follows (note the protocols and ports):

rtmp://server:1935/application/[instance]

rtmp://server:443/application/[instance]

rtmp://server:80/application/[instance]

rtmpt://server:80/application/[instance]

In contrast, specifying a port is a signal to the Flash Player that prevents it from automatically attempting connections on other ports should the specified port fail. For example, this connection string would only result in a single connection attempt on port 1935:

rtmp://server:1935/application/[instance]

Tunneled Connections

While the aforementioned port rollover sequence ensures a high success rate for server connections, you can use another technique to boost this figure to close to 100%. Some firewalls not only block certain ports but also detect what type of traffic is sent over those ports. These firewalls only expect to see HTTP traffic passing through (or HTTPS traffic on port 443) and will block any other type of traffic, such as RTMP.

To work around these very tight firewalls, Flash Media Server uses a feature called HTTP tunneling, which uses the HTTP protocol to send RTMP data, effectively wrapping the RTMP packets into HTTP or HTTPS.

RTMP Tunneling (RTMPT) can also circumvent connection problems caused by certain HTTP proxy servers. The procedure for this is specified with RTMPT in the connection string. When deployed, the Flash Player will try an RTMPT connection on port 80 if all other attempts using RTMP fail.

To explicitly establish a tunneled connection, use this syntax:

rtmpt://server:80/application/[instance]

Secure Connections

Flash Media Server supports a third and final protocol, RTMPS, or secure RTMP. RTMPS connections (which are essentially HTTPS connections) use port 443 by default and use Secure Sockets Layer (SSL) to enable secure communications; this is often used for encrypting live broadcasts and data-only transmissions such as text chats. FMS supports incoming and outgoing SSL connections.

Here is a sample connection string to establish a secure connection to Flash Media Server:

rtmps://server/application/[instance]

To use SSL, you must configure port 443 on Flash Media Server as secure. You do this by modifying the server's Adaptor.xml file, specifying port 443 as secure by adding a minus sign in front of it. You also need to generate the required SSL certificates via a library such as OpenSSL.

That's all I can cover without going beyond the scope of this book. To learn more on this topic, I suggest you consult the Flash Media Server LiveDocs, and in particular the chapter on SSL support in Flash Media Server, part of the Managing Flash Media Server guide at *http://tinyurl.com/ylnsta*.

Connections Summary

To recap, Flash Media Server currently supports three protocols:

- RTMP (standard RTMP)
  The default protocol usually on port 1935.

- RTMPT (tunneled RTMP)
  The protocol for tunneled connections usually on 80.

- RTMPS (secure RTMP)
  The protocol for secure RTMP connections usually on port 443.

You can configure all three to run on other, nonstandard ports. As a best practice, I recommend to configure your server to run on ports 1935, 80 and 443. That way, the Flash client can roll over to port 80 or 443 if port 1935 is blocked. You can use Port 443 for secure connections, in which case FMS needs further configuration.

Note that HTTP tunneling may have a negative effect on application performance, especially with live audio and video transmissions, as all data to and from the server must be encrypted.

Connection Tips and Examples

Let's take a closer look at how to establish a connection to Flash Media Server in ActionScript. To follow along with this example, you must have access to Flash Media Server, either installed locally on your machine or on a remote server. I am assuming that the server is installed locally on a Windows OS and will use connect to localhost in the following examples.

Creating the Simpleconnect Application

Before you connect to FMS, you must create an application. To do that, follow these steps:

1. Locate your server's applications directory, which you can find inside your installation directory, which on Windows is usually C:\Program Files\Macromedia\ Flash Media Server 2.

2. Navigate into the applications directory and choose File > New > Folder to create a new directory and name it simpleconnect. **Figure 16-14** shows the directory structure on my machine. Note that my applications directory also contains three other applications that you don't need for this example.

Figure 16-14
The applications directory with the newly created simpleconnect application.

Now that you have created the simpleconnect application, let's make sure that the server is running.

3. Choose Start > Control Panel > Administrative Tools > Services from the Windows Start menu. The Services Console appears.

4. Scroll down to Flash Media Server and make sure that the Status column shows "Started". If it doesn't, click Flash Media Server to select it, then right click and choose Start from the menu.

Establishing a NetConnection

Now that Flash Media Server is up and running, you can attempt to establish a connection. To do this you need the file simple_connection.fla, which you can find among the sample files for Chapter 16, in a subfolder called connection_examples.

1. Choose File > Open from the menu bar to open the file simple_connection.fla in Flash 8 or Flash CS3.

2. Click frame 1 of the actions layer, and choose Window > Actions from the menu bar to open the Actions panel. You will see the following code.

```
var nc:NetConnection = new NetConnection();
nc.onStatus = function (info)
{
    trace(info.code);
    if (info.code == "NetConnection.Connect.Success")
{
    trace("connection successful");
}
}
nc.connect("rtmp://localhost/simpleconnect");
```

This code establishes a connection to Flash Media Server. The first line creates a NetConnection instance by the name of nc.

I then added an onStatus handler, which is a special function that gets automatically invoked when certain events occur on the NetConnection—for example, when the connection succeeds, fails or gets rejected. In this example, I am only interested in a successful connection and while I trace every possible onstatus message via this line

```
trace(info.code);
```

I only take further action when the message equals the string of NetConnection. Connect.Success. If and when that happens, I run another trace statement:

```
trace("connection successful");
```

This signifies a successful connection to Flash Media Server. In a more complex application, this would be my entry point into further application logic, such as, setting up a NetStream instance to begin streaming video (more on this in the next chapter).

3.   To see the trace statements in the Output panel, you must test the application in Flash by choosing Control > Test Movie from the menu bar.

Flash will compile the FLA to a SWF and run it inside the standalone Flash Player, and the Output panel will show the following trace statements:

```
NetConnection.Connect.Success
connection successful
```

This indicates a successful connection to the server. You might also try checking for a failed connection by stopping Flash Media Server from the Services Console and running the application again. Now, the Output panel will (after 5 to 10 seconds) display:

```
NetConnection.Connect.Failed
```

If you do test for a failed connection, you may notice that it takes several moments to receive the NetConnection.Connect.Failed statement. This is because the Flash Player will make allowances for network problems and wait a few seconds before concluding that the connection will never succeed. This leads me on to the next section and tips for establishing a connection as quickly as possible.

The Shotgun Approach

While the native port rollover of the Flash Player (when encountering a failed connection) is a great feature, it's sometimes more efficient to use a connection routine that is geared towards minimizing the time to establish a connection.

As you have seen in the previous example, the Flash Player will sometimes take a substantial amount of time before flagging a connection attempt as failed, due to the fact that it will try to connect on several ports (1935, 80, 443) using two protocols (RTMP, RTMPT), one after the other. This can be a lengthy process and some users may not wait around for the end of it.

A common workaround is to emulate Flash Player's procedures and accelerate the connection process by trying to establish multiple NetConnections on several ports and protocols in quick succession.

The Flash Player will utilize the first successful connection (to serve video, for example) and terminate the other, pending connections. This approach is very robust and widely used by many major providers. Usually the routine involves two connections, a standard RTMP connection on port 1935 and a tunneled RTMPT connection on port 80 (you can add other ports and/or protocols if needed). Between those two connections, it is highly likely that virtually all users will quickly connect to your Flash Media Server.

I have prepared a file to illustrate this functionality. Here's how to proceed:

1.   Create a new application in your server's application directory, this time by the name of shotgun_connection.

2.   Locate the file shotgun_connection.fla among the Chapter 16 sample files, which should be in a folder called connection_examples.

3. Open the file shotgun_connection.fla in Flash 8 or Flash CS3 and click frame 1 of the actions layer.

4. Choose Window > Actions from the menu bar to open the Actions panel and reveal the following code:

```
var host:String = "localhost";
var application:String = "shotgun_connection";
var protocols:Array = [{protocol:"rtmp", port:1935}, {protocol:"rtmpt",
port:80}, {protocol:"rtmp", port:443}];
var connect_ID:Number;
var conn_count:Number = 0;
var ncs:Array = new Array();
var nc:NetConnection;

function doConnect()
{
    var connStrings:Array = new Array();

    for (var i=0; i<protocols.length; i++)
    {
            var conn_string = protocols[i].protocol + "://" + host + ":"
+ protocols[i].port + "/" + application;
            connStrings.push(conn_string);
    }
    clearInterval(connect_ID);
    attemptConnect(connStrings);
    connect_ID = setInterval(attemptConnect, 500, connStrings);
}

function attemptConnect(connStrings)
{
    ncs[conn_count] = new NetConnection();
    ncs[conn_count].index = conn_count;
    ncs[conn_count].payload = 0;

    ncs[conn_count].onStatus = function(info)
    {
            trace(info.code);
            if (info.code == "NetConnection.Connect.Success")
            {
                    clearInterval(connect_ID);

                    for (var i = 0; i<connStrings.length; i++)
                    {
                            if (i != this.index)
```

```
                              {
                                      trace("closing connection attempt to
    " + connStrings[i]);
                                      ncs[i].close();
                                      ncs[i].onStatus = null;
                                      ncs[i] = null;
                                      delete ncs[i];
                              }
                      }
              }
      };
      trace("trying "+connStrings[conn_count]);
      ncs[conn_count].connect(connStrings[conn_count], true);
      conn_count++;

      if (conn_count>=connStrings.length)
      {
              clearInterval(connect_ID);
      }
}
doConnect()
stop();
```

I heard that sigh. But don't worry; it's not as bad as it looks. Before reviewing this listing in detail, test the application.

5. Choose Control > Test Movie from the menu bar. If your Flash Media Server is running locally, you should see the following trace statement in the Output panel:

```
trying rtmp://localhost:1935/shotgun_connection
NetConnection.Connect.Success
closing connection attempt to rtmpt://localhost:80/shotgun_connection
closing connection attempt to rtmp://localhost:443/shotgun_connection
```

The traces indicate that the connection to

```
rtmp://localhost:1935/shotgun_connection
```

succeeded and that both other connection attempts (which weren't actually started yet) have been closed. At this stage, your application is connected to the server and ready for use.

Had the first connection not been established within the first 500 milliseconds, then the second one would have been initiated 500 milliseconds later. This also indicates that the initial connection in this example succeeded within half a second.

Rather than detailing the entire code listing, I'd like to point out the most important parts. The first three lines of code are essentially the configuration.

```
var host:String = "localhost";
var application:String = "shotgun_connection";
var protocols:Array = [{protocol:"rtmp", port:1935}, {protocol:"rtmpt", port:80},
{protocol:"rtmp", port:443}];
```

The host variable specifies, you guessed it, the host or server address. In this case it is local-host but it may also be an IP address or domain such as *fms.mysite.com*.

The application variable contains the name of the application that you want to connect to, and an optional instance name. In this case it is shotgun_connection, corresponding to the folder inside the server's applications directory. If you want to connect to a specific application instance, then you could change this line to

```
var application:String = "shotgun_connection/myinstance";
```

The third line creates an Array of objects, each holding a protocol string and port number. These values specify all the protocols and port combinations that the script will attempt to connect to, using the host name and application specified on the first two lines. In this particular example these values, as assembled by

```
var conn_string = protocols[i].protocol + "://" + host + ":" + protocols[i].port +
"/" + application;
```

would be:

```
rtmp://localhost:1935/shotgun_connection
rtmpt://localhost:80/shotgun_connection
rtmp://localhost:443/shotgun_connection
```

You should be aware that the entry point to your application would be following the if state-ment, which checks for a successful connection.

```
if (info.code == "NetConnection.Connect.Success")
```

It is generally not necessary to know which protocol and port actually produced a connec-tion; all your application needs to know is that one of the connection attempts succeeded.

For more details on the shotgun connection approach, I recommend that you check out Will Law's article "Streaming Through Firewalls and Proxies: From the Client's Perspective" which you can find at *http://www.adobe.com/devnet/flashcom/articles/firewall_streaming.html*.

Conclusion

By now you should feel comfortable about installing Flash Media Server and you know some important details about its inner workings. The information on pricing and licensing should also assist your implementation decisions, like whether to buy Flash Media Server yourself or choose an outsourced solution.

That's the theory out of the way and I am sure you are ready to finally see some streaming video. With your newly gained RTMP skills, you should be well prepared for the next chapter in which you will learn how to stream Flash Video via FMS using a variety of approaches.

CHAPTER 17

Streaming Video with Flash Media Server

As you've already learned, Flash Media Server is currently the only solution that can stream Flash video content to connected clients. There are several advantages of using Flash Media Server over a progressive download approach, some of which include:

- **Bandwidth efficiency** – The video is served as needed by the remote viewer, minimizing wasted bandwidth if the viewer clicks off before the end of the video

- **Fast start-up** – An initial small buffer can provide fast video start-up and the buffer can be increased during playback

- **Advanced seeking capabilities** – Users can navigate to any part of the video at any time, without having to wait for a download, which is well suited for long files

- **Security** – Native SSL support and the lack of local content caching make it harder to copy streamed content

- **Maximum reach** – Video streaming in Flash is supported since Flash Player 6 (latest version is Player 9)

- Ability to detect user bandwidth (even midstream)

- Support for live video and video capture.

In this chapter you will learn how to stream Flash video using a basic, ActionScript-centric approach, as well

Author's Tip

The fact that streamed video is not cached can be a disadvantage in some scenarios. Users on slower connections are able to wait for progressive video to download and can (eventually) watch the content in high quality. With streaming delivery, this can only be achieved by using a very large buffer—something that is rarely used. It is therefore important to match a streaming video to the user's bandwidth and if that isn't possible—for example, because the bandwidth is just too low—provide alternative content. Note that you cannot serve Flash video progressively via Flash Media Server.

as the most commonly used deployment method of using the FLV Playback component, including the use of SMIL files. I will also cover the specifics of streaming Flash video over a Content Delivery Network (CDN), more specifically called a Flash Video Streaming Service Provider, using Akamai as an example.

Then, we'll examine Flash's live streaming capabilities.

Here's a summary of what's coming up:

- On-demand streaming using ActionScript
- On-demand streaming using the FLV Playback component
- Using a SMIL file with the FLV Playback component
- Streaming Flash video using a Flash Streaming Service Provider (FVSS)
- Producing live Flash video.

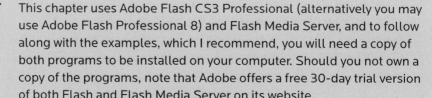

ALERT This chapter uses Adobe Flash CS3 Professional (alternatively you may use Adobe Flash Professional 8) and Flash Media Server, and to follow along with the examples, which I recommend, you will need a copy of both programs to be installed on your computer. Should you not own a copy of the programs, note that Adobe offers a free 30-day trial version of both Flash and Flash Media Server on its website.

Also, note that you can find the files referred to and used in this chapter, including completed skins, at *www.flashvideobook.com*. Consider downloading these files now, so they'll be available once I start referring to them.

On-Demand Streaming Using ActionScript

In Chapter 11, you learned how to serve an FLV video file progressively using both Action-Script and the FLV Playback component. Now, we'll walk through a similar exercise with the key difference being the delivery method, which in this case is streaming.

Preparation
Before you can attempt to access and play a streaming FLV file, you first need to deploy it onto your Flash Media Server. To do that you will need to:

- Create an application on the server
- Create the necessary folders to hold your FLV files
- Upload (or copy) files to the correct location.

If you followed along in the exercises of Chapter 16 and haven't deleted any of the created folders, then your Flash Media Server's applications directory should still contain a streamvideo folder/application with a streams subdirectory with added subfolders _definst_ and room1. If not, go back to the section *Examining the Server's Folder Structure* in Chapter 16 and create the application and subfolders.

In the following steps you will copy several videos into the _definst_ folder (you will be connecting to the default instance) and stream one of the videos into a Flash application.

1. Locate the sample files for this chapter. If you haven't yet downloaded them, please get them now from the book's website at *www.flashvideobook.com*.

2. The source files for Chapter 17 contain a folder called videos. Copy the files snippet_56kbps.flv, snippet_250kbps.flv and snippet_550kbps.flv from the videos folder into the streamvideo\streams_definst_ folder on your Flash Media Server, as shown in **Figure 17-1**.

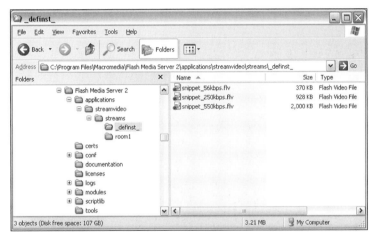

Figure 17-1
The _definst_ folder which holds the video files.

You will work with just one FLV file (snippet_550kbps.flv) for now, but later in the chapter you'll need all three files.

3. Open the file streamvideo_as.fla in Flash. You can find it in a folder called stream_actionscript.

4. Click frame 1 of the actions layer and choose Window > Actions from the menu bar to open the Actions panel. The Actions panel contains the following code:

```
var nc:NetConnection = new NetConnection();
toggle_pb.enabled = false;
restart_pb.enabled = false;

nc.onStatus = function (info)
{
```

```
        trace("#NC# " + info.code);
        if (info.code == "NetConnection.Connect.Success")
        {
                toggle_pb.enabled = true;
                restart_pb.enabled = true;
                init();
        }
}
function init()
{
    ns = new NetStream(nc);
    vid.attachVideo(ns);
    ns.onStatus = function (info)
    {
            trace("#NS# " + info.code);
    }
    ns.play("snippet_550kbps");
}

restart_pb.onRelease = init;

toggle_pb.onRelease = function()
{
    ns.pause();
}


nc.connect("rtmp://localhost/streamvideo");
```

5. Before looking at this code in more detail, let's compile and run the application. Note that if the server isn't running locally, you should update the RTMP address on the last line of the code to reflect your server location. Choose Control > Test Movie from the menu bar.

6. The application compiles and starts streaming a short video, as shown in **Figure 17-2**. If it doesn't run:

    •   Check to make sure the server has started.

    •   If the server is not local, check the RTMP address.

    •   Make sure the video files are stored in the correct location, as described in step 2.

Figure 17-2
After compiling the application, a short video starts to stream.

The code to achieve streaming playback in Flash is very similar to the progressive download example.

The first line of code

```
var nc:NetConnection = new NetConnection();
```

creates a new NetConnection instance. This will be used to connect to the server.

I have also placed two button components on Stage to pause and restart the application. Initially both buttons are disabled by setting their enabled property to false:

```
toggle_pb.enabled = false;
restart_pb.enabled = false;
```

The NetConnection's onStatus handler will give feedback about the connection status. For this reason I have set up the necessary code to respond to an info.code value of NetConnection.Connect.Success.

```
nc.onStatus = function (info)
{
        trace("#NC# " + info.code);
        if (info.code == "NetConnection.Connect.Success")
        {
           toggle_pb.enabled = true;
           restart_pb.enabled = true;
           init();
        }
}
```

Once the NetConnection.Connect.Success string is encountered, I enable both buttons and call the init function, which sets up the NetStream.

Author's Tip

NetStreams are needed for playing back FLV videos in Flash and this object is used for both progressively downloaded and streamed content.

Within the init function I first create a new NetStream instance (note that I am passing a reference to the NetConnection instance nc to the NetStream's constructor) and then attach this NetStream instance to the video object vid on Stage. This ensures that you can actually see the video once it starts streaming. Failing to attach the NetStream instance to the video object would result in audio-only playback.

```
ns = new NetStream(nc);
vid.attachVideo(ns);
```

The NetStream object also provides an onStatus handler similar to the one that the Net-Connection Object provides. This allows you to check different playback status messages, as I covered briefly in Chapter 11.

Here is the Netstream's onStatus handler, which simply traces these messages to Flash's Output panel.

```
ns.onStatus = function (info)
{
        trace("#NS# " + info.code);
}
```

Finally two button handlers are added before the NetConnection is established.

The following line of code restarts video playback by again invoking the init function:

```
restart_pb.onRelease = init;
```

The toggle_pb button calls the NetStreams pause method, which acts like a toggle: if the stream is already paused, then it unpauses it and vice versa.

```
toggle_pb.onRelease = function()
{
        ns.pause();
}
```

Arguably, the most important line of code is right at the end:

```
nc.connect("rtmp://localhost/streamvideo");
```

This invokes the NetConnection's connect method and passes it the server RTMP address and the application name. Note that omitting an instance name (as I do in this case) connects the application to _definst_, which is why you earlier copied the video files to the corresponding location of /streamvideo/streams/_definst_.

This application provides you a barebones example of connecting to and streaming video from Flash Media Server. Those who know a bit of ActionScript will have no problems improving and extending this example.

If you're new to ActionScript programming and feel a bit challenged by this code, then you'll find the next section more suitable, as it covers streaming video using the FLV Playback component, which makes the entire process accessible even to Flash novices.

On-Demand Streaming Using the FLV Playback Component

Streaming Flash video with Adobe's FLV Playback component is very straightforward, as the video-import wizard walks you through the necessary steps. For this example, I will use the local server at *rtmp://localhost* with the application called streamvideo from Chapter 16.

I will play the same video used in the previous section, and the location requirements for the FLV Playback Component and ActionScript are (of course) identical. Please refer to the previous section for details on which folders to create and where to copy the files.

If you are using a remote server or created a different application, then you will need your server's RTMP address and the application name before you can proceed.

The Importance of Main.asc

Flash Media Server applications often utilize server-side ActionScript to process incoming connections and other events. The FLV Playback component requires a file by the name of main.asc, which ships with Flash, and you can find by searching in Flash help for main.asc or in your Flash application folder under /Samples and Tutorials/Samples/Components/ FLVPlayback/main.asc.

To use the FLV Playback component, you must deploy this file to your Flash Media Server application, specifically (in this example) into the folder streamvideo, as shown in **Figure 17-3**. I have included a copy of this file among the source files for Chapter 17 in a subfolder called stream_flvplayback. Again, you can download all source files from the book's website at *www.flashvideobook.com*.

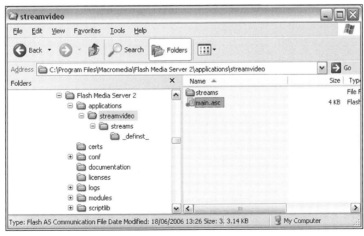

Figure 17-3
For the FLV component to operate, you must deploy main.asc into the streamvideo application folder.

Technically, the main.asc file facilitates bandwidth detection and provides a method for requesting the stream length from the server. The FLV Playback component takes care of these features automatically, but I will also cover a way of manually detecting bandwidth in Chapter 18. The manual approach is useful for more customized applications that require features that the FLV Playback component doesn't provide.

ALERT The FLV Playback component will not work without this particular main. asc file. Most problems that arise when trying to stream video using FLV Playback relate to the lack of this file and even experienced developers tend to forget about this from time to time. I know this from my own bitter experience. Usually the video will simply fail to play when you try to import it from an RTMP address using the Flash import wizard. In that case, double-check that the required main.asc file has been deployed.

Building the Client-Side Application

Now that the server is set up for connections from the FLV Playback component, it's time to build the client side application.

1. Locate the file streamvideo_flvplayback.fla among the source files for Chapter 17 and open it in Flash. The file is completely empty and you will now add the FLV Playback component to it using the Import Video wizard.

2. Make sure that Flash Media Server is running.

3. Choose File > Import > Import Video from the menu bar. The Import video wizard opens.

4. Select the second option Already deployed . . . and enter the following address into the URL field: *rtmp://localhost/streamvideo/snippet_550kbps.flv* (see **Figure 17-4** for reference). Remember to adjust this address if your server is not running locally. Click Next.

5. Choose a skin and click Next.

6. The next screen will summarize the procedure again. Click Finish.

    Once the wizard exits, you'll return to Flash with an instance of the FLV Playback component on Stage. The component is now already configured and you can review the settings from the Parameters tab of the Properties panel. Make sure to click and select the component on Stage to view its parameters.

    Should the wizard show an error, please ensure that:

    •   You've deployed the FLV file to the correct location (streamvideo/ streams/_definst_)

    •   You've deployed the main.asc file to the streamvideo folder

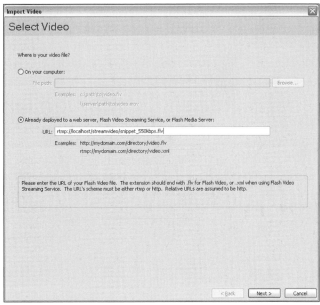

Figure 17-4
The URL field showing the configured RTMP path.

- Flash Media Server is running

- You have specified the correct RTMP address for your server.

7. Choose Control > Test Movie from the menu bar to test the application. The file will compile and start playing as shown in **Figure 17-5**.

Figure 17-5
The video being streamed from Flash Media Server.

Author's Tip

You may remember from earlier chapters that the name of the `contentPath` property has changed to `source` in ActionScript 3. If you are using the AS3 version of the FLV Playback component in Flash CS3, then remember to substitute `contentPath` with `source`. The examples used throughout the book use the ActionScript 2 based version of the component.

Author's Tip

Do not delete the streamvideo application from the server once you have completed this lesson. You will use it again in Chapter 18.

Should you need to change the contentPath parameter (to swap the video for another) then you can simply double-click the appropriate entry in the Parameters tab of the Property panel (**Figure 17-6** shows you where to find it).

You can then modify the FLV path to point to another file, for example to snippet_250kbps.flv which (if you have followed the instructions in the previous section) should be deployed in the same location.

You are probably wondering why I asked you to copy three files over to the _definst_ directory. The answer is easy: in the next section you will use a SMIL file to control multi-bitrate playback of several FLV files.

This wraps up the example on simple streaming video with the FLV Playback component. The next section uses the component again, not to target an FLV file directly but instead use FLV Playback's bandwidth-detection features in combination with a SMIL file.

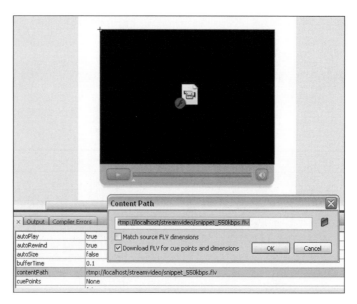

Figure 17-6
Use the contentPath parameter (or source parameter if you are using the ActionScript 3-based component) to update the video path.

Using SMIL and the FLV Playback Component for Bandwidth Detection

The FLV Playback component in combination with the deployed main.asc facilitates a mechanism for bandwidth detection. This detection happens automatically and transparently to both the developer and user watching the video.

I detail the specifics of the detection routine in Chapter 18. For now, it's sufficient to know that this detection happens by default when you use a SMIL file that contains links to several bitrates of the same FLV file, making it very easy to use.

Briefly, SMIL stands for Synchronized Multimedia Integration Language and it is a form of XML document that describes multimedia content. The FLV Playback component supports a subset of SMIL that allows it to process properly formatted SMIL files to serve the content (in this case FLV videos) described within. Here, we'll use SMIL to serve a particular file based upon the bandwidth detected by the FLV Playback component.

When used to serve multiple bitrate files, the information contained in a SMIL file specifies the location from which your streams are served (the RTMP address) and the file names of the FLV video files, in multiple bitrates. Here are the contents of the SMIL file used in the following example:

```
<smil>
      <head>
         <meta base="rtmp://localhost/streamvideo" />
      </head>
      <body>
         <switch>
             <!-- bitrate is in bits (550kbps, 250kbps) -->
             <video src="snippet_550kbps" system-bitrate="563200" />
             <video src="snippet_250kbps" system-bitrate="256000" />
             <video src="snippet_56kbps" />
         </switch>
      </body>
</smil>
```

As you can see, a SMIL file is structured similarly to an HTML document, containing head and body tags. The <head> tag may contain meta and layout tags, although layout is not used in this example, since we already know the size of this particular video. Moreover, the FLV Playback component is able to size itself automatically to the actual size of the video as long as this option has been selected via the Parameter tab of Flash's Property Inspector. An existing layout tag would contain information about the width and height of the video content, yet I personally rarely use it.

The <body> tag accepts either a single link to an FLV video or—as is the case in this example— links to several versions of the same FLV in multiple bitrates nested within a <switch> tag.

The <video> tag within the <switch> tag supports an src attribute to specify FLV files. It also accepts a system-bitrate attribute to specify the minimum bandwidth required to play the FLV file. This allows the FLV Playback component to automatically serve a video that matches the user's detected bandwidth most closely. If only a single FLV is specified, then no bandwidth matching takes place.

You can find a copy of this file (called smil.xml) among the source files for Chapter 17 in a folder called stream_smil.

Configuring the FLV Playback Component with SMIL

Now that we've looked at the SMIL code, let's learn how to use it. Specifically, let's examine how to use the FLV Playback component alongside a SMIL file, facilitating bandwidth detection and bitrate matching in a single line of code. The required steps are straightforward. Instead of passing an FLV address as the component's contentPath property, you will now point to the SMIL file instead. The code contained within the component will take care of the rest.

1.   Open the file smil.fla in Flash. You can find this file among the source files for Chapter 18 in a subfolder called stream_smil. The FLA source file contains an FLV Playback component on Stage with an instance name of vplayer.

2.   Click frame 1 of the actions layer and choose Window > Actions from the menu bar to open the Actions panel. It contains the following single line of code:

```
vplayer.contentPath = "smil.xml";
```

This code sets the component's playback property to the value of smil.xml, a file residing in the same folder as the FLA (and soon to be compiled SWF) file.

3.   Open the file smil.xml in your favorite text editor. You can find the file in the same location as the FLA you just opened.

4.   Make sure that the SMIL's meta base attribute correctly reflects the location of the streamvideo application. If your Flash Media Server is running locally then the RTMP address of *rtmp://localhost/streamvideo* should be correct.

5.   Be sure that your Flash Media Server's applications directory contains a streams subfolder with a _definst_ subfolder within it. The _definst_ folder should contain the FLV files snippet_56kbps.flv, snippet_250kbps.flv and snippet_550kbps.flv.

Refer to the section "On-Demand Streaming using ActionScript" earlier in the chapter for details on how to create the directory structure, which is shown once again in **Figure 17-7**.

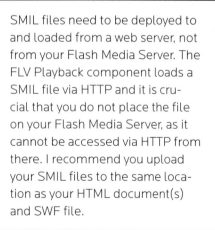

Author's Tip

SMIL files need to be deployed to and loaded from a web server, not from your Flash Media Server. The FLV Playback component loads a SMIL file via HTTP and it is crucial that you do not place the file on your Flash Media Server, as it cannot be accessed via HTTP from there. I recommend you upload your SMIL files to the same location as your HTML document(s) and SWF file.

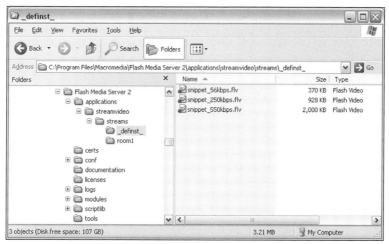

Figure 17-7
The _definst_ folder contains the same file in multiple bitrates.

6.   Back in Flash, choose File > Publish Preview > Default (HTML) from the menu bar to test the application in your default browser. Flash will compile the FLA to a SWF and launch your browser to play it within an HTML document, as shown in **Figure 17-8**.

Leave the browser window open for now, as you will need to refresh the application during the next section.

Figure 17-8
After loading the SMIL file and matching its contents to the detected bandwidth, the FLV video starts to play.

You will note that the process of loading the SMIL file, carrying out the bandwidth detection and serving the appropriate FLV file is totally transparent to the user. It's also very fast.

To deploy this application, you would upload the contents of the stream_smil folder (minus the FLA source file) to your web server and create a link to the smil.html document from another page of your website. Users accessing smil.html will then be able to see the stream. Note that, in this case, your Flash Media Server must be accessible from the Internet for the stream to function.

Just to be clear, Flash will produce the smil.swf and smil.html files for you if you choose the HTML publish option as described earlier (Flash CS3 will also produce a JavaScript file). You're in charge of creating the smil.xm file, or equivalent, and of making sure that whatever skin you use ends up in that directory.

A Look Behind the Scenes

How can you be sure that the component has actually carried out the assigned tasks? How can you check which file is playing? Fortunately, that's very easy.

In Chapter 16 you learned about the Flash Media Server's Management Console and you will use it now to check on the FLV Playback component, as outlined in the following steps.

1. Open the Flash Media Server Management Console in a new browser window. On a Windows system you will typically find it by choosing Start > All Programs > Macromedia > Flash Media Server 2 > Management Console. If you are not using Windows or cannot find the console via the Start menu, then find a file called fms2_console.htm, which is located in your Flash Media Server's installation directory. Once you open that file, it will provide browser-based access to the Management Console.

2. Enter your server admin username and password to log in to the Console.

3. Click the View Applications button in the top navigation bar.

4. Leaving the console view open, return to the browser window containing the video player and refresh it by pressing F5 (it's the browser window shown in **Figure 17-8**).

5. In the console, click the Live Log button if not already selected.

   You should see a trace statement similar to the one shown in **Figure 17-9**. The message in the Live Log window indicates a connection from the FLV Playback component and also shows the detected bandwidth figures.

6. Click the Streams button within the console. The Streams view opens.

7. You should be able to see the name of the FLV file that's playing. In my case, the file snippets_550kbps.flv is being served (see **Figure 17-10**) as it most closely matched the detected bandwidth—unsurprising, if you consider that my server runs locally and would have detected an extremely fast connection when checking my bandwidth.

Figure 17-9
The Management Console showing bandwidth detection figures.

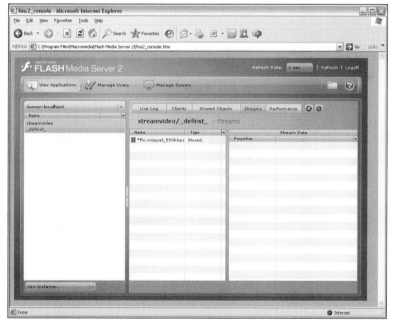

Figure 17-10
The FLV file snippet_550kbps.flv is being served and shown in the console.

Streaming Flash Video Using a Flash Streaming Service Provider (FVSS)

If you're streaming to large numbers of simultaneous viewers, your audience is scattered around the globe or you simply want to ensure that your visitors get the best possible experience, then you should consider hosting and serving your video content through a Flash Video Streaming Service Provider (FVSS).

Author's Tip

What Is a CDN?

CDN stands for content delivery network and it is essentially a system of networked servers that are located around the world. When a user requests a piece of content, such as an image or video clip, she will not connect to one particular server, as is the case for most smaller websites, but the request is intelligently routed to a server that's best suited to serve that content at that particular time. The best server could be one that is geographically proximate to that user or simply a server that is running under its current capacity limit and is therefore quick to respond.

Some CDNs maintain huge networks with literally thousands upon thousands of servers, and most large sites such as Lastminute.com, Apple, eBags or Yahoo (to name but a few) serve their content over a CDN. With ever-dwindling bandwidth costs and increased competition, CDN delivery is no longer an exclusive service that only major brands can afford.

How can you tell if CDN delivery of video content is something you should consider? This is a tough question, but it's fair to say that if you are running a single server or even a shared web-hosting account and you rarely receive complaints about your site's performance, then you are unlikely to be in need of CDN delivery.

In contrast, if you're serving several hundred or even thousands of gigabytes of data each month or if spikes in viewer traffic frequently slow your server, denying some users access to the content, then it's probably worthwhile to consider a CDN. In addition, if you're hosting an event that will put a high demand on your server, you should also consider a CDN.

A Flash Video Streaming Service Provider is essentially a content delivery network (CDN) that also offers streaming Flash video services. There are currently four Adobe-certified partners offering this service and they are VitalStream, Akamai, Limelight Networks and Mirror Image Internet. The main advantage of using an FVSS, apart from the fact that you don't need to maintain your own hardware and network, is the unrivalled performance and reliability that a CDN can offer.

What are the technical requirements for using a CDN? Of course, no two CDNs are identical and I cannot review each and every individual provider. However, I have used Akamai in the past to serve Flash video content and there are a few particular points worth noting, as you may encounter them on other CDNs, and with certainty on the Akamai network.

RTMP Addresses

The first thing to note about using a CDN is that the syntax of RTMP addresses may vary somewhat from the format that we just learned. With your own Flash Media Server, an RTMP address would take the format of

rtmp://host.com/application/instance

Akamai uses a similar syntax and you must still connect to a server and application. The first difference you may notice is that you will always connect to the same application, as will every other customer that uses on-demand Flash streaming with Akamai. The first part of the RTMP address is normally comprised of the customer's CP code, an Akamai naming convention, followed by the server name of edgefcs.net.

For example, if your CP code was "12345," then the RTMP address to the on-demand streaming application on Akamai's network would be

rtmp://cp12345.edgefcs.net/ondemand

Note that the domain cp12345.edgefcs.net does not resolve to a particular server. Instead, this request will be intelligently routed when the request is made, and may resolve to many different servers, depending on the current user's location and time of the request. This is how a CDN's service distributes traffic to many locations around the globe.

The second part of the RTMP address (which basically points to a particular FLV video stream) is also slightly more complex than what we learned above.

On Akamai, the `ondemand` application is again followed by a CP code (numeric part only) and followed by the path to the video file. A complete RTMP path to a particular video therefore typically looks like this:

rtmp://cp12345.edgefcs.net/ondemand/12345/somefolder/video.flv

The key takeaway is that RTMP addresses may vary in complexity depending on where you host your content. Don't be intimidated by long RTMP strings and instead try to break them down into the individual elements you learned about (server address, application name, file names) to better understand how and why they resolve to a particular location. Doing so will make it easier to debug any playback problems that you may encounter.

Circumventing Client Proxies

Of course, distributed networks such as those used by most CDNs present their own unique set of problems. One such issue is posed by certain client-side proxy servers when used in combination with a Flash video application.

As mentioned previously, a CDN will route traffic to the most suitable server at the time of the request. Certain proxy servers will reestablish this initial connection throughout the lifetime of a session, which, depending upon the distribution logic used by the CDN, may reconnect the user to a different server, potentially interrupting or even restarting Flash video playback, either way resulting in a bad user experience.

A web browser avoids this problem by retaining the IP address reference to the initial server and directs all subsequent requests to that same IP and server. In contrast, the Flash Player does not retain such an IP reference and may reconnect to a new destination when going through a proxy server, thereby losing the session.

ALERT   The routines outlined in this section are unique to Akamai. Other CDNs may or may not deploy similar procedures and connection routines. Please consult the documentation of your provider for more information.

To circumvent this problem, Akamai has deployed a system that allows Flash applications to request the IP address of the ideal server. This IP address can then be used to build the RTMP string and connect to that IP directly, rather than using a hostname that may resolve to a different IP at different times. Should the proxy server re-establish the connection during the session, it will reconnect to the original IP and server, avoiding any loss of session-related information. **Figure 17-11** shows the flow of obtaining the IP information and establishing the RTMP connection.

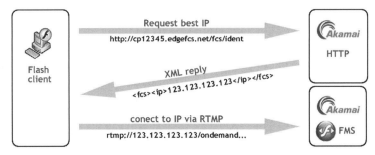

Figure 17-11
Akamai's implementation of determining the best IP address to serve Flash video from.

I am providing a sample ActionScript class file, named FindAkamaiServer.as, you can use to facilitate this IP lookup in a subfolder named Akamai in the sample files for Chapter 17. The accompanying file getip.fla demonstrates the use of the class. Because this file is very specific to the Akamai network, I will not describe it here in any more detail.

Live Flash Video

Contrary to common belief, it is entirely possible to stream live Flash video using Flash Media Server. In fact, this feature has been supported since the initial release of Flash Communication Server 1.0 back in 2002. There are several reasons why live Flash video has been adopted slowly in the marketplace.

Firstly, there are some scalability issues. It can be challenging to build a cluster of Flash Media Servers that would support live webcasts on a large scale—even with stacked licenses there comes a point when a single server is not sufficient. You could, of course, opt for an Origin/Edge set-up, but this is very costly and quickly dismissed when compared to the deployment costs of other technologies, like Windows Media Server. For these reasons, many CDNs have implemented Flash Media Server on a large scale but not many are actively pushing the use of live Flash streaming at this point in time.

The second issue was the lack of a high-quality codec. The Flash Player currently only supports the Spark codec for live encoding, making it less suited for high-quality streams. On2's VP6 codec is only available as a decoder for watching but no VP6 encoder is present in the Flash Player.

A Flash application is also not ideally suited to serve as a professional encoding solution. Professional webcasters expect a turnkey solution that doesn't involve the added learning curve of Flash application development. Running inside a browser, the Flash Player is also not making optimal use of system resources.

Finally, there were no Flash applications that enable multicasting, allowing one stream to serve many in intranet or even Internet applications. This reason, in particular, is a significant competitive disadvantage when compared to mature streaming technologies like Windows Media, Real and even QuickTime.

For these reasons, live Flash video streaming has traditionally been confined to consumer-type applications such as browser based e-learning applications (Breeze is a good example) or video chat applications.

The good news is that several shortcomings of live Flash video are being addressed. On one hand, many large Flash video providers like Akamai are planning to increase their Flash video capacity in the near future. This reliability and scalability will make it easy to deploy and run large live Flash video webcasts.

At the same time, there are now two desktop encoding applications available, which allow even Flash novices to broadcast live Flash video using the VP6 codec. The first program is Adobe's own Flash Media Encoder (FME); the other one is Flix Live by On2, the company behind the VP6 codec.

Adobe Flash Media Encoder Overview

Adobe Flash Media Encoder (FME) is a free Windows desktop application which enables webcasters to stream high quality Flash video content to a live audience using On2's VP6 codec in combination with Flash Media Server or the Flash Video Streaming Service (FVSS). It is therefore ideally suited for users who would like to explore Flash's live video capabilities when delivering broadcasts of sporting events, general webcasts, elearning content or concerts (although the latter may not be such an ideal use case, as I'll explain in the section on audio codecs). Let's examine the application in more detail.

The user interface is simple and effective, being divided into two main parts. The top part contains—in its standard layout—previews of video Input and Output (see **Figure 17-12)**. Note that the Output window does not reflect the chosen bandwidth and thereby output video quality until broadcasting starts. For this reason, you should run a few test encodings to determine a satisfactory video quality setting.

The collapsible bottom part of the application contains the encoding options for video and audio, as well as Output parameters, with a dropdown menu that doubles as an entry form

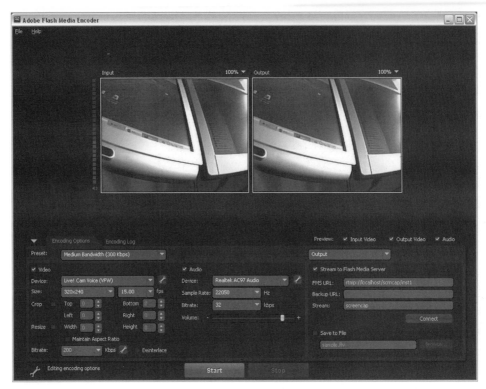

Figure 17-12
Adobe Flash Media Encoder.

for video metadata. The fact that video and audio can be enabled or disabled individually is nice, as it allows audio-only broadcast. Likewise, the audio portion can be omitted from a video broadcast.

You will like its price too: FME is completely free. The EULA does, however, tie its use to Flash Media Server or FVSS (Flash Video Streaming Service). You may wonder why this is; after all, the encoder is useless without a server. The answer lies with other emerging platforms such as Wowza Media Server and Red5, both of which could potentially be used in conjunction with FME.

For a more in-depth review of the Adobe Flash Media Encoder, please check out my article at *http://www.streamingmedia.com/article.asp?id=9519*.

On2 Flix Live Overview

Flix Live is a Windows-only application that enables live Flash video broadcasts using the On2 VP6 codec. Just like the Flash Media Encoder, On2 Flix Live can directly connect to Flash Media Server via RTMP, which previously only the Flash Player itself was able to do. Both encoding tools, therefore, open up a new channel to push audio and video data to FMS in a way that is independent of the Flash Player. **Figure 17-13** shows the application in its Advanced view.

17. Streaming Video with Flash Media Server

Figure 17-13
On2 Flix Live.

Operation is simple but lacks configurability. For example, the user selects a canned publishing profile that sets total bandwidth of the outgoing stream, but can't adjust parameters like frame rate, audio and video bitrate or capture size.

While some of these settings are accessible via a file called *bitrates.xml* located in the application's install directory, this is neither obvious nor very user-friendly. After all, On2 Flix Live tries to address Flash webcasting requirements for users who are not necessarily familiar with Flash and who may feel uncomfortable editing raw XML files. A 'custom' option for publishing settings would have made this a lot easier to manage.

Other settings include a field for the RTMP address of the Flash Media Server application that's used for the broadcast, alongside a stream name. On2 supplies a main.asc file for the server side application, which is not required but can be used as a starting point for further functionality.

Like FME, On2 Flix Live has an option for saving a copy of the live broadcast locally, which is handy if you plan to make the footage available on demand at a later date. Unfortunately, local copies can only be saved in FLV format, which shuts the door on any editing or meaningful post production of the saved footage.

You select video and audio sources via list boxes, but apparently can't switch sources during a broadcast, which would have been a nice option. You can test the On2 Flix Live application by signing up for the trial at *www.on2.com* (remember this application as well as FME is Windows-only).

The main difference between FME and On2 Flix Live is price, as the features of both applications are about equal. While FME is free, On2 Flix Live is currently priced at USD $999 per year. For this reason, I wouldn't hesitate to recommend FME to my clients, although On2 Flix Live did a fine job for us while it was the sole live VP6 encoding option.

Inside the Industry

Audio Codecs

I haven't discussed the audio codecs used in FLV files yet and the reason is simple: there is no real choice at this time. Video encoding tools such as Flix 8 Pro or Sorenson Squeeze only offer MP3 or uncompressed audio during encoding, with uncompressed audio obviously unsuitable for online delivery.

Live Flash video broadcasts face similar if not even tighter restrictions. When broadcasting with the Flash Player, FME or On2 Flix Live, you automatically use the Nellymoser codec, an audio codec that is optimized for voice, and produces reasonable quality. As with many voice-oriented audio codecs, however, music quality is sub-par, making Nellymoser a poor choice for concerts and other music-oriented webcasts.

The Nellymoser codec is also nearly impossible to transcode to other audio formats, which shuts the door to many interesting applications like user-submitted recordings that would work well if distributed in the form of a podcast and as MP3 files. Odeo.com is one site that has overcome this problem, and can transcode FLV recordings to MP3, presumably by licensing the necessary transcoder from Nellymoser. Adobe has promised a tool to transcode Nellymoser audio to MP3, but at the time of writing, hasn't announced a release date for this tool.

Alternatives for Deploying Live Flash Video

If you want to use the On2 VP6 codec for a live Flash video broadcast, then FME and On2 Flix Live are currently the only two options.

Digital Rapids, a well-known developer of professional hardware and software solutions for encoding and webcasting, has announced that they are adding support for live VP6 encoding to their Stream family of media encoding solutions. This will undoubtedly be a package that will satisfy professional webcasters and video encoding specialists, adding features to live VP6 broadcasting that have long been available on other webcasting platforms.

Last but not least, the Flash Player offers live encoding capabilities out of the box. As mentioned previously, it currently supports only the Spark codec, which offers lower quality than VP6, but has lesser system requirements.

Accordingly, if you are considering a consumer Flash application to enable users to simply 'plug and play' with their webcam and microphone, the Flash Player is an ideal platform. While it is beyond the scope of this book to implement a live webcasting application in

Flash, you might enjoy an Adobe Developer Center article that I wrote in 2005 which covers exactly this topic. The name of the article is "Building a Simple Live Video Broadcaster and Receiver." The URL for it is *http://www.adobe.com/devnet/flashcom/articles/broadcast_receiver.html* and it also contains all source files.

Conclusion

You should now have a good understanding of the different delivery methods for streaming Flash video, both on demand and live. Getting to know Flash video concepts such as NetConnections and NetStreams and feeling more comfortable with SMIL files as a configuration option will help you make decisions for your own application. It should be easier to understand and decide if you can tackle a particular task yourself or if it may be better to get help in the form of a third-party developer, hosting provider or even CDN.

While live Flash streaming with the VP6 codec is still in its infancy, the coming months and years should see a significant uptake of the technology as new tools and services are developed around it.

In the next chapter you will learn about several features that will help you improve the user experience, such as bandwidth detection (this time without SMIL) and automatic Flash Player detection. I will also cover Flash Media Server's logging features, among other things.

CHAPTER 18

Advanced Flash Media Server Techniques

Now that you know the basics of Flash Media Server, it's time to move on to more advanced features, most of which are focused on improving the user experience. For example, I will detail how to deploy a bandwidth-detection routine that enables you to serve an appropriately encoded FLV video targeted at a particular connection speed, matching file bandwidth to connection speed. You will see this routine working in ActionScript, without the use of a playback component or SMIL file.

Next up is Flash Media Server's virtual keys feature, which allows you to serve a video that fits the user's Flash Player capabilities, and in particular to match the VP6 codec to Flash Player 8+ while serving users with Flash Player 6 and 7 a Spark-encoded video. All this detection routine runs server side and removes complex Flash Player version detection logic from your SWF movie.

After deploying your Flash videos, you'll probably want to know how well they're performing—and if not *you*, then certainly your boss or client will want to. Fortunately, Flash Media Server now supports W3C-compliant log files in text format, which simplifies reporting, and also features a much improved admin console so you can monitor your server's vital health issues in real time.

I will conclude the chapter by looking at some additional Flash Media Server features that enable it to be a conferencing platform, multiuser game server or notification system (anyone remember push technology?), to name but a few.

To sum up, here's a list of what I will cover in this chapter:

- Using virtual directories to organize FLV files
- Serving streams according to Flash Player version using virtual keys
- Using bandwidth detection

- Logging and reporting
- The power of SharedObjects.

Let's jump right in.

ALERT This chapter uses Adobe Flash CS3 Professional (alternatively you may use Adobe Flash Professional 8). To follow along with the examples, which I recommend, you will need a copy of the program installed on your computer. Should you not own a copy of the program, note that Adobe offers a free 30-day trial version on its website.

Also, note that you can find the files referred to and used in this chapter, including completed skins, at *www.flashvideobook.com*. Consider downloading these files now, so they'll be available once I start referring to them.

Using Virtual Directories to Organize FLV Files

Virtual directories in Flash Media Server allow you to share resources like FLV files between applications and application instances. They are essentially a mapping of a keyword to a location on the server's hard drive, attached storage device or even a network storage location. This allows several different video players access to a large library of video content and is often essential for large-scale deployments.

You may recall from the last two chapters that by default a Flash Media Server application can only access resources that are stored in a specific folder, which is named according to the current application instance (which by default is called _definst_). If you can't remember where FLV files are stored on the server, then now is a good time to skip back to Chapter 16 and the section titled "Examining the Server's Folder Structure."

Virtual directories allow you to break out of this strict folder structure that the default set-up imposes. Now that you understand the default set-up and basic streaming techniques, you can work up to a finer tuned configuration.

Updating the Server Configuration

To make use of virtual directories, you must configure them in a file called vhost.xml, which is located in the server's installation directory. The path to this file (from your installation root) is /conf/_defaultRoot_/_defaultVHost_/Vhost.xml as shown in **Figure 18-1**.

Follow these steps to configure a virtual directory for your FLV videos:

1. Create a new folder myvideos on your primary hard drive. In my case this is the C: drive. You may create this folder in another location and/or give it a different name; note, however, that in this example I will refer to the location of C:\myvideos and I recommend you follow this naming convention to make the example easier to follow.

Figure 18-1
Vhost.xml shown in its default location.

2.   Locate the folder videos among the sample files for this chapter. Again, you can download all example files for the book from *www.flashvideobook.com*.

3.   Inside the videos folder, you will find a file sample_250kbps.flv. Copy this file into the newly created folder C:\myvideos, as shown in **Figure 18-2.**

Figure 18-2
You created C:\myvideos to contain video files and copied in the file sample_250kbps.flv.

4. Open the Vhost.xml file in your favorite text editor.

5. Find the `<VirtualDirectory>` tag by scrolling down to around line 65. Note that any text contained between `<!–` and `-->` is a comment and has no effect on server configuration.

6. Locate the `<Streams></Streams>` tag nested within the `<VirtualDirectory>` tag.

7. Modify the `<Streams>` tag so that it reads:

```
<Streams>mymapping;C:\myvideos</Streams>
```

You have now created a mapping by the name of mymapping, which resolves to the location of C:\myvideos. This means that every time a Flash application requests a stream starting with the name mymapping, the server will look in C:\myvideos for the file.

8. Restart the server by logging on to the admin console and choosing the Manage Servers option (consult Chapter 17 for details on how to access the admin console). Then click the restart button on the bottom left, as shown in **Figure 18-3**.

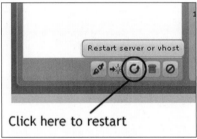

Figure 18-3
Click this button to restart the server.

The server must restart to reload the XML configuration files and for the changes to take effect. You can now test the newly created virtual directory in Flash.

9. Open the file virtual.fla in Flash. You can find it among the source files for Chapter 18 in a folder called virtual_directory.

10. Click frame 1 of the actions layer to select it.

11. Choose Window > Actions from the menu bar to show the Actions panel if it is not already showing.

12. Inside the Actions panel, scroll down to line 25 to the following line of code:

```
ns.play("mymapping/sample_250kbps");
```

The path to this video file starts with the name of the virtual directory mapping that you have just created. This means that when this application executes it will instruct the server to check in C:\myvideos for a file called sample_250kbps.flv (note that the .flv extension needs to be omitted from the FLV name when using ns.play in ActionScript).

Testing the Configuration

OK, we've got it all set up; now let's test.

1. Choose Control > Test Movie from the menu bar to test the application. Flash will compile and run the file and the video should start playing.

    Should the video fail to play, verify that the RTMP address on line 35 points to a valid application on your server. Also make sure that the server is running and that you have followed the previous steps correctly.

Verifying the Mapping

To verify that the server can access files outside the default location of the applications directory (which is normally /streams/instancename), you can modify the RTMP string on line 35:

```
nc.connect("rtmp://localhost/streamvideo");
```

Currently this line of code will connect the application to the default instance _definst_.

2. Add an instance name by appending "myinst" to the RTMP address so that it reads `nc.connect("rtmp://localhost/streamvideo/myinst");`

3. Test the application again by choosing Control > Test Movie from the menu bar.

    You will see that the same video plays, unrelated to which instance name you are connecting to. Note that the mapping is available to all other applications on the same Vhost (and in most cases this means to all applications on the entire server). As long as any requested stream name is mymapping/sample_250kbps then the server will find and play that file, regardless of the application's name. This is very different from the standard set-up, which ties the location in which streams are stored to a particular application.

You have now successfully created and configured a virtual directory mapping and have used it to break out of the default directory structure, enabling you to share video files among applications and application instances. In the next section you will build on this knowledge and use a feature called virtual keys to expand on the functionality of virtual directories.

Author's Tip

Mapping Network Drives
You can also use virtual directories to map to storage locations that are not on the same physical machine as Flash Media Server. A common set-up is to map locations on network drives, enabling large amounts of storage space to be added without requiring hard-drive space on the server itself.

You should note that the syntax used to map a network drive is crucial. You should avoid using external drive letters or network share names, but instead use the IP address of the device that you are mapping. The correct syntax to map a network drive is therefore: `<Streams>mymapping;\\192.168.0.5\foldername</Streams>` (you need to substitute the IP address used in this example with the actual IP address of your device). You must also make sure that the Flash Media Server has read and write permissions for the location you are mapping.

Serving Streams According to Flash Player Version Using Virtual Keys

The virtual keys feature in Flash Media Server enables on-the-fly mapping of stream directories to match the user's Flash Player version. Using virtual keys in combination with virtual directory mappings enables you to deploy a custom stream-delivery feature that will serve Spark-encoded videos to users who have not installed the required Flash Player to view VP6-encoded videos. Likewise VP6-encoded videos can be served to those users who have the appropriate Flash Player installed. The Flash Media Server manages the entire detection and mapping routine on the fly.

Server-Side Flash Player Detection

Each Flash Player (which represents a user) that connects to Flash Media Server is automatically assigned a virtual key (once configured) based on the detected Flash Player version.

The server can read the Player version based on a parameter that is automatically passed to it in the form of a FlashVar string. The specifics of this process needn't concern you; you only need to be aware of the fact that the server can "read" the Flash Player's version number.

Configuring Virtual Keys

For the purpose of this exercise I will presume that you want to detect and divide your users into two groups: those who can view video encoded with VP6, the later and higher-quality Flash video codec, and those who can't, who will be served Spark-encoded footage. This is also the most commonly used configuration.

The earliest Flash Player to support VP6 playback, progressive or streaming, was Flash Player 8. You therefore need to create two virtual keys, one covering Flash Player 8 and above and another covering Flash Player 6 to 7, both of which support Spark-encoded video when streamed.

To set up virtual keys, you first need to create the appropriate directory and key mappings in the server's XML configuration. Here's the procedure:

1. Create a new folder called virtualkeys inside the folder C:\myvideos, which you created in the previous section. If you haven't followed along with the previous section, then I suggest you now refer to step 1 of the previous exercise.

2. Locate the sample files for Chapter 18, which contain a directory by the name of virtual_keys.

> ### Author's Tip
>
> Just as a reminder: while Flash Player 6 supports streaming video playback using Spark, it does not support progressive playback. To support progressive Flash video, your users need to have a minimum of Flash Player 7 installed.

3.   Open the virtual_keys directory where you will find two folders, player6_7 and player8.

4.   Copy both folders including contents into C:\myvideos\virtualkeys.

Figure 18-4 shows the correct set-up. Of course, you may create these folders in a location of your choice as long as the mapping you create in the next steps reflects this location.

Figure 18-4
Your mappings will target these newly created directories.

You've probably already guessed that the folder player6_7 would contain videos targeted at Flash Player 6 and 7 (encoded using Spark) and the folder player8 would hold videos targeted at Flash Player 8, encoded using VP6. Currently each folder contains one video called sample_250kbps.flv.

Note that only the names are identical; the actual content is different so you can later distinguish and test which folder is serving the files. In a production environment, both directories would normally hold identical footage, the only difference being the codec used for encoding the footage.

5.   Open your server's Vhost.xml file in your favorite text editor. This file can be found in Flash Media Server's default installation directory in the subfolder /conf/_defaultRoot_/_defaultVHost_. **Figure 18-5** shows this location once again.

6.   Find the <VirtualKeys> node at around line 42. You will now create two keys, A and B, to match the Flash Player versions you want to detect and redirect.

Figure 18-5
You can find Vhost.xml in this location.

Author's Tip

Assigning Virtual Keys at Runtime

Virtual keys can also be set in a server-side main.asc script. This allows you to inject more advanced logic into the assignment of virtual keys, for example setting a virtual key based on the user's detected bandwidth. For more information on this, please consult the Flash Media Server documentation.

As previously mentioned, Content Delivery Networks do not allow for a custom main.asc to be deployed and the on-the-fly assignment of virtual keys is therefore not possible when using CDN delivery.

7. Add four key tags to the VirtualKeys node so that it reads:

```
<VirtualKeys>
<Key from="WIN 6,0,0,0" to="WIN 7,9,9,9">A</Key>
<Key from="WIN 8,0,0,0" to="WIN 20,0,0,0">B</Key>
<Key from="MAC 6,0,0,0" to="MAC 7,9,9,9">A</Key>
<Key from="MAC 8,0,0,0" to="MAC 20,0,0,0">B</Key>
</VirtualKeys>
```

This creates two virtual keys, A and B, for both Windows and Macintosh platforms. Key A covers Flash Player 6 and 7 while key B covers Flash Player 8 to 20. I've used a figure of 20 to make this configuration compatible with future Flash Player versions.

8. Scroll down in Vhost.xml to around line 65 and find the <VirtualDirectory> node. You will now configure two virtual directories to map to the keys and folders you created in the previous steps.

9. Add two new \<Streams\> nodes to the \<VirtualDirectory\> node so that it reads

    ```
    <Streams key="A">playermap;C:\myvideos\virtualkeys\player6_7</Streams>
    <Streams key="B">playermap;C:\myvideos\virtualkeys\player8</Streams>
    ```

    Make sure to restart Flash Media Server if it has been running while you were making these configuration changes. Otherwise, start it up via the Services panel or choose Start > All Programs > Macromedia > Flash Media Server 2 > Start Flash Media Server 2.

Testing the Application

I have created a simple player that will allow you to test the newly created configuration. The application is essentially identical to the player from the previous exercise, which in turn is based on the file streamvideo_as.fla from Chapter 17.

You can find the application among the sample files for this chapter. The filename is virtual_keys.fla and it's located inside the virtual_keys folder.

1. Open the file virtual_keys.fla in Flash 8 or Flash CS3. The main differences in this file compared to the previous example on virtual directories are:

    •   The mapping name you will be using now is playermap:

        ```
        ns.play("playermap/sample_250kbps");
        ```

        Remember that the name of the mapping is entirely up to you. For this example I chose playermap simply because I want to make it clear that this mapping is a different one from the one used in the previous section.

    •   The FLA's publish settings have been changed to Flash Player 6 as this is the minimum version required to play the Spark-based video files.

    •   I've made some minor code changes to make the ActionScript compatible with Flash Player 6, as this is the lowest Flash Player version that this application needs to support.

Let's remind ourselves what is going to happen when you compile this application.

    •   Flash Player will automatically notify the server about its version and platform.

    •   Flash Media Server will notice the mapping playermap that is passed in when a stream is requested and look for (and find) a mapping pointing to two virtual key mappings, defined in Vhost.xml.

    •   The server will match the Player version to either key A or B, resulting in an automatic streams directory mapping to either C:\myvideos\virtualkeys\player6_7 or C:\myvideos\virtualkeys\player8

    •   The server will then serve the appropriate file.

2. Test the application in your default browser by choosing File > Publish Preview > Default (HTML) from the menu bar. The application compiles and runs in your

Author's Tip

Note that this exercise presumes that the previously created stream-video application is still present. However, any other application will also work fine for testing this file due to the fact that stream mappings work independently of the application name.

default browser. If you have Flash Player 8 or above installed in your browser, then you should now see a video of Jan talking about green-screen lighting. If your Flash Player version is 6 or 7, then you should see a short advertising snippet.

Testing with a Different Flash Player

You probably realize now that this application is tricky to test unless you uninstall and reinstall different Flash Player versions—otherwise, how can you verify that the mapping switches to the correct location? If you are using Firefox as your preferred browser and Windows as your operating system, then you can very easily overcome this by installing a great extension called Flash Switcher by Alessandro Crugnola. It allows for easy and painless switching of Flash Player versions at the click of a button. You can download Flash Switcher at *http://tinyurl.com/ylmet9*.

If you are not using Firefox on Windows and haven't got access to a different machine for testing purposes, then you may have to uninstall and reinstall the Flash Player. You can download archived Flash Player versions from *http://www.adobe.com/go/tn_14266*.

If you have Flash Switcher installed and test the application using both Player 6 and Player 9, then you will see two different videos depending on your chosen Flash Player, as shown in **Figure 18-6**.

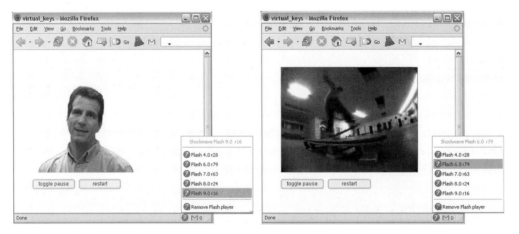

Figure 18-6
The same application plays a different file depending on the current Flash Player version.

Let me remind you once more: you normally would not serve different video but rather the same source video encoded with either Spark or VP6. The point of the exercise is to use Flash Media Server's virtual keys feature to redirect requests to the correct virtual directory on the fly.

Using Bandwidth Detection

In Chapter 17, you learned how to use SMIL files in combination with the FLV Playback component and a SMIL file to detect the user's bandwidth and to stream files to the user that are matched to that bandwidth. While this approach works well, it requires the FLV Playback component, which may not be suitable for some custom applications.

Other use cases for manual detection may include gathering bandwidth data for statistical purposes without actually serving any video content at all. And lastly, such data can also be useful for live video broadcasts—for example, to inform a dial-up user that her connection will not be sufficient to experience the event fully.

Fortunately, you can easily hook into the existing bandwidth detection scripts with a few lines of ActionScript and use the detected data however you see fit. Not only that, since the same scripts are used by most Content Delivery Networks, it is also a solution that works in a globally distributed network. All you need to do is call the right server-side functions and let the server do the rest.

Requirements for Manual Bandwidth Detection

Flash Media Server uses a server-side ActionScript file (usually called main.asc) to provide certain functionality to a connecting client. This main.asc file also contains the bandwidth detection logic, so you therefore need to deploy it like you did when you used it in combination with SMIL files and the FLV Playback component.

Author's Tip

To refresh your memory on the significance of the main.asc file, you can skip back to Chapter 17 and read the section titled "On-Demand Streaming Using the FLV Playback Component."

Creating the Application on the Server

The detection routine you will soon deploy must connect to a server-side application and you will use the streamvideo application from Chapter 17 for this exercise. If the streamvideo application still exists in your Flash Media Server's applications directory, then you're ready to go on the server side.

If you deleted the streamvideo application, or haven't yet set it up, then please refer to Chapter 17 and the section titled "On-Demand Streaming Using the FLV Playback Component," which details where and how to create the application.

Also make sure that the main.asc file is still present and, if not, then copy it back into the streamvideo folder. You can find the file among the sample files for Chapter 18 in a folder called manual_bandwidth. This main.asc is identical to the one used with the FLV Playback component in Chapter 17. Finally, make sure that Flash Media Server is running before moving on to the client-side application.

Using ActionScript to Detect a User's Bandwidth

The ActionScript requirements that enable your application to detect and process bandwidth checking are very simple. All you need to provide are two functions in your Flash applications, which are defined on the NetConnection Object.

When the application connects to Flash Media Server, it will pass a flag (of true or false) indicating whether or not the server should detect connection bandwidth. If the flag is set to true, the server will call a function called onBWCheck several times to obtain an average bandwidth figure based on those calls. The onBWCheck function looks like this:

```
nc.onBWCheck = function()

{

        trace("onBWCheck called");

        return;

}
```

As you can see, it is extremely simple and does nothing more than return the call to the server. The trace statement will notify you during testing that the function has been successfully invoked.

Once the bandwidth check is complete, the server will call another function called onBWDone. This function is passed several arguments, one of which is the detected bandwidth in Kbits per second. The complete function looks as follows:

```
nc.onBWDone = function( kbitDown, deltaDown, deltaTime, latency )

{

        // more logic here

}
```

The developer can add any further processing logic to this function. Additional parameters that are passed to onBWDone are deltaDown, deltaTime and latency. The delta figures can usually be ignored but the latency figure give some insight into how responsive a user's connection is. Latency is measured in milliseconds and the lower figures indicate a healthier Connection.

Putting It All Together

To see this code in action, you can use a file named bwcheck.fla that you can find among the sample files for Chapter 18 in a folder called manual_bandwidth. Let's do this together:

1. Open the file bwcheck.fla in Flash 8 or Flash CS3. This file contains nothing more than the ActionScript needed for bandwidth detection and a text field on Stage to display the results.

2. Click frame 1 of the Actions layer to select it.

3.   Choose Window > Actions to open the Actions panel if it isn't already showing. The completed code looks as follows:

```
nc = new NetConnection();
nc.onStatus = function(info)
{
    trace(info.code);
    if (info.code == "NetConnection.Connect.Success")
    {
        startTime = getTimer();
    }
};


nc.connect("rtmp://localhost/streamvideo", true);


nc.onBWDone = function( kbitDown, deltaDown, deltaTime, latency )
{
    now = getTimer();
    endTime = now - startTime;
    trace("onBWDone: kbitDown = " + kbitDown + ", deltaDown= " + del-
taDown + ", deltaTime = " + deltaTime + ", latency = " + latency);
    stats.htmlText = "Bandwidth check completed in " + endTime/1000 + "
seconds<br><br>Detected speed: " + kbitDown + " Kbit/sec<br><br>";
}
nc.onBWCheck = function()
{
    trace("onBWCheck called");
    return;
}

stop();
```

Most of this code should look familiar to you by now. After creating a NetConnection and associated onStatus handler, the code will connect the application to the locally running streamvideo application.

```
nc.connect("rtmp://localhost/streamvideo", true);
```

The last parameter true is a signal to the server (and to the code in main.asc that gets invoked) to run a bandwidth detection routine.

The line `startTime = getTimer();` captures a time marker which later allows us to calculate how long it took to complete the bandwidth-detection process. This step is optional and not needed for a speed result.

What follows is the previously described code consisting of the `onBWCheck` and `onBWDone` methods, which are defined on the NetConnection instance `nc`.

4. Choose Control > Test Movie to compile and run the application.

Once the Flash Player connects to the server, the bandwidth-detection routine will automatically run and display the results in the text field on Stage, as shown in **Figure 18-7**.

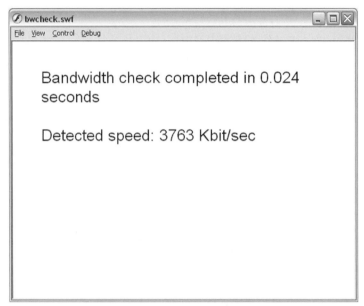

Figure 18-7
Detected bandwidth speed and time taken are displayed upon completion.

Author's Tip

Alternative detection routines can involve either a JavaScript-based approach or a timed file download. While this latter approach also works quite well, one drawback is that it involves the transfer of large chunks of data, which makes it tricky to deploy if detection is required throughout the user's session.

It can also be problematic for dial-up users because of the time it takes to complete the test. In contrast, Flash Media Server's detection routine does not involve large amounts of data and is easy to use at any stage throughout the session.

Of course, the connection speed is very high because the Flash Media Server is running locally; over the Internet, this figure would be much lower. Remember that this test measures how quickly data can flow between the server and the currently connected client at the time of the test; it does not detect the maximum speed that the client's Internet connection may support.

Your application is now ready to further process the gathered data, for example by requesting a particular video file. Other options could include a call to a remote script that might log this data to a database for later processing. The particular implementation depends on the specifics of the application that you plan to develop.

Logging and Reporting

Log files are essentially text files containing information about system events, errors or simple process workflows. These events can include data about successful and failed connections, data flow, system state, bandwidth usage and a multitude of other data. Most servers and computer systems support some kind of logging mechanism and the data it produces is commonly used for troubleshooting and security analysis.

Author's Tip

W3C stands for World Wide Web Consortium, which is the main international standards organization for the World Wide Web. The W3C's mission is "To lead the World Wide Web to its full potential by developing protocols and guidelines that ensure long-term growth for the Web."

Before the release of Flash Media Server 2, the only format in which the server would write log files was FLV. That's right—logs were captured inside what is essentially a video file and written as data tracks, which made it tricky to process the logs efficiently.

Luckily, all this changed with the release of FMS as it introduced a text file format for all logs and, better still, produced W3C-compliant logs, which is the most common format for most web and streaming servers. This made the log files easier to process using several readily available log readers and data-mining programs.

Log Files and Storage Locations

Flash Media Server writes its logs to several different files, depending on which part of the server triggered the event being logged. Log files are, by default, written to the server's logs directory, which is a subdirectory of the installation directory (on Windows this is most commonly C:\Program Files\Macromedia\Flash Media Server 2).

The logged events are split into the following files:

- **Access log file (access.log)** – This file includes information about client connections (usually web users connecting to your application) as well as stream activity. It details user activity and can be used to produce reports that detail consumed bandwidth for a session, accessed resources and viewed streams, among other things.

- **Application log file (application.log)** – Application logs log data about a particular application instance. These logs are commonly used for debugging, and also capture trace messages within any server side ActionScript files (.asc). Application logs are stored in a subfolder of the logs directory named after the vhost, application name and application instance. Using the SMIL application of Chapter 17 as an example, the path to the application logs would normally be *C:\Program Files\Macromedia\Flash Media Server 2\logs_defaultVHost_\smil_def*inst_.

- **Diagnostic logs** – Diagnostic logs include several files, which are master.log, edge.log, core.log, admin.log and httpcache.log. Their names are fairly descriptive and these logs are most likely used to debug uncommon events that occur but are not captured by the operating system's own logs. All of the diagnostic logs are located in the logs directory inside the installation directory.

Logging Configuration

The server's logging behavior and configuration are controlled by two files, Logger.xml and fms.ini. Both files are located in the server's conf directory, which under Windows you can usually find at *C:\Program Files\Macromedia\Flash Media Server 2\conf*.

The fms.ini file contains substitution variables used throughout the server's XML configuration files, so it is not solely used to configure logging features. All configuration entries using a dollar sign and curly bracket syntax, like ${LOGGER.LOGDIR}, are configured in fms.ini. Fms.ini therefore offers a single point of configuration for the most commonly used options, while finer control is offered by modifying the XML files directly.

The LOGGER.LOGDIR directive is incidentally also the only configuration option in fms.ini that is related to logging. By default, this entry is empty, which means the logs are written to the default locations.

In contrast, the Logger.xml file offers more options than just the log-file location. It includes multiple configuration options, including specifying an external logging server to send logs to (handy for larger server clusters), maximum log file size, naming masks, events to be logged and loads of other options. For more information on this, you can consult your server documentation. You can find the online version at *http://tinyurl.com/yhew62*.

Producing Reports

It is unfortunate that Flash Media Server does not provide any reporting capabilities outside the live view enabled by the admin console. It is therefore quite challenging to produce detailed reports based on the generated log files.

Even worse, I have yet to find a tool that can digest FMS log files reliably. For example, most web-server log parsers seem to choke on FMS log files, presumably because these tools are targeted at web-server logs and not Flash Media Server.

Introducing Microsoft Log Parser

One powerful but technically challenging option for producing reports from FMS log files is a free tool from Microsoft, called Log Parser. Currently in version 2.2, Log Parser provides universal query access to text-based data such as log files, XML files and CSV files. Since FMS writes its logs in W3C compliant format, Log Parser can read and access the data contained within its log files and create reports, charts or statistics based on it. One downside of Log Parser is (of course) that it only runs on Windows.

Log Parser also supports output targets, so you can use the utility to insert the results into a database, among other things. It uses a SQL-like syntax, similar to the language used to access databases.

You can download Log Parser at *http://tinyurl.com/5uoxz* and, once installed, access it via Start > All Programs > Log Parser 2.2. I can't go through all of Log Parser's capabilities, but I will show you the most commonly used features with a sample script for each use case.

Producing Charts

Assuming that you have installed both Log Parser and Flash Media Server in their default locations, you can use the following syntax to produce a 3D column chart that lists all played videos contained within the log file access.02.log (note the use of `-i:W3C` to specify the W3C log format):

> **Author's Tip**
>
> If you are outsourcing your Flash video delivery to a third-party hosting provider or CDN then you needn't worry about reporting and logging, as your provider should handle this for you. The level of reporting varies from vendor to vendor, with more detailed reporting usually available at additional cost and basic statistics free of charge.

```
C:\Program Files\Log Parser 2.2>logparser "SELECT x-sname, COUNT(*) as videos into
chart.gif FROM 'C:\Program Files\Macromedia\Flash Media Server 2\logs\access.02.
log' GROUP BY x-sname" -i:W3C -chartType:Column3D
```

Log Parser will save the chart into its installation directory under the name of chart.gif, which you can see in **Figure 18-8**.

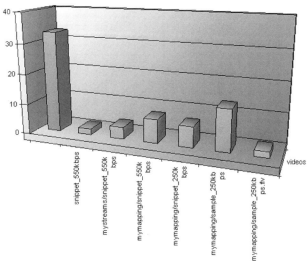

Figure 18-8
Accessed video streams are displayed in a column chart.

To process all access logs contained within the logs directory, you would simply alter the syntax to read:

```
C:\Program Files\Log Parser 2.2>logparser "SELECT x-sname, COUNT(*) as videos into
chart.gif FROM 'C:\Program Files\Macromedia\Flash Media Server 2\logs\access*.log'
GROUP BY x-sname" -i:W3C -chartType:Column3D
```

Generating Reports

Log Parser usually displays its query results right inside the output window, which isn't very handy when your goal is to produce easy-to-manage reports. Fortunately, the tool supports a variety of output formats, including CSV, XML, SQL and others.

It can also write the generated output directly to a file, as the following example shows. It produces a spreadsheet report.csv (saved into Log Parser's installation directory), which contains date and time information about each connect event across all access log files stored in FMS's default logs directory:

```
C:\Program Files\Log Parser 2.2>logparser "SELECT x-event as logons, date, time
INTO report.csv FROM 'C:\Program Files\Macromedia\Flash Media Server 2\logs\ac-
cess*.log' WHERE x-event='connect'" -i:W3C
```

You can see the resulting spreadsheet in **Figure 18-9**.

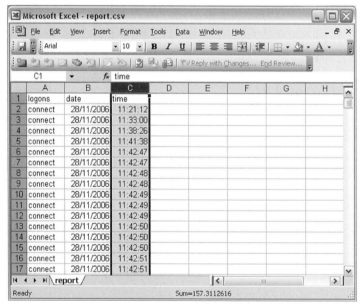

Figure 18-9
This spreadsheet lists connect events and their date and time.

While these are very basic examples, they nicely demonstrate Log Parser's capabilities. It wouldn't be too difficult to build upon this or other examples to gather any type of information required, format it, filter it and output it to a specific file format and location.

Searching for Data

The power of SQL is ideally suited to search for specific pieces of information across an entire directory, or individual files if required. The following example shows how to search for all events generated by a specific IP address, in this case 127.0.0.1, which is the localhost IP that I used during testing.

The query is run against a single access log file named access.03.log but you could also query an entire directory if needed. Again, Log Parser saves the results to report.csv as a spreadsheet.

```
C:\Program Files\Log Parser 2.2>logparser "SELECT * INTO report.csv FROM 'C:\
Program Files\Macromedia\Flash Media Server 2\logs\access.03.log' WHERE c-
ip='127.0.0.1'" -i:W3C
```

Figure 18-10 shows the output that this query generates.

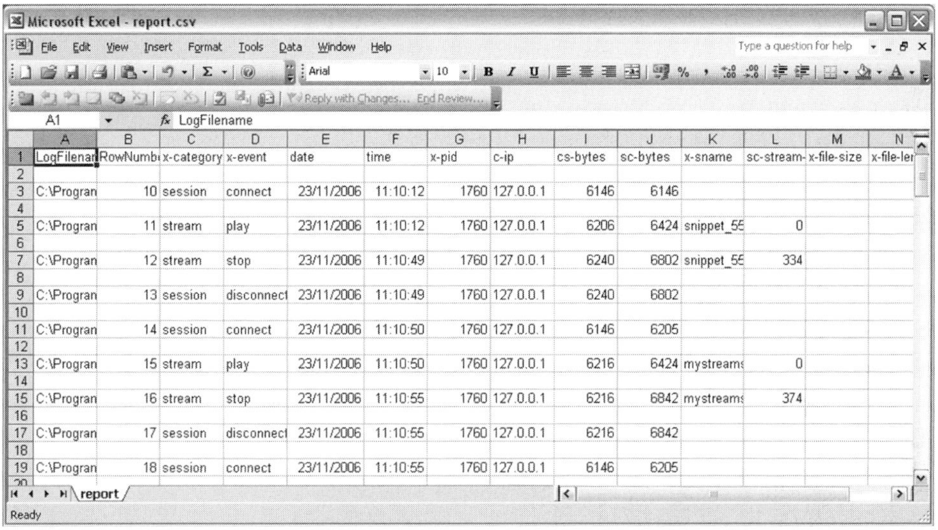

Figure 18-10
The spreadsheet lists all activity generated by IP 127.0.0.1.

This type of SQL syntax and output capability makes Log Parser an immensely powerful tool. At the same time, it also poses a distinct learning curve to users new to SQL.

To find out more about this tool, note that the Log Parser installation directory contains a variety of sample files and help documents. A quick Google search also yields some interesting results.

The Power of SharedObjects

Flash Media Server does a lot more than just stream video. In this section, I will provide a brief overview of some of its capabilities and associated features so you can identify additional potential uses. Leveraging these features will help you to take your next video-on-demand project to a new level, by offering a depth and richness of features that is unparalleled by other platforms.

Author's Tip

Most of the features listed here are only available when using a dedicated Flash Media Server or shared Flash Media application hosting. They will likely be disabled when using CDN delivery for your video files. It is, however, possible to combine CDN delivery of video with dedicated Flash Media Server features inside a single application.

Use Cases

SharedObjects are, in my opinion, the coolest feature of Flash Media Server after video. SharedObjects are somewhat similar to a mini-database where your application can store information, be it related to connected users, the state of the application or pretty much anything else that you see fit.

SharedObjects are nothing new to Flash; they are available as Local SharedObjects to any Flash application and are mainly used like traditional browser cookies—for example, to store a username between visits.

When used with Flash Media Server, however, you can access Remote SharedObjects, stored on the server and accessible (if you want them to be) to all connected clients. This may not sound like a big deal, but it offers immense possibilities. It is, for example, fairly trivial to create a text chat application using just a single SharedObject.

Whenever a user submits a message to the server, this data is stored in a Remote SharedObject and relayed back to all connected clients. This process happens virtually automatically, using a method on the SharedObject called onSync. This method fires automatically once the data inside the SharedObject changes, and it eliminates the need for clients to poll the server for new information. Instead, any new data is automatically sent to the connected users. My website features a few examples of this, including coMMChat which can be found at *http://www.flashcomguru.com/commchat.cfm*.

To take this concept a step further, you could create an application where the server queries an external data source for information—for example, stock data. As soon as the external data changes, the server can write this information to the SharedObject, which in turn propagates it to all connected clients. The application could even offer online and offline modes that would synchronize a disconnected client once they come online.

Inside the Industry

Alternatively (and where video features are less of a priority), the newly released Flex 2 Data Services, part of the Flex 2 platform, is using features derived from Flash Media Server to deliver data synchronization, data paging, publish/subscribe messaging and more to allow developers to build the next generation of rich Internet applications.

Flex 2 is a rich Internet application framework based on Flash that enables developers to create highly scalable, data-driven applications that can reach virtually anyone on any platform. For more information on Flex check out *http://www.adobe.com/products/flex/*.

I am sure you can think of many other ways to combine video and data features to enrich the user experience. A simple text chat running alongside a video can really enhance an otherwise fairly standard video player, allowing for co-browsing features and a community-like experience in which several visitors are connected on a single page.

Or why not enhance the display with a slideshow running alongside the video? It is a real bonus that Flash Media Server can deliver all this without the need for third-party technology, and that it can all be delivered within a single Flash application.

Where to Go from Here

As you probably guessed, I have barely scratched the surface of SharedObjects's capabilities. Moreover, they constitute just one of many additional Flash Media Server features and it would take another book to describe them all in detail.

To learn more about Flash Media Server and its capabilities, visit *http://www.adobe.com/products/flashmediaserver* or check out the Developer Center at *http://www.adobe.com/devnet/flashmediaserver.*

Lastly, do not hesitate to subscribe to the Flash Media List, a mailing list that is frequented by many Flash developers and video professionals and where your questions will swiftly be addressed. The address is *http://www.flashcomguru.com/flashmedialist.*

Conclusion

Flash Media Server is a complex beast, no doubt about it. But don't be intimidated by its wealth of features.

Instead, concentrate on the parts that you and your project require. If streaming Flash video delivery is your only requirement, then consider outsourcing your hosting requirements and get on with the job at hand.

Likewise, if your goal is to create more customized and integrated online experiences, then you are now armed with the basic knowledge required to get up and running with Flash Media Server and can even set up some of its more complex features.

Keep in mind, however, that this book concentrated mainly on the server's video features and that there is a multitude of other features waiting to be discovered. Do feel free to get in touch via the book's website at *www.flashvideobook.com* and tell us about the applications you are building.

The next chapter contains several case studies detailing fun and interesting applications of Flash video creation and distribution.

CHAPTER 19

Case Studies

Case studies provide an interesting glimpse into how real-world websites get it done. Here we present five case studies, two from Stefan and three from Jan.

Stefan's case studies are from his consulting work, and discuss nitty-gritty goals, requirements and implementation details. Jan can't match the cache of Stefan's client base, so turned journalist and reported on some of the most high-profile uses of Flash video on the web today.

Enjoy.

The Roanoke Times

The *Roanoke Times* and *roanoke.com* is the leading daily newspaper in Roanoke, Virginia. The team runs a daily video webcast called the TimesCast, covering upcoming news stories with a mix of local news, weather, sports, and entertainment information. The paper publishes TimesCast on their own website and distributes it via some well-known video portals, including YouTube.

Implementation

The *Roanoke Times* already had a basic video production workflow in place when they approached me (Stefan) in 2005. They had identified Flash as their chosen delivery platform due to the wide reach it offers and they also realized that the existing Real Server was no longer a good fit for their needs.

After developing a few basic Flash video applications in house, the *Roanoke Times* quickly recognized the need for third-party help in order to take the TimesCast (see **Figure 19-1**)to the next level. The requirements for the new application were fairly advanced, including:

- The ability to run pre-roll video ads before the main feature content
- The ability to support multiple, configurable advertisements, randomly presented
- A traditional banner ad synced to the currently playing video ad
- Configuration via XML

- Graphical elements inside the player should sync with the video content (think cue points)

- Video and graphical content should be easily updateable by the team at the *Roanoke Times* and *roanoke.com*

- The ability to track ad impression, video plays and user interaction

- Bandwidth detection and serving of an appropriately encoded version of the video content.

Figure 19-1
The TimesCast at *http://blogs.roanoke.com/vlog*.

The videos are shot and produced daily in front of a green screen by the team at the *Roanoke Times* and *roanoke.com*. After keying out the background using Grass Valley's Edius 3 and adding custom graphics, the source video is encoded to FLV using Sorenson Squeeze.

Working closely with Seth Gitner, the multimedia editor at the *Roanoke Times*, we quickly established a list of deliverables for version 1 of the TimesCast player. Some features turned out to be a little trickier to implement than others, with the main one being a custom implementation of cue point functionality that allowed for a series of graphics inside the player to be synchronized with time codes of the video itself.

Navigation or event cue points were quickly dismissed, as it would have been fairly inflexible to add the cue points during encoding, a requirement with both navigation and event cue points. ActionScript cue points were also out of the question, as one key requirement was the ability for the player to receive its configuration from an XML file, while ActionScript cue points are usually inserted before compiling.

Instead, we decided to implement our own cue point routine, which uses a series of XML nodes, each specifying the required time-code information. The player continuously monitors the playback time and compares it with the cue-point list loaded from the XML file. If there's a match, it will show the required graphic on screen. Other features of the completed player included:

- A bandwidth-detection routine utilizing Flash Media Server, with the actual video then delivered progressively via a standard web server
- Banner synchronization through Flash's built-in LocalConnection Object
- Impression and user interaction tracking.

Results

Since its launch over a year ago, the TimesCast has grown in popularity with daily viewing figures ever increasing. And for viewers that are on the move, the site now also offers the TimesCast in a downloadable MP4 (iPod) format.

Rather than recreating a TV news show, the TimesCast is a great example of a new type of online content that is quickly emerging and which constitutes a great addition to existing media.

Video on the web and Flash video in particular is now both easy to implement and quick to deploy, with production and broadcast of the TimesCast happening on the same day. Through the use of short and unintrusive advertising, some of the production costs can easily be recovered—not to mention all the positive publicity that this particular use of the technology has received.

The *Roanoke Times* and *roanoke.com* has since won the top award for General Excellence in Online Journalism for medium-sized sites from the Online News Association and the TimesCast was thought to have secured them the top spot. It also received an Eppy Award and was named Best Overall Newspaper-Affiliated Internet Service in the category serving under 1 million unique monthly visitors.

No surprise then that one viewer wrote in to say that the TimesCast was "Better than the Naked News".

You can check out the TimesCast at *http://blogs.roanoke.com/vlog*.

CNET UK

CNET is well-known for its focus on technology and the site has been deploying a lot of its video content through Flash in recent years. As far back as 2004, CNET deployed live Flash video broadcasts using Flash Communication Server for their "Help Desk Live" feature.

When CNET UK contacted me (Stefan) in 2006 to upgrade their existing video players to ActionScript 2 and for help with migrating their existing content to the Akamai network, I quickly agreed.

Implementation

CNET already had a massive library of video content and needed a way to transition their existing video players to the Akamai network, using streaming Flash video. A simple switch to Akamai wouldn't have been very complex; however, the migration was seen as a good opportunity to also rewrite the existing players in a more up-to-date, ActionScript2-based format, which promoted the ability to reuse parts of each player in other scenarios.

The first step involved creating a few connection classes that queried the Akamai servers for the ideal IP address to play the video stream—you may remember this routine from Chapter 17. Once the ideal server IP was received, another class would handle the actual connection.

Apart from basic playback controls such as play, pause and volume scrubber, the player also needed to provide support for:

- A sponsor graphic that was optionally clickable

- A pre-roll video ad, again optional

- A JPG image that could be shown before playback

- Configuration via XML

- Product link for more details.

Figure 19-2 shows the player on CNET UK's homepage.

Figure 19-2
CNET UK's well-known Flash video player.

An ActionScript2 class to handle the loading and parsing of the XML configuration file was also required and created. The approach used in that class is very similar to the implementation I detailed in Chapter 14, where an external XML file is loaded into Flash for configuration.

Results

The transition to CNET's updated player, which is now serving streaming video from the Akamai network, went smoothly. Not long after the first player was completed, two more followed. One of these included a playlist feature to continually play up to five videos sequentially, while another one allows users to switch from a JPG gallery view to a video player or vice versa.

CNET continues to be one of the major destinations for technology-related information and the large amount of video content on the site makes a visit a very engaging experience. I personally visit the site almost daily—and once you've watched a few of Chris Stevens's video reviews I bet so will you.

My (Jan's) case studies are more journalistic and reveal some of the nitty-gritty deployment decisions made by a couple of high-profile, high-volume sites.

ESPN

With over 350 million page views in August 2006, ESPN.com (**Figure 19-3**) is by far the most popular sports site in the US. Sports fanatics come for scores, they come for news, they come for commentary, and they come for Flash video.

Figure 19-3
Millions of Internet viewers visit this website daily.

According to Paul Gavalis, ESPN's director of video technology and operations, the site posts videos originally shot by the broadcast arm, as well as original video shot by a dedicated production team specifically for the website. Video is integrated into the site's editorial content, allowing contextual viewing, and also presented within a video-only Flash-based interface containing all videos available on the site (**Figure 19-3**). There are multiple video packages, including the basic ESPN Motion, which is advertiser supported and available free to all visitors, and ESPN 360, an expanded service, and pay-per-view sporting events.

Choosing Flash as their primary streaming was an easy decision, according to Gavalis, because of three factors. First, their primary goal was to make the video easy to access and play, which they can easily do with Flash. Second, they wanted to serve the widest possible audience, and felt they could leverage Flash's near ubiquity. Finally, they wanted to give their product managers as much flexibility as possible regarding the user interface for their respective products, another Flash strength. Since the site was already Flash intensive, Gavalis already had multiple Flash designers and engineers on staff, so ramping up to support Flash video wasn't a major undertaking.

All new video content is captured with digital camcorders and edited on Windows workstations, with some animation and other content created on Macs. Though ESPN has developed their own proprietary encoding systems, they licensed technology from On2 for Flash encoding.

ESPN publishes most video at between 400–600 kbps, depending upon subject matter, usually at 440×330 resolution. Gavalis reported that ESPN used single pass, constant bit rate encoding for time-sensitive video, or video with low-motion content, but produced most high action video using two-pass variable bit rate encoding.

Digital Life TV

If you know Patrick Norton as the host of DL.TV (which he calls "Mouseketeers for geeks"), it's easy to dismiss him as just another pretty face. As "head of podcasts" for Ziff Davis Media, however, he's charged with producing all video programs produced by the consumer group of Ziff Davis, and affordably distributing them in both live and downloaded formats. This makes him a virtual encyclopedia of codec features, benefits and foibles.

If you surf over to DL.TV (For Tech Fans by Tech Fans), you'll immediately notice that all shows are offered in five video formats (Flash, Windows Media, Quicktime H.264, Video iPod and DivX) and MP3 for audio only download. Here's an overview of the production cycle.

Norton shoots all shows live with three Sony FX1 camcorders mixed via a NewTek Tricaster. The show is available for viewing live, but only via Windows Media, with a Windows Media server distributing the video. After the show finishes, DL.TV encodes a Flash 7 video file streamed via Flash Media Server (**Figure 19-4**). Or, you can download the video or audio in any of the other listed formats.

Figure 19-4
Pat Norton of DL.TV in the Flash version of the show (One of seven available streams).

Norton encodes all video to a maximum of about 500 kbps, with at least 64 kbps devoted to mono audio. Resolution depends upon format, with iPod video produced at 320×240, H.264 at 640×480 and all the rest output at 480×360. Norton uses dual-pass, variable bit rate encoding when available in all formats, with H.264 MOV rendered by QuickTime Pro by far the most time consuming, taking about 4–5 hours to encode per show.

Norton reports that 40% of viewers download the iPod-formatted video, which he encodes with iSquint, which he says is faster than QuickTime Pro. Flash is the second most popular format, with 20% of viewers, while 15% watch the Windows Media stream and another 15% download the H.264 MOV file. The remaining 10% is split between DivX and MP4.

Obviously, user preference drives DL.TV's codec decision making, but Norton pegged H.264 as the quality leader, though impractical for those running older computers without the processing power to decode the stream. Interestingly, Norton is closely watching the MPEG-LA licensing group to make sure that his use of MPEG-related codecs accrues no charge, which should be a concern for producers who charge for their videos (DL.TV is supported by advertising, with no charge per stream).

Norton says Flash is the easiest for viewers to use, but warns that it's much more costly to distribute, primarily because you need a Flash Media Server to get benefits like advertising insertion and comprehensive back end statistics. Norton also found Flash challenging to work with and advised small-budget shops to check programming and distribution costs before committing to the format.

Norton said that Windows Media was great for Windows users with no "ax to grind," and DivX slightly behind the quality of the other codecs at his encoding parameters, though great if you can "throw masses of bandwidth at it." According to Norton, RealVideo was never in the picture because of its "intrusive player" and the fact that while he's had requests for video formatted for PSPs, cell phones and low-res formats, no user has ever requested RealVideo.

While admitting that web distribution eliminates many of the barriers of broadcast TV, Norton warned wannabe video producers to be careful what they wish for, because they just might get it. He was referring to the bandwidth costs of distributing video, which he states can be "prohibitive" if you're moving large amounts of video. His best advice is to shop around for the best price from your ISP or CDN.

He recounted a story of one producer whose video "got viral" and, several hundred thousand downloads later, received a bill from their ISP of about $17,000. He advised producers to consider distribution sites like youtube.com or blip.tv rather than hosting their own videos, since they shoulder these distribution costs and deal with the pain of configuring and maintaining the player.

Blip.TV

If you're looking to emulate Oprah or Dr. Phil, but lack the network connections, blip.tv has got a deal for you. They'll post your videos, help you find sponsors (for a 50% split) and assist your promotional efforts. Sound far-fetched? Perhaps, but CEO Mike Hudack reports that some shows are grossing more than $10,000 a month.

Though blip.tv looks a lot like youtube.com to the untrained eye, the goal of the site is different—it's seeking independent, highly branded serial shows from sources like star video blogger Amanda Congdon (**Figure 19-5**).

While producers can upload video to blip in almost any format, with MOV and WMV preferred (and MPEG-2 and DV discouraged), blip automatically encodes all videos to Flash format, at a resolution as high as 600×450 and data rate of 512 kbps, including 96-kbps audio. Uniquely, blip also lets publishers make their originally uploaded video available to their viewers. Hudack reports that many of their publishers upload in iPod-compatible QuickTime format so their viewers can download the file to their desktops or watch it on their iPods.

According to Hudack, blip chose Flash because video quality was very good, the Player near ubiquitous and because they could customize the player and viewing environment to their liking. One downside of the current version of Flash, however, is the lack of a Linux player. Interestingly, blip does not distribute Flash with a Flash Media Server, due to the high per-unit cost. Instead, blip distributes their video via HTTP using Apache servers running on Linux computers.

Figure 19-5
blip.tv, and star video blogger, Amanda Congdon.

One of the downsides of this approach is that the files lack the interactivity provided by the Flash Media Server, which allows viewers to drag their sliders through the file. With blip.tv, your only option is to play the video file straight through from start to finish. Also missing are higher-end features like closed captions.

Hudack noted that QuickTime was the second favorite format among their user community, and that they may start automatically transcoding video files uploaded by their publishers to QuickTime as they do to Flash now.

blip rejected Windows Media because it doesn't work well on Macs, which obviously didn't sit well with their creative community. Hudak commented that Real was "not even on the radar screen in any way, shape or form." Reasons included high licensing costs, that Real had a bad reputation for bundling software with the Player, and lack of support among aggregators or video distribution sites like iTunes or Akimbo.

Hudack said that blip might consider using H.264 as the primary distribution format in the future, citing excellent video quality and better QuickTime player distribution via iTunes. Today, however, it can be hard for lower-powered computers to playback in real time.

Another codec on the horizon is Ogg Theora, an open-source video codec originally developed by On2. Hudack bemoaned the lack of an "MP3 codec for video," commenting that the lack of a standard confuses viewers and slows market acceptance. Though admitting that Ogg Theora wasn't quite ready for primetime, he felt that it held great promise as a royalty-free codec that could work across systems and platforms without the need for a supporting business model.

Conclusion

There are plenty of great Flash video stories out there waiting to be told. Good luck in creating your own.

Index